Empire of Knowledge

D1557511

Empire of Knowledge

Culture and Plurality
in the Global Economy

Vinay Lal

Pluto Press

LONDON • STERLING, VIRGINIA

First published 2002 by Pluto Press
345 Archway Road, London N6 5AA
and 22883 Quicksilver Drive,
Sterling, VA 20166–2012, USA

www.plutobooks.com

British Library Cataloguing in Publication Data
A catalogue record for this book is available from the British Library

ISBN 0 7453 1737 5 hardback
ISBN 0 7453 1736 7 paperback

Library of Congress Cataloging in Publication Data
Lal, Vinay.
  Empire of knowledge : culture and plurality in the global economy /
Vinay Lal.
    p. cm.
Includes bibliographical references and index.
  ISBN 0–7453–1737–5 — ISBN 0–7453–1736–7 (pbk.)
  1. Social history—20th century. 2. Economic history—20th century.
3. World politics—20th century. 4. Developed countries—Relations—
Developing countries. 5. Developing countries—Relations—Developed
countries. 6. Equality. 7. Knowledge, Sociology of. 8. History—Philosophy.
I. Title.
  HN16 .L35 2002
  306'.09'04—dc21
                                                          2002002247

10   9   8   7   6   5   4   3   2   1

Designed and produced for Pluto Press by
Chase Publishing Services, Fortescue, Sidmouth EX10 9QG
Typeset from disk by Stanford DTP Services, Towcester
Printed in the European Union by Antony Rowe, Chippenham, England

For
Avni Sunaina
to whom the future belongs
and
Teshome Gabriel
who has enabled the futures of many young ones

and
to the memory of
Elisabeth ("Lilo") Difloe
who had her future snatched from her

Contents

Acknowledgments

There are many friends, fellow travelers in politics and ideas, and other well-wishers to whom I have owed a book – indeed, this book – for a very long period of time. There is, to begin with, my brother Anil, with whom I have been conversing on matters touched upon in this book for over two decades. Roby Rajan was present when these conversations first transpired, and I am not certain that over time he has become less cynical and more temperate. But he remains an intellectual soul-mate, delightfully scornful of communalists, troglodytes, and – most significantly – academics who have come to think too much of themselves. Among my friends in Chicago, I am grateful, in particular, to Bernard Cohn and Dipesh Chakrabarty. It is with immense pleasure that I recall being Barney's student, but it is not only colonial India with which I became intimately acquainted through his writings, anecdotal meanderings, and rambling reminiscences. Barney, among other friends, has been a true example of a radical democrat. I am deeply appreciative of Dipesh's interest in my work.

At the University of California, Los Angeles, where I have been ensconced for nearly a decade, I am grateful to Esha De, Russell Leong, Don Nakanishi, Peter Nabokov, and Michael Salmon for their keen support of my work. Daniel and Arundhati Neuman have been wonderful friends, and scarcely any words are adequate to describe the friendship and intellectual camaraderie I have shared with Teshome Gabriel. With his learning, wisdom, and patience, not to mention his capacity for unstinting friendship, his near indifference to the tyranny of clock time, his emphatic repudiation of that menacing excuse of being "busy," his intellectual playfulness, and his ability to elicit thought with a mere gesture or a carefully chosen *mot*, he has endeared himself to me and doubtless to many who have come to see him as an inspirational figure.

For their intellectual friendship and help in numerous other ways, I am truly beholden to Ravindra Jain (Delhi), Frederique Apffel-Marglin (Northampton, Massachusetts), Makarand Paranjape (Delhi), Henry Ranjeet (Chennai), Manu Kothari (Mumbai), Douglas Lummis (Tokyo/Okinawa), Anne Beech (London), and Akira Usuki

(Osaka). Chieko Otsuro made possible the four-month-long trip to Osaka during which the outlines of this book first took concrete shape. I am thankful to her for her laborious efforts in making my trip comfortable and productive. Likewise, I am immensely grateful to Anne Beech not only for her encouragement, but for her willingness to take a risk with an author unknown to her. While much of this book was being written, Avni – and more recently Ishaan – were comfortably settled in at night with Anju, and I am extremely thankful to her, as well as to my in-laws, Ram Dhan and Krishna Relan, and to my parents, Kishori Lal and Shanno Devi, for material and moral support of various kinds.

Over the years, Ziauddin Sardar and his family have invariably opened up their house to me in London. Zia's hospitality is exceeded only by his acerbity and his penchant for conversation as well as a relentless drive to probe the limits of interpretation. This book, I am hopeful, will appeal to him. It has gained immeasurably, as well, from the sustained conversations over the last 15 years with Ashis Nandy, whose intellectual insights have been critical to my thinking. His friendship, too, has been exemplary.

Bits and pieces of this book have been published elsewhere, generally in a different form. Chapter 1 is a greatly expanded and highly revised version of a short article that was first published in *Humanscape* (Bombay) as "Relocating Time: The Politics of Time at the Cusp of the 'Millennium,'" Vol. 6, no. 12 (December 1999): 6–13. From a career as successful stockbroker, Jayesh Shah, the journal's founder and publisher, has traveled a long distance to become an activist and imaginative player on the NGO scene in India. His friendship, and his interest in repeatedly publishing my work, are gratefully acknowledged.

Portions of the section entitled "Total Violence" in Chapter 2 were previously published in the article "The Globalism of Modern Knowledge Systems: Governance, Ecology, and Future Epistemologies," *Emergences* 9, no. 1 (May 1999): 79–103, and similarly the section on "Human Rights" partly draws upon "The Imperialism of Human Rights," *Focus on Law Studies* 8, no. 1 (Fall 1992): 5 ff.

Some of the paragraphs in Chapter 3 on sanctions draw upon an earlier version published as "Sanctions and the Politics of Dominance, Multilateralism, and Legalism in the International Arena," *Social Scientist* 25, nos. 5–6 (May–June 1997): 54–67.

Portions of Chapter 4 on development draw upon the aforementioned article in *Emergences* on "The Globalism of Modern

Knowledge Systems." The concluding section on the disciplinary structures of knowledge has appeared in a different version as part of a larger paper in *Futures* (February 2002).

The pages on Gandhi and ecology in Chapter 5 are adapted from "Gandhi and the Ecological Vision of Life: Thinking Beyond Deep Ecology," *Environmental Ethics* 22, no. 2 (Summer 2000): 149–68, and several paragraphs in Chapter 6 are adapted from various articles published in *Humanscape*.

Introduction

They make war and call it peace.[1] So wrote Tacitus in the first
Christian millennium. When I first entertained some concrete
thoughts about this book, in the early summer of 1999, these words
appeared to resonate chillingly: the will of a Western empire – call
it the United States, the North Atlantic Treaty Organization (NATO),
the European Union – was once again asserting itself as the universal
history of mankind. Bombs were being rained down on Yugoslavia,
or what remained of it after secessionist and liberation movements
had shrunk it down to much less than half its former size. As this
book was being completed, in the infancy of the third Christian
millennium, one might have been forgiven for thinking that the
hullabaloo over the millennium was much ado about nothing: now
superbombs, some weighing as much as 15,000 lb apiece, were
creating firestorms around the strongholds of the Taliban. A little
more than two years had elapsed, and the war machine was still at
work, the Tomahawks and Stealth Fighters now supplemented by
"special ground forces" and a new generation of bombs which
apparently can puncture the walls of caves dug deep into the hills.
Amidst the promise of commitment of troops from Germany, Italy,
Australia, and Canada, NATO remarkably had invoked, for the first
time in its history, provisions of its charter to the effect that any
assault upon the United States would be considered an attack upon
the member nations of NATO.

No reasonable person could have failed to applaud the "peace" of
Yugoslavia, when we think of the immense suffering inflicted upon
its people, but the manner in which this peace was negotiated made
it appear to be another name for coercion and, even, state-sponsored
terrorism. Now one awaits with similar foreboding the "peace" of
Afghanistan, and again one suspects that the acquiescence of even
the harshest critics of the American conduct of the war would have
been purchased with the thought that the people of Afghanistan
would no longer have to suffer another night of air raids. A peace
that imposes a new form of hegemony, and that brings into power
an alliance of soldiers, among whom are many whose thuggish
behavior previously threw Afghanistan into chaos, may look like an

1

attractive option after months of bombing have made impossible any other kind of solution.

Exactly 100 years ago, the United States was acquiring an overseas empire, and in southern Africa the Boer War was to introduce new forms of orchestrating death. The British Empire then covered nearly one-fourth of the globe, and scarcely anyone could have imagined that by the middle of the twentieth century all the European powers would have been divested of their empires, retaining possession only of scattered colonies and entrusted with trusteeship responsibilities over small islands. Decolonization, to intellectuals and political activists in the Third World, appeared as the most promising development to overtake colonized people, and for a moment it must have seemed that the true meaning of freedom, namely an awareness of the conditions of oppression under which people labor, was on the verge of being realized. Nationalist resistance movements everywhere contributed to the demise of colonial rule, though geopolitical theorists were doubtless more inclined to view the two world wars as instrumental in the decline of the great European powers. Since many Western political commentators and other intellectuals considered the colonized to be incapable of producing a genuine or "good" nationalist movement, they proposed that the European powers were retreating from sheer exhaustion, the apprehension that their benevolent work in the colonies would elicit no appreciation from ungrateful natives, and the necessity of repairing their own war-torn economies. The colonized could now be put to better use in the metropoles: in retrospect postcolonial theorists may like to describe this phenomenon as "the empire striking back," but Indians, Pakistanis, and Indonesians, among others, were viewed as furnishing the necessary labor force.

As the era of decolonization receded, and the communist nations fell into disrepair, leading eventually to the dismemberment of the Soviet Union and the transformation of the countries behind what was once the Iron Curtain, the Americans proclaimed the arrival of a "new world order." But the disparities between the First World and the Third World continue to grow apace, and successive United Nations Human Development Reports have highlighted the seemingly intractable problems – poverty, dwindling resources, unemployment, illiteracy, "brain drain," environmental devastation, gender inequities, pollution, exponential growth of the urban population, and lack of medical care and facilities, among numerous others – that continue to afflict much of the formerly colonized world. Yet the brute fact of poverty hides more than it reveals, and social science discourse, which has arrogated to itself the responsibility of defining, articulating, and managing poverty, is largely without the awareness that the affluence of some is the most glaring sign of poverty. If modernizers, liberals, and Marxists had been less mocking of Gandhi's espousal of poverty, which was seen as obscuring his dalliances with the bourgeoisie, they might have recognized his heroic endeavor to reintroduce the notion of voluntary poverty and (to use Majid Rahnema's phrase) convivial poverty while offering a resounding critique of modernized poverty. But scholarship has often had little time for such distinctions, since to embrace any notion of poverty is to invite attention to one's "backwardness." Moreover, the economist's only rejoinder to poverty is a plan to engender "growth," in obvious indifference to the fact that growth generates its own forms of poverty. With respect to all the other principal orthodoxies of the day, the story is a similar one. The critique of development is barely tolerated, since nothing is construed as more heretical than the supposition that underdeveloped countries should not, with some obvious qualifications, emulate the developed countries. These terms point to an evaluative scale, which in substance is no different than the nineteenth-century tale that the colonized nations, by virtue of being colonized, were markedly inferior to the colonizing powers, which had attained superiority in the arenas of material attainment, morality, and intellectual reasoning.

In the new world order, the primitives, the backward, and the rebels are largely being eliminated by kindness, since the conventional pieties of the day generally do not allow for open and racist abuse, or for the unabashed celebration of Western civilization as the greatest good ever bestowed upon humankind. While certain sections of the academy have been buzzing with discussions of hegemony, the great powers have been finding new uses for it, and the apparatus of oppression has taken on more insidious and invisible forms. Though the bombing of Iraq in 1991 decimated the country and pushed it back, in the words of an official UN document, to the medieval period, the casualties on account of sanctions have been immeasurably greater. Yet the then Secretary of State, Madeleine Albright, considered that the containment of Hussein was "worth the price" of the lives of the over half a million Iraqi children who have died from starvation and lack of medical care since the sanctions were first imposed upon Iraq. The fatalities have continued to multiply since then. Sanctions, ironically, are even championed as a non-violent and charitable form of intervention, one designed to teach recalcitrant nations the moral consequences of their actions.

Thus, placed as we are at the threshold of a new epoch, the only thing that might well be "new" is forms of social engineering that obliterate the remnants of knowledge systems and cultural practices which have so far not been assimilated into the worldview of modernity and its numerous practitioners. Nothing is as much global as the knowledge systems that perform the interpretive, political, cultural, and managerial work which characterizes modernity in the era of globalization, and consequently it becomes imperative to provide a cartography of the global framework of knowledge, politics, and culture, as well as of those paths which open up alternative frameworks to a more pluralistic future. If human beings have the uncanny ability to devise the most extraordinary forms of oppression, they are equally endowed with the capacity to find ways of freeing themselves from oppression. Similarly, while many scholars and academics have lent their services to the state or other dominant institutions of civil society, the true function of the intellectual is to be resistant to dominant epistemologies and political practices, and to investigate precisely that element of knowledge which gives it the quality of being taken for granted. To do otherwise is to abdicate the responsibilities of the intellectual. Much academic writing, it remains to be said, has rendered itself opaque, not least of all that writing which claims to speak in the voices of the powerless and the marginalized. The postcolonial scholar has found new modes of self-indulgence.

This book is intended to be an intervention in numerous contemporary debates and offer a dissenting perspective on the politics of knowledge. There is, as I suggest, an empire of knowledge, perhaps far more considerable than the empires we associate with Euro-American imperialism or with the large corporate undertakings that have divided much of the world among themselves, and it has shaped the categories through which we view the world; and since many of these categories are largely invisible, or bathed in the language of kindness, good intentions, and progress, they are more insidious in their operation than the forces and agents through which naked domination is exercised. This book, in keeping with my stance that intellectuals cannot but be forward-looking, is also prospective in outlook, though that should not be understood as indicating an interest on my part in policy-making, much less any suggestion that readers should expect a blueprint for the future. It is perfectly illustrative of my argument that our futures should have been hijacked by policy-makers and management gurus. Earlier generations, particularly before the advent of Enlightenment discourses, knew of another "specialist" dealing with the future, namely the prophet. This is scarcely to say that I am interested in prophecy, or that the prophetic mode should substitute for the interpretive mode, interesting though prophecy is as one of the numerous ahistoricist forms of knowledge which have been suppressed in our times; rather, it is to suggest that, if the future is not to become hostage to those very ideas that, in the twentieth century, led us to total forms of domination as much as to modern knowledge systems which are global in their reach and appetite, it becomes imperative to work for dissenting futures.

Though the special provenance of this book might be characterized as an excursion into the politics of knowledge, besides furnishing a broad and, I daresay, somewhat different canvas for the understanding of politics, extending beyond party politics, electoral struggles, and even identity politics and multiculturalism, my work also seeks to understand the intersections between politics and knowledge. In Chapter 1, I consider what it means to have moved into the twenty-first century, and to have heralded the arrival of a new millennium. Though there are many histories of clocks and calendars, and the philosophical consideration of time has an honorable trajectory in Western thought, from Augustine to Heidegger and Ricoeur, few commentators have paused to consider the cultural politics of time itself, and the ubiquitousness of certain of its categories. To read accounts of the underdevelopment of the Third World is to be reminded of the snide observation that "natives" in the southern hemisphere have insufficient respect for the clock and do not make good use of their time, though they have almost uniformly submitted to the norms of the Western calendar.

At a different macro level of interpretation, it becomes necessary to inquire about our deployment of the categories "century" and "millennium," and the politics that is disguised by the apparently neutral meanings attached to these categories of time. If, as is frequently encountered in common parlance, considerable parts of India, Africa, and especially the Muslim world – the "especially" apparently underscored by the events of September 11th – are said to be living in medieval times or in the nineteenth century, then it is transparent that categories of time have also been spatialized, just as categories of space have, by the act of displacement, temporal effect. Consider, too, that as we were poised to enter into a new millennium, we scarcely stopped to ask for whom it is that the millennium struck, and by what sleight of hand the Christian millennium became the benchmark for all peoples. For (say) Muslims, it may serve as an unpleasant reminder of the overwhelming hegemony of the West. As one reflects upon the unease and anxiety among the Muslim leadership in the last decade of the twentieth century, whether in Algeria (where civil war has left 80,000 people dead), Malaysia (where the Prime Minister, Mahathir Mohamad, squashed the reform movement and had its most promising figure, Anwar Ibrahim, arrested and convicted on what are widely believed to be false charges), Indonesia (where the crash of the economy and the overthrow of Suharto was accompanied as well by violence targeted at the Chinese community), Afghanistan, Pakistan, Bangladesh, Sudan, or elsewhere, one wonders whether the imminence of the new millennium generated within Islam a certain melancholia.

The history of millenarian movements is inextricably tied to prophecies of doom, and the events of September 11th must have appeared to the doomsayers as having vindicated their prognostications. The internet furnishes a generously accommodating home for rumors of global scope and conspiratorial theories of the widest import; and here the millenarians, while not sufficiently attentive to the expansive conception of space entailed by *new* technologies ("newness" itself being a predicate of time), were espousing their own ideas about the end of time. But millenarianism's other self, so to speak, speaks in a different voice and with the expectation of renewal. There may well be other ways of renewing and renegotiating our sense of time, and not allowing it to be compromised by millenarian time, clock time, the time of the Gregorian calendar, and the time of schedules. Being busy, not having the time for others, is itself an evasion of our obligation to treat everyone as an end in himself and herself, and we have not been reflective enough about how busy-ness creates its own forms of oppression. I ruminate, for instance, on the relationship between time and our eating habits, and the conviviality and richness of those meals which stretch time to pleasant albeit temporary extinction. Similarly, the disciplinary notion of time which rules over modern lives is not easily reconciled with the various modes of what might be called BodyTime. The hegemonic conceptions of time are an aspect of the oppressiveness of modern knowledge systems, and to this extent the burden of the discussion is to democratize and pluralize our notion of time.

If Chapter 1 is partly prospective, Chapters 2 and 3 are largely retrospective. We have to begin with the chilling fact that the twentieth century was soaked in blood. Varying estimates have been furnished of how many people may have been killed in wars and other armed conflicts, but the conservative estimate of 110 million is at least indisputable; not less significantly, as a proportion of the total population, the number of casualties for the twentieth century seems to be higher than for any other point in recorded human history.[2] Having left the twentieth century behind us, a century dedicated to the principle of total war and brutalized by exterminationist mentalities, it also becomes necessary to inquire into some of the other principal political developments that shaped the previous 100 years. The preceding century witnessed as well the final enthronement of the nation-state idea, the emergence of the idea of international governance in economic and political spheres, the expansion of human rights – or at least the deployment of the notion in a wide public arena, decolonization and resistance movements, and what I have called the democratic totalitarianism of the United States. It was with the desire of eliminating the scourge of war that the short-lived League of Nations, and subsequently the United Nations, was set up, and it is increasingly under the putative jurisdiction of the United Nations, particularly of its Security Council, that the novel, but by no means incorruptible, idea of *international governance* is taking shape. As I have already suggested, decolonization and resistance movements were to leave their impressions upon large parts of the world, but formerly colonized people could not resist the attraction of the nation-state system, which continues to play havoc with the lives of people in the Middle East, South Asia, and virtually all of Africa.

The UN Charter, numerous international covenants, and movements predicated on the enunciation of ethnic, linguistic, sexual, racial, and religious differences, to which were subsequently added other considerations such as the mode of lifestyle that one might choose to adopt, were together to create a new-found awareness of human rights. Nationalist movements, driven by the notion of cultural difference, and squarely grounded in the rhetoric of human dignity, were equally critical in the emergence of the notion of human rights, which never before has had the salience that it does in our times. The notion of human rights has generated much debate. Some commentators describe it as a new front for Western imperialism, while others are inclined to view it as the indispensable and non-negotiable condition for the flourishing of human societies. As the conflict in Kosovo indubitably established, human rights will, for the foreseeable future, furnish grounds for intervention, but in this respect as in all others, the power of chastisement lies only with some agents. The idea of human rights is particularly appropriable, as I shall suggest, to the democratic totalitarianism represented by the United States. Though one might be inclined to view the Pax Americana as the logical continuum of the Pax Britannica, or be seduced by cyclical theories of history and by narratives derived from political science about shifting balances between great powers, the concentrated power represented by the United States has no comparison with any previous point in history, and it behooves us to understand what "divine dispensation" has driven the US to the helm of world affairs, and what this portends for humanity in the twenty-first century.

If the United States, which has developed a new grammar of conduct and a new lexicon of power, extending from "rogue states" to the international community, has its counterpart in the United Nations, under the auspices of which peacekeeping operations and sanctions have brought ruin to some countries, the third part of the tripartite system of contemporary global governance is occupied by the institutions – the World Bank, the International Monetary Fund (IMF), and the World Trade Organization (WTO), among others – charged with the responsibility of managing the global economy. Not unlike the United Nations, these institutions purport to be independent, but they are severely constrained by the actions and will of the United States.[3] Much ink has been expended on such matters as the consequences of the expanding free trade regimes, the unevenness of the rewards reaped under globalization, the price of patents for the poor, the threat to indigenous knowledge under the pretext of international property rights, and the commodification of lifestyles that are scarcely affordable in developing countries. The literature is immense, and many minds have been trained on the question of globalization, but my own modest endeavor is to cast a critical glance at the settlement dispute provisions in the WTO. What is presumed by these provisions, and how substantively do we assess the presumed parity between nations who come to the tribunal either with a grievance or to defend themselves against charges of the violation of WTO rules?

Alongside the political developments encapsulated in the previous two chapters, the ideology of development was to acquire, following the Marshall Plan and decolonization, near sacrosanct status. This discussion, which takes us directly to the politics of knowledge, initiates Chapter 4. To question the logic of development was to place oneself among primitives and traditionalists, and to be viewed as an obdurate native who refused to be reformed. Though the millions who perished in the Holocaust, or in the killing fields of Cambodia and Rwanda, are recognized as victims of political violence and genocidal impulses, the more numerous victims of development have rarely been accorded the dignity of even being considered visible. The true "unknown soldier" of the twentieth century, invariably lying in an unmarked grave, is the victim of development. At least the unknown soldier at whose altar politicians pay their veneration to the idea of sacrifice had another name – hero, martyr, patriot; the victim of development has no name, and was asked to march to the tune of development, laying aside his and her lands, honor, traditions, and culture in the name of the nation. The victim of development is not even a victim; he or she is a statistic.

It was the insanity of development which fed Stalin's gulags, and created the starving millions in Mao's China – at least 25 million people perished in the paean to progress styled as the Great Leap Forward – and which has since claimed the lives of tribal, aboriginal, and other powerless people throughout the world. This is the intractable problem of modernity, namely that oppression now comes to us in indecipherable guises, often posited as developments for our own good or as acts of humanity and kindness, and few people have considered whether oppression will not increasingly be inflicted upon us through categories of knowledge. Nor is this tantamount to an admission that the military-industrial complex is entirely a thing of the past, or that brute force will not continue to be exercised as the most evident display of domination. The violence in our midst permits no such conclusion. Nevertheless, dominant states can no longer justify their domination predominantly with the rhetoric of the "civilizing mission" so effortlessly employed by colonial states, and it is remarkable that though the conflict with the Taliban has been represented by the US as a war between the "civilized world" and those who hate freedom and democracy, there has been virtually no talk of civilizing the Afghans: the war aims are represented as bringing terrorists and their sponsors to justice and placing a new administration in Afghanistan. The "new world order" is itself framed, not by an explicit contrast between the colonizers and the colonized, superior and inferior races, but rather in the language of laws, the injunction to be moral, the apparent concern for lives (there must be no American casualties, in any case), and the ethic of caring. The imperative to punish and kill is now derived by designating entire states as rogue or outlaw formations, who invite retribution by having stepped outside the pale of the law or what American politicians call the international community.

If development is only one of the more insidious categories that predominates in modern knowledge systems, alongside that cluster of ideas – nation-state, modernity, big science, history and others – which have gained adherents in the farthest reaches of the globe, the persistence of these categories in the face of the onslaught against conventional ideas that has been witnessed in the academy, whether in the US, France, Britain, and even some Third World countries (notably India), is all the more remarkable. Some years after decolonization had been achieved nearly everywhere, the intellectual counterpart of that movement, initiated by French poststructuralism and the critique of Orientalism, was to take apart the assumptions of Enlightenment and colonial discourses. While earlier discourses had taken the subject – the white patriarchal male – for granted, the entire question of how subjects are constituted, while processes of exclusion work to remove certain classes of people from the purview of reason, history, and the nation-state, was now thrown open for investigation. However, notwithstanding the thoroughgoing anti-foundationalism of much of poststructuralism, not to mention postcolonial theory, deconstructionism, and postmodernism, the intellectual ferment of the academy has had little if any relation to the public sphere, and certainly has exercised no tangible influence on the conduct of foreign policy, whether in the US or elsewhere. While I can do little more than gesture at purportedly radical critiques encapsulated under cultural studies, the place of the university in modern life, and the relations between the academy and society, the disciplinary structure of modern knowledge, especially of the social sciences, is subjected in Chapter 4, and in portions of the following chapters, to more rigorous scrutiny. History has become the most widely accepted public voice of the social sciences: consider that there isn't a group of people, whether constituted in racial, ethnic, or linguistic terms, that wishes to be viewed as lacking a history. The practitioners of "radical" histories, which are attentive to the voices of the marginalized and the invisible, and partake of more recent analytical and investigative methods to deconstruct dominant historical narratives, have not paused to consider whether their own triumph does not signify the rather totalizing ascendancy of history. Is history the only language that remains to those forgotten and living at the margins?

A fundamental concern of this book, following on the earlier discussions of political developments and modern knowledge systems, is the future of dissent; and Gandhi, as Chapters 5 and 6 suggest, is supremely iconic of what I would view as an emancipatory politics of the future. There are a great many truisms about how the dissenters of yesterday are the stockbrokers of today, but none of the prevalent formulations should be allowed to obfuscate the centrality of dissent in the imagination of any society. Regrettably, the possibilities of dissent in our times have dangerously narrowed, and we are all compelled to be dissenters in similar ways. Though identity politics, for example, was born in the cauldron of cultural difference, it is extraordinary to what degree advocates of identity politics, whether moved by considerations of race, gender, sexual preference, or (seldom) class, advance claims on similar epistemological grounds. On a different plane, when a civilization like that of India, whose principal architect of independence from British rule was an exponent of non-violence, reduces itself to the lesser status of a nation-state, in the expectation that the explosion of nuclear devices, most tragically on a day celebrated as the birthday of the Buddha, will catapult it on to the world stage, then clearly even less can be expected from nations without those cultural resources that an ancient civilization can husband.

Unless dissent is couched in the rational, civilized, constitutional, and adult-like language recognized by Western parliamentarians and social commentators, it is condemned to oblivion. Gandhi recognized this, when he abandoned the placard, petition, and parliamentary speech in favor of another apparatus of dialogue and resistance, and sought to persuade the British, as well as his antagonistic Indian interlocutors, that fasting, spinning, non-cooperation, and even walking could be construed as forms of dissent. Modernity insists that even the dissenters from modernity should speak in the language of modernity, just as practitioners of women's studies, environmental studies, and gay studies found that they had to stitch themselves into the institutional fabric of the academy, with its attendant paraphernalia, in order to obtain a hearing and not be viewed with more than just a tinge of mockery. It is perfectly possible, and more than likely, that exponents of "queer theory" are also card-carrying members of the National Rifle Association: so much for the dissenters in America. Similarly, though the nation-state is increasingly under assault as a mechanical form of political existence which bears little relation to the cultural histories of many of the peoples upon whom it has been imposed, all its obituaries are premature, as the aspirations of those people without a nation-state, whether Palestinians, Sikhs, Kurds, or the Basque, so starkly suggest. Even these dissenters have been reduced to agitating in the language of a political science which recognizes the nation-state, and its numerous variations (such as associations of nation-states), as the only authentic expressions of political intent or cultural longing. To speak of dissenting futures, then, is to explore, lest our options should be decisively foreclosed, the conditions for radical and emancipatory dissent. As is implicit in my arguments, we shall have to be more attentive to critiques of modernity, more nuanced in our deliberations on the much celebrated ideas of tolerance, democracy, and freedom, and more engaged with what one philosopher, James Carse, has described as "infinite games."[4] In the life and teachings of Gandhi, the consummate player of infinite games, lie some clues about the conditions for dissent.

To speak of dissenting futures, as I do, is to speak of the politics of the future. The days of MAD (mutually assured destruction) seem to lie in the distant past when the "evil empire" was still a force in world politics, but the genocidal mentality behind the thinking of nuclear hawks is equally incarnated in the philosophy of non-nuclear nuclearism. Since nuclear warfare carries with it such immense sanctions, the perpetrators of genocide have embraced new forms of warfare, embodied for the first time in the aerial pulverization of Yugoslavia by US-led NATO forces, that are also predicated on the elimination of all casualties except those on the side of the enemy, the complete avoidance of face-to-face combat, the thorough extinction of civil society, and the elimination of all possibilities of retaliation. Never before in history, except during the atomic bombing of Hiroshima and Nagasaki, has there been a conjuncture of all these circumstances, and Kosovo points the gruesome way to the Great Power Mode of Warfare and Governance in the future. This is only the partial meaning of the "peace of Kosovo"; in the Kosovo agreement one can see the seeds of the reinvention of Europe, the center of the world to which, in Hegelian fashion, all history is fated to return.

I have previously adverted to the growing importance of sanctions, which are illustrative of the fact that international governance will surely continue to evolve new forms. Sanctions are a characteristic feature of the governance of late modernity, since they are created in the kiln of grave inequity. Like most other exchanges in our times, sanctions work unilaterally and unidirectionally. They are imposed against states that are deemed to be outside the pale of humanity, but it is inconceivable that they could be exercised, as perhaps they ought to be, against the United States, which has a prison population of 2 million, more homicides by gun in one day than Japan has in an entire year (a bad year at that), and a proven track record of supporting dictatorships, death squads, and brutal military regimes in nearly every part of the world. Sanctions have this characteristic feature of modernity too: like development, which often takes its toll of humans in piecemeal fashion, and allows them to be chalked up as the victims of food shortages, anomie, displacement, homelessness, joblessness, and landlessness, so sanctions kill slowly but surely, and the dead can be enumerated as victims of malnourishment, starvation, infectious diseases, and invented underdevelopment.

Sanctions, then, compel us into a consideration of the grounds for a truly emancipatory politics of plurality and democracy. Our thinking at this juncture is at considerable remove from being ecological. The word "ecology" is derived from "economy," and economy is not what economists have made of it, namely mathematical models to which the world should render subservience, but rather "household management," and the husbanding of resources. To think ecologically is to think wisely, to be cognizant of the resources available at our disposal, to be sensitive to plurality, and to accept the principle that freedom is indivisible. Far-sighted as the policies of the Sierra Club, for instance, appear to be, they might only be destructive for much of the rest of the world – the ultimate example of this being the policy which advocates the zero cutting of trees in the US, but does not stress the reduction of consumption levels in the US. (It will no longer be coal that has to be carried to Newcastle, but wood to wooded New England.) Nor is this far from being analogous to American-style war, where, as I have suggested before, any number of casualties on the enemy's side is acceptable, so long as one's own soldiers do not have to be brought back in body bags. The problems of inequity and inequality are not yet sufficiently addressed by ecological discourses – construing "ecological" here in the widest sense, as stretching beyond biodiversity and diversity to the very survival of cultural plurality and the restoration of the word "economy" to its proper usages. If a small island nation, Gandhi once remarked with characteristic foresight, had to bleed the world to satiate the needs of its people, then how much exploitation would be required to bring the needs of the many millions more inhabiting India [or China] to the same level? That levels of consumption in the United States exceed those of the developing world by a ratio of 40:1 is only one of the sad verities of our times, and no amount of American philanthropy can even minutely compensate the world for the displays of excess in which the country revels. To think ecologically is to understand that while some parts of the world are undoubtedly underdeveloped, if one is at all inclined to that modality of thinking, it is nonetheless the overdeveloped parts of the world which ought to give greater cause for anxiety. The rich, not the poor, are the problem for humankind and the earth's resources in the long run.

Neither multiculturalism nor free elections, and most certainly not the ecological movements of the West, can stand in place for a more complex and less ethnocentric conception of ecological plurality. While it is desirable to allow a multiplicity of voices, this can only add to the "chic" of the West, particularly when these voices speak in the same register. The language of history, to take one example, has submerged ahistoricist discourses to such an extent that "the peoples without history" are poised now to become peoples without myths.[5] Though, to appropriate T. S. Eliot's language, the modern world is in agreement that a sense of history is an inescapable element of freedom, it may well turn out to be the inescapable condition of servitude. As I argue with greater or lesser force throughout this book, to question the dominant frameworks of knowledge is to open the way to other forms of engagement – the Western "local" with the Gandhian "global," the historicist with the ahistoricist, the finite game with the infinite game. The necessary oppositions are not between tradition and modernity, or between particularism and universalism; rather, the intent is to probe how one set of universalisms, associated with the trajectory of Western reason, came to establish their predominance, and what are those competing universalisms which can claim our allegiance. It is a truism of the 1960s that the activists were inspired by the slogan, "Think globally, act locally": it still resonates strongly with liberal and progressive forces around the world. However, it is the burden of this book that in that slogan lies the charter of our oppression, and freedom from oppression moves us to the realization that we are bound to "Think locally, act globally." This ambition, rather than any predisposition towards postmodernism, which like my friend Ziauddin Sardar I am inclined to view as another wonderful thing for the West,[6] but with little in it to instruct those civilizations where the ground reality and ethical thinking always inclined towards plurality,[7] accounts in part for what might occasionally appear as the disjunctive elements of my writing or the arrangement of this book, with perhaps seemingly odd juxtapositions of Gandhi and Bill Gates, the ecology of equality with the economics of inequality.

I had nearly completed the first draft of this book, and most of the introduction, when the terrorist attacks of September 11th upon the World Trade Center and the Pentagon transpired. Since the subject matter of the book has every relation to many of the issues that arise out of these events, I thought it prudent, indeed necessary, to attach a long postscript. It is my view that the arguments on offer in this book acquire all the more urgency in light of these events and, more significantly, the copious commentary that has issued forth from nearly every country in the last few months. That the world could have been indifferent to the plight of Afghanistan for so long, awakening to the turmoil of that region only when the Empire itself was viewed as being under an invasion, is in itself an illustration of the problems of "dissent" and "categories" with which my book is so concerned. As I point out in the postscript, Afghanistan never fell into the categories through which American scholarship seeks to appropriate or merely understand the world: neither the Middle Eastern specialists, nor the smaller fraternity of experts working on South Asia, ever had any interest in Afghanistan. Suffice to say only that the postscript, while it can be read independently, should also be viewed as an inextricable part of this book and as having a considerable bearing upon its central arguments, suggestions, and assaults upon the dominant frameworks of Western knowledge.

1 Reckoning with the Millennium

The twenty-first century is upon us. While the greater number of millennium-mongers squandered their energies on the "Y2K" problem, often indulging in more esoteric apocalyptic visions, and others were detained by the more pedestrian, though not meaningless, exercise of determining whether 1 January 2000 or 1 January 2001 marked the decisive moment in this turn of history, few paused to consider how "millennium" and even "century" came to constitute such ubiquitous categories of our experience. Like a great many other things, the categories by which time is calculated – hour, week, month, year, decade, century, and millennium – have been naturalized, but there is nothing self-evident about how a week of seven days became the unit by means of which time flows into our lives, or about the calendar that dominates much of the modern world system. Almost nothing is as cliched as the observation that "we are all the slaves of time," though that "we" is at times thought to exclude those of the non-Western world whose management skills at time still fall far short of minimally desirable standards; moreover, this enslavement not only does not evoke much resistance, it is welcomed as the most decisive marker of progress in human affairs and the orderliness of a world always on the verge of slipping into chaos and the chasm of discontent.

The schedule and calendar rule most lives, but there is nothing inevitable about this course of history. It is only in the mid-eighteenth century, with the emergence of industrialization and the factory clock, that the tyrannical discipline of time became a reality for the working classes. Another 100 years were to elapse before the standardization of time was achieved in the West itself, while in much of the rest of the world the Gregorian calendar was becoming paramount, though the "natives" had still to learn the lessons of the clock. If by some accounts the inhabitants of the underdeveloped countries still do not make good use of their time, they are nonetheless largely captive to the norms of the Western calendar. Birthday celebrations, for instance, are one of the most iconic measures of how far modernity and secularism have crept into the sensibility of all cultures, though doubtless the birthday party has been molded and transformed by the idioms of local cultural practices. Doubtless, too, some cultures have retained their own calendars, but from the point of view of the moderns, that is no more than the churlish resistance of tradition-bound nativists and primordialists, or – considering the profound association of many calendrical systems with religion – an attempt to retain a religious space within the secular domain of modernity.

Having entered the new millennium, should we not stop to ask for whom it is that the millennium struck and continues to strike, and by what sleight of hand the Christian millennium became the benchmark for all peoples? What meaning can the millennium possibly have for (say) Muslims, if not to remind them that the entire world now lives in the thralldom of the West, and that no one is safe from the ambitions, to use that phrase fraught with ominous consequences, of the world's sole superpower? Is it the imminence of the new millennium that, in the 1990s, appeared to have generated a certain melancholia in Islamic countries, and which formed the substratum of unease and anxiety among Muslims, whether in Malaysia, Indonesia, India, Pakistan, Afghanistan, Bangladesh, Algeria, or elsewhere? A thousand years ago, a large swathe of the world, from the Atlantic extending across North Africa and the western Mediterranean to west Asia and Afghanistan, was under the sway of Muslim rulers. Today, by contrast, Western domination is supreme, and the derisive term "Islamic fundamentalism" has become commonplace.

Or, to ask questions in a different vein, though we have long understood how European powers effected spatial colonization, are we sufficiently cognizant of the dimensions of temporal colonization?[1] The recent postcolonial incursions into museum studies have alerted us to the exhibitionary complex of colonialism, and the epistemological significance and political thrust of the various "world fairs" that began to proliferate in Europe and North America in the second half of the nineteenth century, but much less has been written on the manner in which museums colonize time. The railroad timetable, the Gregorian calendar, the weekly schedule, the factory clock, and the office timecard inserted themselves with considerable virulence and bloodthirstiness into the culture of colonized peoples, and yet the imperialism of time may well have more deleterious consequences in the years to come. The homogenization of time has not only facilitated the emergence of globalization and a worldwide culture of corporate business and management distinguished only by its extraordinary mediocrity and greed, it has also greatly assisted in narrowing the visions of the future. To speak of the resistance to clock and corporate time, which betoken a mentality nowhere better expressed than in the predictably American formulation that "time is money," is to point not merely to what some may deride as utopian thoughts, but to a cultural politics of time that would enable us to reterritorialize temporality.

MONOLITHIC TEMPORALITY

It is with remarkable prescience that Lewis Mumford, more than 50 years ago, observed that

> the clock, not the steam engine, is the key machine of the industrial age ... In its relationship to determinable quantities of energy, to standardization, to automatic action, and finally to its own special product, accurate timing, the clock has been the foremost machine in modern technic; and at each period it has remained in the lead: it marks a perfection toward which other machines aspire.[2]

Our sensibilities in late modernity are marked by an extraordinary but deadened awareness of time: it has become habitual to speak of having no time, of being too busy, and of being harried by time. Though industrialization and the age of cyberspace are associated with time-saving devices, the overwhelming number of people appear to be extremely short on time, and in countries such as the United States, the working week appears to have become longer for the laboring and corporate class alike. Juliet Schor's acclaimed study, *The Overworked American*, suggests that the working day over the last 50 years has become increasingly longer, and in the two decades between 1970 and 1990, an average of nine hours of extra work were added to most working lives each year.[3]

"What kind of rule is this?" asks Sebastian de Grazia: "The more timesaving machinery there is, the more pressed a person is for time."[4] What does it mean to save time? Or, indeed, to waste time? Is time saved when a phone conversation is conducted from the wheel of a car, and are those who resolutely fail to embrace this innovation thereby wasting time? Is leisure time wasted, or time well-spent? And if well-spent, when does it shade into squandered time, idleness, anomie? What kind of investment does saved time represent, and why is it that this investment has had, demonstrably, such strange and poor returns? More so than in any previous age, lives appear to be tyrannized by clocks, office and airline schedules, and calendars. The story of temporal colonization has been told inadequately. "The invention of the mechanical clock was one of a number of major advances that turned Europe," David Landes remarks, "from a weak, peripheral, highly vulnerable outpost of Mediterranean civilization into a hegemonic aggressor."[5] The pervasive assumption of technological determinism behind this assessment should not obscure the fact that Europe at this juncture of history displayed considerably more interest in the scientific and mechanical keeping of time than most of the Asian, African, and other cultures that Europeans encountered, and both timekeeping and calendrics were among the many domains of social activity in which they claimed superiority. The infamous "lazy native" of colonial discourse, it need not be said, had no use for the watch and seldom kept time, and the clock-towers that are now found in the towns and cities of many formerly colonized nations were built under the dispensation of colonial regimes. European powers colonized, penalized, and traumatized their own dissenters and religious, ethnic, racial, and intellectual Others before proceeding to colonize the non-Western world, and in the matter of how time was reckoned with, the homogenization of the Western world was similarly to precede the entry of a uniform clock-time in the rest of the world.

The Pattern of the Week

Though seconds, minutes, hours, and days – the rising and setting of the sun furnishing the divisions of day and night – constitute the basic units of time, the pre-eminent centrality of the week to the modern organization of time, odd as it is, must be underscored. Patterns of life are generally framed around the week: think of the weekly shopping day, the weekly magazine, the working week (and the ensual of Monday blues), the weekend, the weekly change of films, and so on. It is the weekly schedule which determines the shape of appointments. A year may equally be thought of as 12 months, or 52 weeks; but since recurrent events, such as winter, spring, and summer holidays, or school terms, seldom coincide with an entire calendrical month, one is more likely to think of a one-week vacation or a school term that lasts 10 or 15 weeks. Sociologist Pritrim A. Sorokin has written,

Imagine for a moment that the week suddenly disappeared. What a havoc would be created in our time organization, in our behavior, in the co-ordination and synchronization of collective activities and social life, and especially in our time apprehension ... We think in week units; we apprehend time in week units; we localize the events and activities in week units; we co-ordinate our behavior according to the "week"; we live and feel and plan and wish in "week" terms. It is one of the most important points of our "orientation" in time and social reality.[6]

The precise origin of the seven-day week has never been established with absolute certainty. It is sometimes conjectured that the seven-day week may have been inspired by the lunar cycle, which in fact is not a 28-day or four-week cycle. In the Judaeo-Christian world, the Creation is described as having taken place over six days; "And on the seventh day God finished his work which he had done, and he rested on the seventh day from all his work which he had done." Thus the seventh day, which God "blessed," was "hallowed" because 'on it God rested from all his work which he had done in creation' (Genesis 2:1–3). The observance of the holy day, the Sabbath, was to be the sign that would differentiate the Jews from the non-Jews (Ezekiel 20:12), and it was to assist them in the preservation of their Jewishness amidst the hostile gentiles, particularly during the period of Exile. When Christianity arose out of Judaism, the seven-day cycle was not dispensed with, but rather the Christians tried to mark out their own sphere by eventually electing Sunday rather than Saturday as the day of the Sabbath. Initially, as a persecuted minority, Christians sought to establish a day when they could all congregate in common.

That the Christian Sabbath was deliberately established on Sunday, to help distinguish the Christians from the Jews, is demonstrated by the history of the conflict over Easter, the most important moveable feast in Christianity. In the Eastern churches, the celebration of Easter coincided with the Jewish celebration of Passover, and at the meeting of the First Council of Nicaea in AD 325, it was declared a heresy to celebrate Easter on the same day as Passover. By ruling that Easter be celebrated on the Sunday following the full moon, the two auspicious occasions were severed from each other, since Passover is always celebrated on a full moon. Similarly, though the Nativity, or birth of Christ, was originally celebrated on January 6th, it was only in AD 354 that Christmas was first celebrated on

December 25th, though the choice of that day was scarcely innocuous. Since Epiphany, which marks the appearance of Jesus as the Christ to the gentiles, was also celebrated on January 6th, the Church came to the realization that it was very unlikely that both the birth of Christ and Epiphany had occurred on the same day. In choosing December 25th as Christ's birthday, the Church could not claim to be motivated by biblical evidence or customary practice, if only because the time of the year when Christ was born is nowhere indicated; but since December 25th marked the celebration of winter solstice, it was a day on which the Church marked its determined opposition to pagan rites.[7] In the nexus between religion and the politics of temporality, however, Christianity is scarcely unique. When, in the seventh century, Islam was founded, again the primacy of the seven-day week was not questioned, but Friday, rather than Saturday or Sunday, was chosen as the holy day of the week; indeed, Saturday and Sunday were seen as days of bad omens.[8] In this manner, the Prophet sought to signify the singularity of Islam, and weld the adherents of the faith into a distinct community. If in Christianity Sunday marks the principal day of church attendance, in Islamic countries the importance of Friday is perhaps even more salient: cities with large Muslim populations give pride of place to the Friday Mosque. The singularity of Friday in Islamic countries, it has less often been noticed, resides in the circumstance that it is not, unlike the Jewish Sabbath and Christian Sundays, a day of rest as such, but rather a day on which Muslims are called forth to offer public worship at noon.[9]

Elsewhere, for instance among the Hindus, the seven-day week may have arisen out of the seven planets of ancient astrology – Mercury, Jupiter, Venus, Saturn, the Sun, the Moon, Mars – and it is altogether possible that even in the Western world, the astrological influence was predominant. As one scholar has noted, "the Indian days of the week (*varas*) had already matched their European counterparts many centuries before regular contact between India and the West was established,"[10] and today only places which are outside the orbit of any of the world's major religions, or have arrived at a particular accommodation between a world religion and a vernacular tradition of faith, are likely to have a conception of social organization of life in which the notion of the seven-day week does not play a critical role. However, speaking historically, the week has not always comprised seven days. In many societies, the week generally revolved around the market day, and in societies as varied as those of Peru,

Colombia, Indochina, southern China, and Mesoamerica, the week could extend anywhere from three to ten days. Among the Khasis of northeast India, the market was held every eighth day, and the week was accordingly seen as consisting of eight days; in Togo, the market was held every six days, which became the length of the week.[11]

In the modern period, there have been two notable, but strikingly unsuccessful, attempts to alter the seven-day week, both inspired by the desire to escape what was deemed to be the nefarious influence of bourgeois Christianity. The revolutionary calendar introduced by the French Republic, which marked the year 1792 as Year One, was composed of twelve months, and each month was made up of three ten-day periods of time called decades. This calendar eliminated the traditional Sabbath day, and the weekly rest day, Sunday, was replaced by one rest day every ten days. Much later, the Bolshevik regime, in September 1929, instituted the five-day – and then the six-day – week, in the hope that the illusion of a shorter working week would spur the laboring classes to increased productivity. Both calendar reforms failed, and in France and the Soviet Union alike the seven-day week was restored. It is a mark of the resilience of the seven-day week that the shipwrecked Robinson Crusoe, fearful that he would lose his "Reckoning of Time for want of Books and Pen and Ink," and "even forget the Sabbath Day from the working Days," used his knife to etch on to wood the date of his arrival upon the island of which he imagined himself to be the sole inhabitant, and then for every day made a notch with his knife, "'every Seventh Notch" being "as long again as the rest." When, at long last, Crusoe encountered a native, he named the man "Friday" after the day of the week when he chanced upon him.[12]

The Christian Era and the Gregorian Calendar

The present primacy of the Gregorian calendar has obscured the recognition that different calendrical systems have vied with each other over the greater part of history, and that the Gregorian calendar, a product of the Christian West, has only in the relatively recent past established a nearly worldwide hegemony. Not to speak of the civilizations of China and India, which developed various calendars and complex systems for the measurement of time over long periods, and were fertilized by contact with each other as well as with the Mediterranean, Europe, Africa, and Asia, even the Incas, Mayas, and Aztecs, which developed in isolation from other civilizations, certainly that of the West, invented elaborate systems of

_`,

timekeeping.[13] The first Egyptian calendar, which remarkably had 365¼ days, dates back to 4236 BC, which is also the earliest recorded date in history. Some recent estimates still speak of 40 different calendars presently in use, if only for strictly religious reasons, around the world. Even this number may be vastly understated, when we consider that the Calendar Reform Committee, appointed by Jawaharlal Nehru in 1952, found 30 distinct and well-developed calendars in use in India alone.[14]

As with most other things which the West has succeeded in implanting on to the modern consciousness, largely through the force of colonization, the Gregorian calendar had the advantage of simplicity. The story about the origin of the Gregorian calendar has been told often enough,[15] but this story is usually told in the heroic mode, as the triumph of science, reason, and common-sense alike, not as a narrative which left a gaping hole – shall we say a zero – which might explain why there continues to be an enormous hullabaloo every 100 years about whether a new century begins in the year that ends with a zero or the year that ends with one. Truly speaking, the story – though seldom in its most widely accepted form – also begins not with Pope Gregory XIII, who reformed the Julian [after Julius Caesar] calendar in 1582, but with two Popes who preceded him by a millennium. In the late fifth century, the monk Dionysius Exiguus was retained by Pope Gelasius to translate documents in the papal archive. Some years later, as Dionysius worked under Pope John I, it occurred to him that the old numbering system, Anno Diocletiani, named after the Roman Emperor Diocletian, who had acquired notoriety as a persecutor of Christians,[16] ought to be dispensed with as it rendered implicit homage to an enemy of Christendom. Dionysius marked the new era as 1 Anno Domini, the year (as he incorrectly supposed) of the birth of Jesus: this is the least that could have been done for the founder of a great world religion.

Since history, from Dionysius' standpoint, which the West in its most eminent representatives would share, only effectively began when Christ came into this world, Dionysius was wholly indifferent to the years before the birth of Christ. Not less alarmingly, Dionysius began the new era with one rather than zero – perhaps not altogether surprising, considering that the Romans lacked "zero" in their numbering system and that the idea of zero was appropriated by Western Christendom from India, by way of the Arabs, sometime in the early part of the second Christian millennium. Dionysius was not alone in being encumbered: 200 years later, the Venerable Bede, author of the *Ecclesiastical History of the English People*, initiated the idea of counting the years before the birth of Christ, and in like fashion he began with 1 BC.[17] There may be, in the West's ignorance and repudiation of the zero, more than the usual tale of mathematical backwardness: the word for zero in Sanskrit is *sunyata*, or "nothingness," call it also emptiness, and almost nothing terrifies the West as much as the thought of emptiness. The new worlds encountered by the conquistadors, and later by the puritans and rejects of industrializing Britain who made their way to Australia and elsewhere in the Pacific, were construed as *terra nullis*, as barren lands that could only derive their meaning from the productive labor of the Europeans. So perhaps it is that the purported nothingness of zero strings together a story whose narrative elements include the Gregorian calendar, colonialism, and the depredations caused by the modern keepers of time.

While the Julian calendar continued to be improved upon, the pressing problem of calculating the dates of Easter was not easily resolved. March 21st had been fixed, at the First Council of Nicaea in AD 325, as the date of the vernal equinox, though the true equinox had regressed from March 21st to an earlier day in the month. By the late sixteenth century, the traditional association between Easter and Spring was becoming increasingly difficult to sustain, since the equinox had shifted by ten days.[18] Pope Gregory created a commission to suggest reforms of the Julian Calendar, and its distinguished members decided to act on a suggestion first proffered by Luigi Lilio, also known as Aloisius Lilius, a lecturer at the University of Perugia. Lilius recommended that ten days be excised from the calendar, either all at once or by removing the leap day every four years over a period of four decades. The wise commissioners chose the former course, and by terms of Gregory's Papal Bull of February 24th 1582, the ten days inclusive from October 5th to the 14th were expunged from the calendar. Considering the imperial arrogance behind former Papal Bulls, such as those which had divided the world between Spain and Portugal, or mandated Christians to bring, through none too gentle means, the light of Jesus' teaching to heathens and barbarians,[19] the expulsion of ten days from the calendar appears to be a lesser ethnocentric crime than the expulsion of the Jews and the decapitation of the indigenous people of the Americas. But did the commissioners and Gregory think that the ten days of October had ceased to vanish only for Christians, or for non-Christians as well? How well does it augur for late modernity's notions of ecumenism and pluralism, or for the claims to universalism behind science, that the calendar now most widely in use globally for civil purposes was hoisted upon the world by men acting from narrow sectarian interests and with a fear of the void?

Gregory stipulated as well that January 1st would mark the standard official beginning of the new year. By the 1563 edict of King Charles IX, this had already become the practice in France since 1566: thus the strong association of Easter with the new year was broken.[20] At first the calendrical reform met with acceptance only in Catholic Europe, not extending to non-Catholic Europe until after 1700. Protestant Europe might not have been amiss in thinking that Gregory, a staunch defender of the Counter Reformation, whose Christian conduct can be gauged by his bacchanalian celebration of the St. Bartholomew's Day Massacre, was attempting to impose the Catholic world order upon all of Christendom.[21] Yet, it is quite likely that Protestants may have been eager to reform the calendar: if the traditional narratives about the Protestant work-ethic and entrepreneurial drive are not without some merit, they must have found objectionable in the Julian calendar the large number of saints' days, days of rest and leisure. By the early 1700s, Norway, Denmark, and Dutch and German states had succumbed to the new calendar; when England followed suit in 1751–52, the Gregorian calendar was extended to its colonies in North America. One scholar, who has made a lifetime study of the sociology of time, remarks that the first two non-Christian countries which accepted the Gregorian calendar were Japan and Egypt in 1873 and 1875, respectively, and both were then engaged upon a radical course of "modernization and Westernization;" ever since then the adoption of the Gregorian or European calendar has been seen as a sign of a society's willingness to embrace Western modernity.[22] However, the Gregorian calendar had been introduced into the non-Western world earlier: in India, for instance, it was the calendar used by the East India Company, and by the end of the eighteenth century, a considerable portion of India was under the Company's rule.

To speak of the Gregorian calendar, as does P. W. Wilson, "as international, inter-religious, inter-occupational and inter-racial,"[23] is to belie its origins in Christianity, colonization, and the cant of modernization. One locus of resistance to the Gregorian calendar, as might be expected, is religion: thus, making an eloquent plea for the Jewish calendar as opposed to a Christian calendar, one Jewish commentator has written that the soul of Israel .. is anchored in its time ... Every people has its own time, which ties it to its land and place, and in which its history and holidays are embedded ... Every people that has tried to separate itself from its time has disappeared and is no longer remembered among the living.[24]

The Muslim month of fasting still bears no relation to the Gregorian calendar, and Indians of different religious persuasions – Buddhists, Jains, Hindus, Muslims, among others – mark time with a variety of calendars, though the use of the *Vikram* (*Samvat*) calendar is not confined exclusively to matters of religious provenance; nor is it, in principle, a Hindu calendar, though doubtless its users would have been Hindus. Indeed, it is to reconcile the different Indian calendars in use that Akbar, whose propagation of a new syncretic faith, *Din-Ilahi*, is well-known, also initiated – two years after the Gregorian calendar was drawn up, in the eighteenth year of his own reign, 992 years after the flight of Mohammed, and 1584 years into the Christian era – a new synthetic calendar, the *Tarikh-Ilahi*. This new calendar, Allah's own, drew upon the mainly solar calendars prevalent among the Hindus, and henceforth Akbar's *firmans* (royal edicts) bore the dates of the *Tarikh* as well as *Hegira*.

The sixteenth century of the politics of Christianity aside, the Gregorian calendar has an inextricable relationship to the Christian era, a system of dating which was introduced only in AD 525 [*anno Domini*] or thereabouts, and spread to most of Europe between the eleventh and fifteenth centuries. Once one recalls that the Venerable Bede introduced the notion of BC [Before Christ] more than 100 years after Mohammed had founded a new faith, and the armies of Islam had made swift advances into the Iberian peninsula, it becomes necessary to ask: what necessity was there of thinking conceptually of the years before Christ? If history began, so to speak, with the birth of Christ, why should Bede have bothered at all with what transpired before Christ? The conception of BC was an afterthought: if such events as the flight of Mohammed from Mecca to Medina in AD 622, which marks the beginning of the Islamic era, were to be restored to their proper insignificance, and the Muslim calendar was to be stripped of its claims to a competing universal history, it was perforce necessary to introduce a category to which Islam could anachronistically be confined. The Prophet, it could not be denied, was born in the sixth century, but he was spiritually housed, in the Christian reckoning, in the period before the advent of Christ, in the period of the prophets. Islam belonged, as it were, to the past of Christianity, when in fact it was alarmingly showing itself as the future of Christianity. The modern representations of Islamic fundamentalism and the medieval nature of Islam all belong to this history. We can be certain that in the hullabaloo over the coming of the millennium, it was presumed that the history of Christianity serves as the template for the history of the world.

The Standardization of Time

It is only a little more than a hundred years ago that the synchronization of time was achieved. At that time, Britain was the regnant world power, and it is not surprising that in 1884, Greenwich, just outside London, was chosen by the International Meridian Conference as the location for zero longitude and so came to acquire temporal sovereignty. All timepieces would henceforth have to be set to Greenwich Mean Time (GMT), from which all other temporal standards – Indian Standard Time (IST), Pacific Standard Time (PST), and so on – are derived. France was then the other great imperialist power, and considering that the French were inclined to view Paris as the center of the civilized world, it is predictable that France resisted this attempt at the centralization of timekeeping. Only in 1912, when Paris hosted the International Conference on Time, did Greenwich Mean Time become accepted unequivocally as the universal timekeeper; at least the French could concede defeat with dignity, on their own soil.[25]

This homogenization of time would have seemed anything but inevitable or natural to most people around the world, though in 1848 British railroad companies had set their clocks to Greenwich, where an observatory had been built in the seventeenth century. If one considers the United States alone, by the 1850s, judging from Thoreau's *Walden*, trains were an inextricable part of the American landscape: "I watch the passage of the morning cars with the same feeling that I do the rising of the sun, which is hardly more regular," wrote Thoreau, adding:

> The startings and arrivals of the cars are now the epochs in the village day. They go and come with such regularity and precision, and their whistle can be heard so far, that the farmers set their clocks by them, and thus one well-conducted institution regulates a whole country.[26]

But the punctuality of trains was not to be confused with the standardization of time. A train might leave on time, but by which time did one attempt to determine its departure and arrival? As late as 1870 there were about 70 informal time zones in the country, and a passenger undertaking a train journey from Washington, D.C. to San Francisco would have had to reset his watch at least 70 times if he wished to keep abreast of the local time at every moment.[27] The pressure to standardize time came from weather forecasters, businessmen, and even more so from railroad companies, whose passengers and business clients alike complained of the difficulties in deciphering and interpreting railroad timetables when there was no one uniform standard of time. Finally, in 1883, American railroad companies agreed upon the establishment of the four time zones that are still in use, but not without raising public ire. The *Washington Post* editorialized on the importance of the standardization of time as "scarcely second to the reformation of the calendar by Julius Caesar, and later by Pope Gregory XIII."[28] True to their name, the railroad companies, then the supreme embodiment of industrialization and entrepreneurial self-aggrandizement, railroaded their way into the temporal precincts of the human spirit, and so paved the way for the elimination of alternative conceptions – local, mythic, pastoral, theistic, and countless others – of time.

Disciplinary time

International Business Machines, better known to the world through its acronym IBM, may well be credited with inventing "computer time." However, in its earlier incarnation as the International Time Recording Company, IBM may have played a yet more critical role in inaugurating the modern age of what may be termed *panopticon industrial efficiency*. The panopticon, to follow its earliest theorist Jeremy Bentham, refers to that modality of surveillance whereby all those under surveillance, such as prisoners, are placed under the watchful eye of the jailer, but cannot in turn watch him.[29] In 1894, the International Time Recording Company introduced – what else? – the time recording system, and in less than 15 years all its competitors had been eliminated. Each employee who came to work punched a time card at the time of his arrival and departure, and the company sold its product to businesses with the argument that its clocks would "save money, enforce discipline and add to the productive time." A 1914 brochure commended the company's product to the attention of businesses with the observation that "the time recorded induces punctuality by impressing the value of time on each individual." It is not merely time that would be reined in and regulated; the very actions of men were to be synchronized by time devices, better keepers of time than men. Another publicity piece stated boldly: "There is nothing so fatal to the discipline of the plant, nor so disastrous to its smooth and profitable working as to have a body of men irregular in appearance, who come late and go out at odd times;" the time recorder would assist management "to weed out these undesirables."[30] Yet it is clearly more than a desire to have men of reasonable appearance and demeanor working for them which animated companies that embraced the new time recording system: they assumed, of course, that the working classes, who alone were subjected to the indignity of this mechanism, were prone to dishonesty and deception, and that men and women from ignoble backgrounds were claiming compensation for more hours than they had actually worked.

Though the time recording system could, with proper surveillance, prevent employees from lying about their working hours, it could not stop the pilferage of time from the job itself. Workers could choose to resist through more subtle means, for instance by showing a disinclination towards optimum productivity, or disguising idleness or a resistance to the gospel of extreme efficiency by pretending that what in reality was a three-hour job could not be completed in less than four hours. Thus, it is with the ambition of introducing scientific management into the industrial process that Frederick W. Taylor created the most significant upheaval in the modern workplace. "With scientific management, as formulated by Taylor in 1895," Daniel Bell has written, "we pass beyond the old, rough computations of the division of labor and move into the division of time itself."[31] Taylor introduced the stopwatch and calibrated the movements of workers down to fractions of a second, so that inefficient actions could be eliminated and productivity be maximized. Each person's work was planned out beforehand, and he was given detailed instructions about the manner in which the work was to be accomplished, and the "exact time" that would be allowed for the completion of the assigned task. The worker, stripped of any capacity to influence the outcome of his or her work, was to be reduced to a mere cog in the machine: "in the new scientifically managed factory," Jeremy Rifkin has observed, "the worker's mind was severed from his body and handed over to the management."[32]

It is these Taylorite principles that informed the compilation of standardized times for clerical tasks by the Systems and Procedures Association, to wit: opening and closing of a file drawer, 0.04 minutes; opening and closing of a folder, 0.04 minutes; opening and closing the center drawer of a desk, 0.026 and 0.027 minutes, respectively; getting up from a chair, 0.033 minutes; turning in a swivel chair, 0.009 minutes, and so on.[33] Even as Taylor was devising his principles of scientific management and enabling the standardization of time, the rigors of clock-time were being introduced to the colonized regions of the world. More than one historian of Bengal has written about *chakri*, or the clerical job, which embraced a disciplined notion of time, and towards which Indian men had perforce to gravitate if they wished to find a place for themselves in the newly established administrative and trading offices following the consolidation of British rule in India after the rebellion of 1857–58. "Time acquired new meaning and disciplinary authority through an equally abrupt entry of clocks and watches," writes Sumit Sarkar, "and there was among some a sense of moving forward in consonance with its linear progress."[34] Sarkar even points to literary works which took the disciplinary regime imposed by time-keeping Europeans as their central subject matter: thus in the 1885 Bengali play, *Kerani-carit*, one of the new breed of office workers complains that "we lose the day's salaries if we reach office a minute late ... half the salary goes on fines ... there is not a single gap in our day's routine."[35]

In Africa, the colonial encounter produced similarly oppressive notions of disciplinary time, and in Chinua Achebe's novel *Arrow of God* (1964), one of the more memorable scenes takes place around an appointment that the priest Ezulu has with the colonial District Officer. When the priest fails to turn up on time, the District Officer orders that upon his arrival he should be placed in jail; but before that can transpire, the District Officer himself has to be carried out with a high temperature.[36] Whatever the importance of clock-time in regulating factory labor and disciplining the laboring classes in the metropolitan and industrial centers of Europe,[37] in the colonies time was seen as effecting an altogether necessary disciplinary function upon lazy and unruly natives. It was perforce necessary to give the native a hard time; but to take a leaf from Dickens' *Hard Times*, the association between hardened notions of time and the machinery of wealth was not lost upon the native:

"You see, my friend," Mr. Bounderby put in, "we are the kind of people who know the value of time, and you are the kind of people who don't know the value of time." "I have not," retorted Mr. Childers, after surveying him from head to foot, "the honour of knowing you – but if you mean that you can make more money of your time than I can of mine, I should judge from your appearance that you are about right."[38]

DEMOCRATIZING/PLURALIZING TEMPORALITY

There is no greater cliche, when the West is compared with India, than the observation that time in India – especially in India, but to a very large degree in other allegedly non-progressive, primitive, and premodern civilizations as well[39] – is largely cyclical while it is linear in the West. The Arab geographer and scholar, Alberuni, who accompanied Mahmud of Ghazni on one or more of his raids into India around AD 1000, and apparently spent a few years in the country, devoted a good tenth of his book on India to Indian conceptions of time, but the distinction between cyclical and linear time finds little place in his observations.[40] Alberuni was a careful observer and voluminous recorder of facts, and of what he took to be Hindu practices and beliefs, and the accuracy of many of his findings can be surmised from his correct representation of the difference between the *Vikram Samvat* and *Saka* calendars, two of eight Indian calendrical systems that he enumerated, as 135 years. Alberuni was struck by the fantastic numbers that entered into the calculations of the Hindus, such as the 26,425,456,204,132 years said to have elapsed before his own time,[41] and he wryly observed that "the Hindus do not consider it wearisome to reckon with huge numbers, but rather enjoy it." But he noted as well that the calculation and even invocation of eras involved impossibly large numbers, increasing the possibility of error and creating confusion, and that the Hindus appeared simultaneously to demonstrate a practical bent of mind by confining most of their deliberations to durations of time, extending at most to some hundreds of years, which had a more human scale, or which could be comprehended through a calendar.[42] It is European writers and colonial administrators, eager to propagate a nexus of ideas – the indifference of Hindus to time, the Hindu representation of the material world as *maya* (illusion), and their consequent disinclination towards governance, or at least mindful administration, and the stagnation of Indian society, or the cessation of time – who were assiduous in circulating the claim that the dominant conception of time among the Hindus was cyclical.

In the most characteristic expositions of this purportedly momentous difference, it is apparently the linearity of time which explains why the West has been committed to ideas of progress, development, and change, just as the presumption of cyclical time in India is said to furnish the most cogent explanatory framework for understanding why Hindus believe in karma or the notion of rebirth, are largely hostile to historical change, and are indifferent, in their daily practices as much as in their metaphysics, to considerations of time. Nothing is said to point more decisively to the "lack of common-sense concepts" of temporality among Indians than the frequently encountered observation that in Hindustani, the adverb "*kal*" means both yesterday and tomorrow, just as "*parsoon*" means the day before yesterday as much as the day after tomorrow. The meaning can only be determined by context.[43] This critical narrative of "Hindu time" is music to the ears of Indian modernizers, who curse the manner in which their countrymen waste their time, and are ever mindful that, more than anything else, Indians must be instructed in the right uses of time. These modernizers welcomed the national emergency that Indira Gandhi proclaimed in 1975, on the grounds that for the first time all government employees arrived to work on time, and even the trains ran on time. The timeliness of Indian trains, which run 24 hours late, is a standing joke among seasoned users of the vast railway network, and no Indian who has ever been to a bank could have failed to confront the rejoinder from the clerk that they ought to return the following day for the accomplishment of their errand (*achha, aap kal aa jaana*). The banking staff in India was apparently never acquainted with Benjamin Franklin's advice to a young tradesman, "Remember, that time is money," all the more ironical because money is, after all, the currency of trade in banks. Indians appear to take the view that nothing need be done today which can just as well be accomplished tomorrow; this is, not unexpectedly, a striking contrast to the maxims handed down to Poor Richard by Franklin, who declaimed: "Dost thou love life? Then do not squander time, for that's the stuff life is made of." Indian attitudes are contrasted, almost always unfavorably, with the opposite tendency to prize efficiency, and at times more philosophically with the observation, attributed to the ancient Greek philosopher Heraclitus, that one does not set foot in the same river twice.[44] On the latter view, change is always around us, and time is never still; change is itself the only form of constancy. And yet, as the great ideologues of nineteenth-century European thought – Hegel, Marx, Weber – insistently reminded us, India had remained unchanged over millennia. We have only to recall Marx's famous and much-quoted judgment:

> Indian society has no history at all, at least no known history. What we call its history is but the history of its successive intruders who founded their empires on the passive basis of that unresisting and unchanging society ...[45]

In the face of Puranic conceptions of time, where ages extend into tens of thousands of years, and single kings can be said to have reigned for hundreds of years, the time of history holds little brief. What meaning does the time of human history have for eternal philosophy, or to the student of geology? On encountering Indian texts in the eighteenth century, British writers became persuaded that Indian conceptions of time, dealing not only with small time units but with such impossibly large units as the *yugas*, the four ages – Krita, Treta, Dvapara, and Kali, comprised of 1,728,000; 1,296,000; 864,000; and 432,000 years, respectively – were much too fanciful, the product of overripe imaginations and inattentiveness to the time of human histories. Thomas Trautmann has offered the insightful argument that had knowledge of Indian traditions been derived a century later, British writers might not have been so dismissive of Indian texts. By the second half of the nineteenth century, Trautmann argues, it had become possible to distinguish between the biblical chronology which condensed human history into a few thousand years and the vast expanse of time opened up by prehistoric archeology, geology, and other sciences. Human time was freed from the "narrow limits of biblical chronology,"[46] and yet this enlightenment could perhaps have come much earlier, had British writers devised more thoughtful interpretive strategies for reading Indian texts.

Thus Indian time conceptions may have contributed to the "expanded time horizons for the history of humans, of life, of the earth, and of the cosmos" that now constitute the bedrock of numerous scientific disciplines, but this is only one of the numerous ways in which the West has occluded the origins of its own intellectual histories. Moreover, such notions of time as are found in Indian texts have often been bracketed as special instances of cyclical or at least eternal time: they unfold as specimens of Oriental mysticism, wisdom, the enchantment with the eternal. The real difficulty is that if one could democratize and pluralize time in no more complex fashion than by positing cyclical time against linear time, that would be to surrender the terrain to linear time. The notion of cyclical time is linear time's reinvention of itself, and we have in cyclical and linear time a false opposition which permits linear time to widen its hegemony in the face of seeming dissent, and obscure the multiple notions of time which formerly competed for our attention, and which have not altogether disappeared from the lives of people around the world. (Vacation time, incidentally, is another mode in which linear and clock time recast themselves: as studies of vacations suggest, vacation time is often rushed, and people often emerge from vacations more bruised than rested. Perhaps more so than even the time of the work week, vacation time is marked by lists of things to see and do, each activity allotted a piece of time.) Most common among alternative conceptions of time are those associated with the taking of siestas and the art of idling. Yet there are numerous other conceptions of time, such as mythic time, pastoral time, and the time of mindfulness – the time when everything is attempted with mindfulness, with a full awareness not of the clock and the importance of productivity, but of the necessity of an awareness that every moment constitutes a fullness in itself.[47] But time can be pluralized much further, as brief and merely suggestive considerations of BodyTime, FoodTime, and RailTime show.

BodyTime

In the most affluent countries of the world, and increasingly among the elites of the "underdeveloped" countries, the regimen of time has extended to the body in curious and even novel ways. The temporal rhythms of the body are increasingly ignored, but the body has become the site of worship: penis enlargement substitutes for lingam worship, and breast augmentation or modeling takes the place of the worship of fertility goddesses. One wonders whether the marked decline of breastfeeding in the United States in the 1960s, and gradually elsewhere around the world, is to be attributed only to the relentless marketing strategies and profiteering of baby-food companies, and the desire of young mothers to remain sexually attractive to their spouses or partners, or if the idea that time ought not to be wasted also played a decisive role in heralding this change. A child could be trained to hold a bottle, so freeing the mother's time for other productive work, or the task of feeding the child could be handed down to women whose time could be more easily purchased. As women began to enter the workplace, it must have become apparent that the time of corporate efficiency and the time of breast-feeding are not synchronous. In recent years, a few corporations have set aside time and space for women to breastfeed their children, but it is corporate time here which sets the template, and which constrains breastfeeding within the duration of allotted time.

If one could invert the travel narratives of the last few centuries, where Europeans commented on what they took to be the peculiar and often gruesome customs prevailing in Africa, the Orient, and other exotic places, nothing would strike reasonable people in these places as more peculiar than the practice in the post-industrial nations of walking on treadmills, often in unison and to the tune of music, while the streets themselves are bereft of pedestrians. A modern gym presents a chilling picture of a robotic future, where each person moves – how could one call the identical, measured movements over suspended space walking – to the march of the same drummer. Walking had at one time an intimate relationship with associated practices, such as sauntering, idling, and loitering, but nearly all these ideas have been divested of their rich cultural meanings: either some of these activities have been criminalized, as is true of loitering, or they have been invested with deliberate, purposeful intent, such as the objective, by working on a treadmill, of losing weight. The "lost time" of walking contrasts with the "productive time" of running: not only is a 30-minute investment of time in running more beneficial than a similar 30-minute investment in walking, but running carries with it the cultural capital of athleticism, (relative) youth, and discipline: one also "runs," not "walks," for office.

Though time is routinely and sometimes obsessively set aside for body-building, weightlifting, or working out in other myriad fashions, the fetishization of the body by this apparent valorization of time set aside for it must not be confused with BodyTime. Unlike adults or older children, who have been socialized into the discipli-nary modalities of modern temporality, infants and very young children eat only when they receive cues from their body. They have not necessarily learned to listen to the temporal rhythms of their body, but adults have undoubtedly unlearned these temporal rhythms. The body must have its time for rest, play, idling, and con-viviality, just as much as for work, eating, and evacuation: all this makes up what might be called BodyTime. As scientific research, or what passes for it, has indubitably established, there is much wisdom in the idea that the body is far more attuned to the siesta common in Mediterranean and Asian countries than it is to the mechanical work habits of North America, northwestern Europe, and Japan.[48] Mechanical time is foreign to the pulse of the body.

Women are more sensitized to BodyTime than men, since the female body is bound up with the temporal cycles of pregnancy, reproduction, lactation, menopause, and most of all menstruation. Hence the reference to the biological clock, and the awareness that all of women's cycles are relentlessly timebound. In the prime of her life, for thirty-odd years or more, a woman can time events in her life and in the larger world outside by her monthly period. A woman's monthly period averages 28–29 days, and so largely coincides with phases of the moon. It is said of the Tiv women of Nigeria that they can determine at what point they are in their pregnancies by counting the lunations, though there are no names for lunar months.[49] Yet modern medical and corporate culture attempts to override the BodyTime of women as far as is possible. Thus, the oral contraceptive is always packaged in weekly cycles extending from three or four weeks, as is most common, to five or six weeks, though the menstrual cycles of women cannot be construed merely as multiples of the week. "What essentially takes place here," in the judgment of Eviatar Zerubavel, "is that the perfectly natural menstrual cycle (which is not always 28 days long for all women) is being replaced by artificial cycles that are all mathematical extensions of an entirely conventional social cycle."[50] Though the pill should have adapted to the temporal rhythms of women, it is women who must forgo their own physiology and temporal rhythms to suit the convenience of gynecologists, the pharmaceutical industry, and countless others whose temporal sensibility cannot think beyond the prescribed intervals of time. BodyTime is sustained with great difficulty and must face the incessant assault of all the institutions of modernity.

FoodTime

One biographer of Napolean has noted that the emperor, who saw himself as a world conqueror reincarnated, spent no more than an average of eight minutes on lunch, and thirteen minutes on dinner.[51] One suspects he thought of even this as time wasted, as time necessary only to stoke the engine of ambition and generate the energy that would enable him to grasp the world. Napolean, however, was merely a fast eater, not the inventor of fast food. All such innovations have largely been the handiwork of Americans, who can be relied upon to give the world everything that is bigger and faster than everywhere else in the world. It is the Americans who appear to vindicate, on the macro level, the proposition that cultures in which food is consumed rapidly are more likely to dominate others. Of course this proposition is not borne out empirically, since the Spaniards and the Italians, who are noted among the Europeans for their leisurely meals, were not without their colonial empires. The Spaniards, notably, were dominant only as long as the English and the French had not become maritime powers; the Italians came to the acquisition of their empire at a very late date, when the principal European powers had left precious little for Italy.

Modern civilization has been tarnished with the curse of fast food, and with fast food have come not only the diminution of the culinary experience, the vulgarization of taste, and increased problems with digestion, but the loss of conviviality, the lack of table manners, and the erosion of conversation and what English essayists such as William Hazlitt described as "table talk." Perhaps the halo placed around the American ritual of Thanksgiving – a testimonial to the labor of the pilgrims, but also implicitly to the slaughtering of the indigenous people – should be attributed not to the secular nature of this feast which endeavors to be ecumenical in bringing together family, friends, and even strangers at one table, but to the fact that it is one of the few striking moments in the time of modern American civilization when time is justly rewarded at the table. It is around the dinner table that civilizations take on their richest hues, and the Slow Food movement, which originated in Italy about ten years ago, is dedicated to the proposition that human beings can be considered worthy of their name only if they rid themselves of speed and "oppose the universal folly of Fast Life." As the manifesto of the movement states:

> Our century, which began and has developed under the insignia of industrial civilization, first invented the machine and then took it as its life model. We are enslaved by speed and have all succumbed to the same insidious virus: Fast Life, which disrupts our habits, pervades the privacy of our homes and forces us to eat Fast Foods.[52]

Though the movement may have drawn the support of mainly connoisseurs and gourmands, its manifesto offers the vision of a future where FoodTime will be honored. The conception of FoodTime, as of BodyTime, is civilizational: it incorporates far more than the critique of fast food, poor taste, and fast consumption, for it recognizes that the frenzy of industrial civilization has transformed the very temporal being of homo sapiens.

RailTime

Earlier I had suggested how the invention of the railroad, and in turn the rapid increase of rail traffic, both for transporting goods and conveying passengers from one destination to another, necessitated the standardization of time. Time zones were created, uniform timetables were introduced; time was no longer permitted to be arbitrary, capricious, or whimsical. But the railroads were generative of social uses of time in another, less frequently explored, sense. Earlier modes of transportation had generally been productive of community formation: people moved around together in caravans and convoys. Movement across large tracts of land took time, and the time was spent in conversation, conviviality, commensality – time was a factor in creating cohesive communities. The railroad, while diminishing the amount of time required to complete a journey, nonetheless generated a more expansive notion of time and community. It brought together disparate individuals, who might not otherwise have shared their time with others, into a single space, and though it shortened the travel time for every journey, it facilitated previously uncontemplated longer journeys, and so helped to give rise to a new conception of "social time." There are still train journeys that, whether in India, China, Russia, or even the United States, take 48 hours and even longer. As much as language, racial feeling, or a notion of some common cause, the railways everywhere contributed to the emerging feeling that one belonged to a nation – but to belong to a nation means as well to share in the prevailing ethos of time in that cultural formation.

Considering late modernity's enchantment with speed, and the rapid transformation of time into a commodity, which is sold and purchased in the marketplace, it is scarcely surprising that the most visible degradation of what I have described as RailTime has occurred in the United States. The railway network has virtually disintegrated, and except in a few small pockets, such as the northeast corridor from Washington, D.C. to Boston, where several metropolises are found along the stretch, trains are mainly used by various categories of people with much "time on their hands," such as men and women in retirement or hobos, or by those who wish to signal their dissent from the technological fixations of American society, or by those who construe trains as a romantic leftover from an earlier era of industrialization. Though the most common sociological frameworks attribute, not incorrectly, the decline of the railways in America to the ferocious lobbying of the automobile industry and its corporate partners in the construction, petroleum, and other allied industries, as well as to the American celebration of the atomistic individual, changing conceptions of time played a not inconsiderable role in hastening the decline of the railways. What is singularly distinct about the automobile is that it brackets the time of its occupant(s) from the time of the occupants of other automobiles: it is a running critique of the time of collectivities and cohesive communities. Though its very justification is that it creates social time, keeping (in the jargon emblazoned across the advertisements of more than one corporate giant) the world "connected," the automobile is inherently defiant of social time. The nexus between fast food, the obsession with speed, the shortness of time, and the decline of conviviality is nowhere better demonstrated than in the picture of the atomistic individual drawing up in his or her car to the take-out lane of the fast-food restaurant and being served while seated in the car.

KEEPING WATCH ON TIME

The watchword of our times is undoubtedly "watch." Over the last few decades, a number of organizations that purport to watch the conduct of nations and organizations have crept into existence, such as Human Rights Watch, Asia Watch, and Helsinki Watch. There is even the "BJP Watch, a group – where else but in the diaspora – which purports to monitor the activities and policies of the Bharatiya Janata Party, the Hindu nationalist party that has dominated Indian politics over the last few years. By this reckoning, there should be a Bush Watch, to monitor the activities of the world's most potentially dangerous individual, as well as an America Watch, to keep a watch on the country that poses the greatest danger to ecologically aware livelihoods and radically dissenting politics. To keep watch is to stand guard, and we might recall one older usage of "watch," namely the contingent of sentries that took their turn at standing guard at the king's palace or fortifications, being replaced at appointed times by a fresh contingent. These days, the keepers of the watch – most of the Watch organizations are located in the United States – are self-appointed guardians, which fact behooves us to watch them and clock their activities.

That the English language (and it is not singular in this respect) allows the metaphors of watch and clock to be extended so far testifies to the extraordinary dimensions of temporality that persist across a wide spectrum of discourses in virtually every culture. The geographer Robert Levine, who has made a comparative study of conceptions of time across cultures, relates that on a recent trip to India he encountered a sign on the narrow-gauge Darjeeling railway that reads: "'Slow' is spelled with four letters; So is 'life.' 'Speed' is spelled with five letters; So is 'death.'"[53] This macabre sense of humor seems not at all out of place in a culture where the bus driver plows his vehicle through the streets at breakneck speed, mercilessly casting aside smaller vehicles and pedestrians alike only to arrive at his destination with nothing on his hands but time. To arrive at a richer conception of time, or rather of life where time is not a commodity, modern culture has perhaps had to make a cult of time, and massacre all those who stood in the path of time's relentless drive. If modernity's encounter with time is any gauge, we have become creatures largely of sense rather than sensibility.

At the start of the twenty-first century and the new millennium, it has become imperative to think about the possible ways in which the reterritorialization of temporality might be achieved. The dominant conceptions of time have been located in the modern bureaucratic, financial, and corporate institutions of the West, as well as in those intellectual practices encapsulated under the disciplines of physics, history, anthropology, and others. The iconic representations of the mechanical view of temporality remain the Gregorian calendar, the stopwatch, the factory clock, the weekly schedule, the appointment book, the Christian era, and such units of time as the century and the millennium. Jeremy Rifkin's sketch of the "Time Wars" which he has predicted will overtake the modern world's concern with spatiality may perhaps be somewhat overdrawn, but there can be little doubt that the temporal dimensions of human life, which the study of history, as it has so far taken shape, is vastly ill-equipped to comprehend, will acquire renewed importance in the future. To reterritorialize temporality, and to make it work in the cause of humanity rather than as an affront to the spirit of humankind, is to relocate time in the body, in foodways and lifeways, and in such cultural practices as walking, writing letters, idling, and conversing. The politics of time is yet to open itself to us, but the time when we shall be let in to its secrets is not so far removed.

2   Politics in Our Times

In the midst of the immense discussion over the coming of the new millennium, comparatively little attention was paid to the contours of global politics in the twentieth century. Doubtless, anyone living in Western Europe at the time of the Reformation must have thought of his or her own times as especially charged with change, just as those who witnessed the industrialization and brutalization of the English landscape must have thought that they were living amidst the most enormous transformations in human history. It is something of a truism that to each generation, at least in the last few hundred years when recorded history has had a more marked presence in human affairs, its own era seems particularly significant. The twentieth century has seemed notably full of cataclysmic moments, and at least one school of thought, which speaks of the "end of history," sees in the emergence of globalization and the achievement and diffusion of American-style democracy the desired fulfillment of human destiny. It has long been an American dogma that countries which moved towards capitalism were also likely to embrace free elections as the political form most compatible with market reforms. "In America," Benjamin Barber writes, "the confidence in the omnipotence of markets has been transformed into a foreign policy that assumes internationalizing markets is tantamount to democratizing them and that human freedom is secured the minute nations or tribes sign on to the dogmas of free trade."[1]

The fall of the Soviet Union, and the end of its hegemony over the Eastern bloc, have furnished to some commentators ample proof of the centrality, not to mention inevitability, of the ballot box and the supermarket aisle to civilization. All else appears to fall by the wayside: both on the right and the left, much contemporary writing offers variations on the argument that we inhabit a globalized information and consumption economy whose nodal points are no longer nation-states. The liberation of the capitalist economy from political and economic constraints alike is celebrated by some; others see in the advocacy and embrace of unencumbered free trade and jingoistic capitalism a recipe for totalitarian capitalism, the complete demise of ideals of egalitarianism and economic justice, and the unchecked reign of large conglomerates or multinational corporations.[2] One recent, widely applauded, book captures the idea of global capitalism as the highest form of imperial power in its title: *Empire*.[3]

It is striking how far contemporary political literature and social commentary, while being fixated on nationalism, political democracy – the discussions generally being confined to elections, psephology, and the constitutional arrangements in various states – and globalization (under the general rubric of which one could also include the so-called information revolution in all its manifestations), and while being attentive to the concerns voiced by growing women's, ecological, social, and human rights movements, has nonetheless occluded some of the principal trajectories of twentieth-century political life from its purview. The twentieth century, as I shall presently discuss in greater detail, was pre-eminently the century of total violence and its impress is everywhere visible – the images of concentration camps, lynchings, cities under fire, mass graves, incinerated bodies, and human remains are burned deep into the mind. As early as 1924, warfare and militarism appeared to have transgressed all known limits to such a degree that one pacifist, Ernst Friedrich, published a volume of 200 pages of captioned photographs to convey with gruesome honesty the horrors of modern violence.[4] It may, then, seem rather strange to suggest that violence is the great unmentionable of contemporary political writing and unthinking: the Holocaust is everywhere remembered, and in Germany it is an offence punishable under the law to deny that it occurred; memorials to the war dead, especially soldiers, proliferated following the two world wars and now dot the landscapes of many countries; and the rise of identitarian politics, as well as critiques of dominant histories, with the concomitant attention lavished on suppressed histories, have sensitized hundreds of racial, ethnic, and linguistic minorities – Australian Aborigines, African-Americans, Native Americans, the Indian populations of central and south America, the so-called criminal tribes of India, among many others – to the extreme violence inflicted upon them and their ancestors. And yet every chapter of this history of total violence is treated as a discrete chapter, placed within some narratological framework which cannot tolerate a more expansive outlook. Thus the Rwandan genocide of 1994 is put down to age-old African hostilities, to the barbarism of tribal politics; the massacre of Bosnian Muslims is described as part of the history of intractable Balkan conflicts shrouded in myths and half-truths and conducted by fanatics; and the Cambodian genocide unleashed by Pol Pot and his acolytes is cast aside as a unique form of auto-genocide, besides being a spectacular demonstration of the evils of anti-modernist and anti-industrial communist utopian thinking. It may well be that these episodes of violence are grounded precisely in these kinds of historical sociology, but their relation to each other and to the history of violence in the twentieth century is generally overlooked, just as they are disassociated from the ideologies of modernization and development which led millions to their graves in Russia, the Ukraine, China, and elsewhere. Descriptions and interpretations of particular phenomena of violence are permitted, precisely because each particular history implicates particular collectivities and exonerates all others. One has only to recall the supreme confidence with which Hitler declared that he could proceed with the extermination of the Jews since so little fuss had been made over the killings of mass number of Armenians. As he told his generals on the eve of the invasion of Poland, "Who still talks nowadays of the extermination of the Armenians?"[5]

Alongside the total violence of the twentieth century, one might also remember the century as a period of decolonization, the consolidation of the nation-state system, and the emergence of an expansive notion of human rights. The United Nations, at least on the formal level, formed the common link between the three: it encouraged the nation-state system and welcomed new entities into its fold; it introduced various international frameworks for the promotion of universal human rights, and has since its inception in 1945 continuously endeavored – though not without resistance – to widen the scope of what are construed as human rights; and it instituted an apparatus to assist in the process of decolonization. Most people living in Asia, Africa, the Middle East, and the Caribbean in the mid-twentieth century would have awoken one day to find that they had been liberated from the colonial regime that was functioning the previous night and had been placed under the rule of a government led by nationalists. The nation-state did not emerge in the twentieth century, but the inventory of this political formation grew spectacularly in the period following World War II as the European powers were divested of their colonies; and again, following the demise of the Soviet Union, the nation-state system witnessed a new breath of life, despite various prognostications about its death.

It has often been argued that the change in power did almost nothing for the vast majority of colonized people, and that life continued unaltered, and perhaps even worsened under independence, but that can be no reason for supposing that people do not generally prefer to be governed by their own, howsoever unenlightened, countrymen and women. There are yet much stronger objections to those who relegate decolonization to the margins of a century filled with extraordinary changes. The presumption that decolonization has offered no consolations to those who were to have benefited from the end of colonial rule is only another way of reinstating an older argument, namely that politics and history have meant nothing to "the masses," who have ever been content to be under one ruling system or another, just as long as they could be furnished with the basic necessities of life. Moreover, the characterization of rural landscapes as unchanging and untouched by politics generally emanates from urban dwellers, whose appetite for living in those areas is not only remarkably thin, but who tend to view the formerly colonized countries as devoid of any indigenous political traditions save that of absolutism. The theory of Oriental Despotism, in whatsoever shade of color it appears, whether as Samuel Huntington's thesis on the "clash of civilizations," as Bernard Lewis' "Muslim rage," or as an argument about Western exceptionalism,[6] remains the refuge of metropolitan urbanites, latter-day eugenicists, and forthright advocates of hierarchy invested in some notion of biological and racial superiority.

TOTAL VIOLENCE

In 1900, the world was witness to a new form of warfare in the shape of the Boer War; 100 years later, the air bombing of Kosovo brought a new generation of fighter aircraft into the sky whose introduction was predicated on a form of terror grounded in the view that indiscriminate bombing of enemy country is permissible so long as one's own soldiers are immune from attack. The Boer War was a quintessentially colonial war in many respects, not least in that its politics was derived not only from the internal squabbling of English politicians but from the self-aggrandizing ambitions of two European populations, and from the circumstance that as the Dutch and the British settlers attempted to settle their conflict, the interests of the various suppressed populations, including the numerically preponderant Africans and the Indians who had been brought into the country largely as indentured laborers, were viewed as wholly inconsequential. Though the term "collateral damage" had not yet come into existence, the non-Europeans were just that, the flotsam and jetsam of white warfare.

The Boer War yet calls to mind the conduct of Western powers in more recent years, and no one ought to be allowed to forget that the seeds of Afghanistan's recent descent into madness and its political and cultural disintegration lie to a very considerable degree in its transformation into a Cold War battleground between the United States and what was then the Soviet Union. Everything was done in the name of the natives, and the Mujahideen were even photographed at the White House, where they were hailed as "freedom fighters"; and yet, as is the habit of colonial powers, all was left to seed. Once Soviet rule had become untenable, the Americans were wholly prepared to allow Afghanistan to self-destruct: the scenario was certainly as acceptable as watching the two dominant hostile powers in the Middle East, Iran and Iraq, smother each other to death with brotherly Muslim love. Not long after the conclusion of the Boer War, those intrepid lovers of freedom, the European men of plenty, became the architects of an institutionalized system of racism that matched slavery in its brutality and dehumanization of the black person; and in Afghanistan, likewise, the much feted liberators of the country from Soviet rule would proceed to author a rigorously segregationist regime and institute an apparatus of terror calculated to stifle all dissent.

The Boer War speaks, then, to the present in chillingly prescient ways, and yet its signal contribution to the shaping of the twentieth century and late modernity resides in its foreshadowing of the idea of total violence. Though trench warfare is more commonly associated with the prolonged battles of World War I, it was introduced during the Boer War.[7] It decimated the idea of the heroic warrior, of the face-to-face combat and the glorious death; during the Great War, soldiers were more likely to die from disease, mud, "trench foot," or the shot from a sniper's rifle as from combat. Dug into their trenches, soldiers saw their adversaries only infrequently.[8] World War I transformed trench warfare into industrial-scale killing. Similarly, World War II revived a British innovation in the Boer War, the concentration camp, and turned it into perhaps the most horrific symbol of man's inhumanity towards man. The puritanical Boers, sitting atop the richest gold deposits in the world, did not merely put their trust in God: they evaded the enemy, harassed British soldiers and supply lines, and pioneered modern guerrilla warfare.

Though the British might trumpet their unique devotion to the notion of fair play, and imagine that they gifted the idea of good sportsmanship to the world, their precise rejoinder to the Boers consisted in herding their women, children, and elderly into large enclosures behind barbed wire that were euphemistically termed "camps of refuge" where the initial annual mortality rate was 34 percent.[9] Their manliness had nothing more noble to show for itself than the concentration camp: as A. J. P. Taylor remarked of the Boer War, "Even forty years afterwards, every European, though few Englishmen, recognized the taunt in the Nazi 'concentration camps,' which deliberately parodied in name and nature the British 'methods of barbarism.'"[10]

At the other end of the century, 100 years removed from the Boer War, NATO's pulverization of Serbia stands forth as brutal testimony to the twentieth century's relentless advocacy of the concept of total violence. The largest force of aircraft ever brought into service against an enemy since World War II pounded Serbia and Kosovo with single-minded intent, and eventually compelled the defiant Slobodan Milosevic to render unequivocal submission to the American mandate. But the distinctiveness of this aerial campaign lies much less in this fact, or even in the argument – which has been heard at other times – that international law makes provision for humanitarian interventions, than in the entirely anonymous and faceless enterprise of cold-blooded killing which this war came to express. No previous war (though American adventurism in Iraq – where ground forces were deployed, suggesting that the Americans were prepared, as indeed one must be in war, to forfeit lives – comes perilously close) has ever been waged from the debased standpoint, raised in the NATO–American action in Serbia to an elevated principle, that the loss of lives on the enemy side is totally acceptable, but that not one of one's own soldiers is to die. Consequently, in an effort to prevent the loss of NATO lives, aerial bombardment from a height where aircraft could not be shot down by Serbian missiles or anti-aircraft fire was resorted to as the only acceptable course of action, though this meant that civilian and military targets could not properly be distinguished. This distinction, which in principle has guided the conduct of modern warfare, was deliberately repudiated on the pretext that there were no "pure" civilian domains: power plants, bridges, water reservoirs, and other infrastructural elements of daily life had potential dual use and were therefore legitimate military targets. Death lies on one side, life on the other: this is the new ontological dualism of the non-nuclear nuclearism unleashed on the world by the West.

Sandwiched between the Boer War and NATO's military crusade in the Balkans, the twentieth century presents a grim picture of a period visibly marked by genocide, large and small wars of expansion and separatism, state terrorism, ethnic cleansing, bureaucratic exercises in massacre, and various kinds of holocausts that are seldom recognized as such. The evidence is unimpeachable, the corpses are there to be seen; the catalog is vast. The bulk of the colonial wars were, no doubt, fought in the nineteenth century. The holocaust perpetrated on the indigenous populations of the Americas had, following the brutality of the initial encounters, been carried out over decades, and in the United States lasted well into the nineteenth century.[11] So the exceptionality of the twentieth century might seem in doubt, except insofar as each of the two world wars was unprecedented, gigantic in scale and in the loss of lives. But the twentieth century as a whole scarcely lacked ingenuity in exceeding the casualty rate of previous centuries. In the midst of World War I, the Armenians could be dispatched to their death by the hundreds of thousands, not as legitimate targets of wars or as hostages to the war effort, but as a matter of deliberate state policy – and all this largely in the space of one year. Estimates of the number killed vary from 600,000 to 2 million, though a United Nations subcommission report released in 1985 arrived at a figure of "at least one million."[12] Similarly, in Rwanda in 1994, it took the Hutus a mere summer to eliminate as many as 800,000 Tutsis, whose extermination as "cockroaches" was openly encouraged on radio broadcasts.[13]

Raymond Aron wrote of "the century of total war" in 1954,[14] and he had not yet witnessed the war of liberation in Algeria, the war against communism in Indonesia and the brutalization of East Timor, the Vietnam War, the genocides in East Pakistan, Cambodia, and Rwanda, the wars in Somalia, Sudan, and Ethiopia, the eight-year long Iran–Iraq conflagration, the twenty-year old conflict in Afghanistan and the ten-year-old insurgency in Kashmir, the periodic rounds of violence in Palestine, the rout of Iraq by American-led forces, the various wars and genocides accompanying the disintegration of Yugoslavia and Serbia, and the hundreds of other strifes of more than ordinary proportions in the last five decades. But it is not only in this respect that Aron's portrayal of the twentieth century is inaccurate, if only inadvertently: he made the mistake of supposing that war is the most authentic, visible, dramatic, and consequential embodiment of violence. Much is made by Aron of the economic achievements of the Soviet Union and Stalin's desire for world conquest,[15] but Aron has nothing to say of the millions of Ukrainians, and other inhabitants of the North Caucasus and the Lower Volga, who were viewed as enemies of collectivization and starved to death.[16] It is reasonable to suppose that Aron, had he been writing two decades later, would similarly have ignored 30 million or so deaths that can be attributed to the Chinese Community Party's genocidal policies of labor-intensive development and rapid industrialization encapsulated under the slogan of the Great Leap Forward,[17] though remarkably these deaths attracted almost no attention outside China.

In considering what I have termed "total violence" in the twentieth century, then, two considerations come to the fore. First, it remains customary in political and social commentary to confine violence to conventional categories, such as the violence of warfare, genocide, or armed political insurrection, or – on a different sociological scale – the violence that often accompanies spousal and child abuse, or the violence, as in the United States, of random school shootings. I have tried to suggest, and will dwell on this point at other moments in this book, that even categories that have largely been taken to be beneficial, such as the idea of development, are deeply invested in the idea and act of violence. In the name of development, nation-states have thought nothing of sacrificing millions of people who were considered expendable. If tribal people, for instance, required to be displaced by large dams, then they were to be seen as doing the bidding of the state in the interest of the "common good." The history of famines provides another case in point of the excision of violence from these narratives. In what remains the most widely accepted though scarcely unchallenged body of work on famines, Amartya Sen argued that famines were caused by people not having enough to eat, not by there not being enough to eat: the problem of famine was one of food ownership, not of food supply. Or, in Sen's language, a person's entitlements to food depended on the social relationships that constituted the web of a person's life.[18] Although Sen's work was instrumental in establishing a correlation between famines and the lack of open and democratic political regimes, it is instructive that entitlement theory is criticized because it has "no place for violence"; where for Malthus famines were natural disasters, for Sen they are economic disasters, and better management is offered as the solution to famines.[19] More recently, the violence that inheres in the practice of sanctions, such as those which have been in force against Iraq for over a decade, where an estimated 5,000 children every month over the last ten years are said to have died on account of acute shortages of medicines and surgical equipment, besides infrastructural problems in the delivery of medical care, is finally beginning to attract attention.[20] But it is understandable that sanctions should never have been seen as a form of violence and category of knowledge; indeed, in advocating economic sanctions against Germany at Versailles in 1919, Woodrow Wilson described it as an "economic, peaceful, quiet, lethal remedy" which would obviate the need for "force. It is not such a painful remedy."[21]

Second, it is commonly assumed that the development of technologies of extinction, from concentration camps and trench warfare to air power and nuclear weapons, made possible the unprecedented violence and brutality of the twentieth century. This is a particularly comforting thought for those whose vision of the future is resolutely technological, who assume the neutrality of technology, and who would in consequence also rely upon technology to redeem the ills of society. "Hardly any piece of fiction," one political theorist has written, "has contributed more to hiding the true nature of technical civilisation than that of seeing in modern technology nothing more than a mere tool, even if a particularly advanced one."[22] The prevailing common-sense about technology is that it can serve humankind for good or for ill; those more resolutely wedded to the technocratic vision of life argue that the shortcomings of technology are best resolved by better applications of technology, or – as in those instances when technology is described as having fallen into the wrong hands, whether construed as errant individuals or rogue states – by regulating its use and forestalling its wider dissemination. Stealth Fighters in the right hands are beacons of freedom, but in the hands of tyrants and despots they are messengers of death. Thus the only country to have deployed nuclear bombs, and now easily possessed of the largest stockpiles in the world of chemical and biological agents of warfare, confidently goes about the business of orchestrating world opinion to the acceptance of the view that only in the hands of the civilized nations of the West are macabre agents of death disguised forms of deliverance. The world should implicitly trust the United States, and perhaps its allies, to act judiciously in the interest of all humankind, though nothing in the conduct of these states warrants their being taken seriously as trustees.

The spectacular nature of the modern technology of death has, besides, obfuscated the recognition that the total violence of the twentieth century may have no intrinsic and necessary relationship to the development of massively efficient or awe-inspiring weapons of destruction. While the Holocaust perpetrated against Jews, gypsies, and homosexuals by the Nazis was aided by experiments in biological and chemical warfare, such as the development of the gas Zyklon B (hydrogen cyanide), it owed a great deal more to that bureaucratization of violence which permitted systematic and widespread transgressions of moral barriers. The theologian Richard Rubenstein has argued, in a brief and chilling rumination on the Holocaust, that it is best understood as an "expression of some of the most profound tendencies of Western civilization in the twentieth century."[23] Whether at Dachau or Auschwitz, guards were forbidden by camp commanders from laying hands on prisoners or having conversations with them. The infliction of arbitrary punishments was sought to be eliminated, so that the clockwork precision of the machinery of elimination should not be compromised; and the gas chambers similarly honored, most perversely, the principle of total anonymity. The sociologist Zygmunt Bauman goes beyond the idea of the Fordization of the murder of Jews to suggest that the Holocaust, far from being a mere "German malady," was the violent expression of the pathology of "rationality."[24] But when we turn from the Holocaust to the Rwandan and Cambodian genocides, it becomes emphatically clear that neither superior technology nor a complicated bureaucratic apparatus, inspired by ideas of efficiency and modernization, is required to operate a regime of death. The vast majority of the Tutsis were killed by machetes, axes, and shovels, wielded by men who set up roadblocks and attacked residences in large groups. In Cambodia, though there was more central planning, routine methods of torture, police brutality, and simple execution-style shootings sufficed to decimate the population.

DECOLONIZATION

The watchword for much political activity of the twentieth century has been nationalism, but decolonization furnishes the more arresting framework for understanding what might be distinct about the twentieth century. Why modern political literature has been shaped largely around nationalism, on which many minds have been trained, rather than decolonization is an interesting question which is seldom discussed.[25] European powers recognized Third World nationalisms as their own creation, even when these nationalisms were disowned as inauthentic, fanatic, or somehow evil. The founding fathers of these nationalisms were seen as men who had imbibed the lessons of Milton, Mill, and Mazzini, and who spoke the language of liberty, though in their practice they might falter and revert to models of Oriental Despotism. The modular form for nationalism was, of course, the nation-state, and any aspirant for a nation-state in the colonized world was rendering homage to European thinking. Even though nationalisms were felt as betrayals by European powers, they could take pride in them as the proper intellectual and political inheritance of the West.

Decolonization, on the other hand, pointed to a different epistemic framework and held out the possibility of a dissenting and emancipatory politics of knowledge. European powers scarcely understood decolonization, except in the language of nationalism; their own experience provided no precedence to locate this phenomenon. They also understood it at the guttural level, as a visceral experience that pointed to the loss of greatness; stripped of their colonies, the European powers recognized themselves as second-rate powers in a world being shaped by superpower rivalry and the rapid ascent of Japanese business enterprises. Though nearly fifty years apart, both Curzon and Churchill understood that bereft of India, Great Britain would cease to be a world power. But decolonization nonetheless remained an alien category of thought in relation to nationalism. The white or settler colonies had gradually been eased into Dominion Status, and it is not instructive to speak of decolonization to describe this transition, since they were understood to have a special relationship to Britain. Nor can one intelligibly speak of the American colonies that tore themselves away from the mother country to constitute themselves as an oppressive power in their own right as having decolonized themselves: not only did Britain remain the cultural and intellectual fount of American intellectual life, but down to the present day it is perfectly reasonable to speak, as politicians often do, of a special relationship between the US and Britain.

As for the non-white colonies, which constituted the bulk of the empires of European powers, the reasons why their decolonization has never been a visible subject of social and political discourses are still more complex. But one must begin with the observation that the absence of decolonization as a category of modern political commentary stands in sharp opposition to the bare facts of the formal decolonization of a greater part of the world in the post-World War II era. In the middle part of the nineteenth century, the most noticeable British possessions included India, Australia, Canada, and the Cape Province; 50 years later, on the eve of the Great War, slightly more than a quarter of the world was under the Union Jack. The "scramble for Africa," as it is commonly described,[26] had added Egypt, Sudan, Kenya, Uganda, Nigeria, Rhodesia, South Africa, the Gold Coast, Sierra Leone, and other territories to the British Empire. Elsewhere, from Singapore and Malaya in southeast Asia to Jamaica and Trinidad & Tobago in the Caribbean, Britain exercised sovereignty.[27] Throughout the nineteenth century, Britain added 100,000 square miles to its empire every year.[28] Yet this was only one aspect of the empire, and only one of several European empires of varying dimensions: the British commanded an "informal empire," such that even in China and much of Latin America its influence was predominant, and elsewhere around the globe the other European powers did their two bits' worth, as they imagined, to civilize the natives and bring all humankind within the orbit of progress. The other dominant imperial power, France, accounted for north Africa and a good deal of central Africa, Indochina, and scattered territories around the world; it, too, had its spheres of influence. The latecomers to the quest for empire, such as Germany, grabbed whatever they could lay their hands on – in this case southwest Africa, the Cameroon, and what is present-day Tanzania – and their turn towards fascism appears to have been inversely proportionate to the size of their possessions. Japan was doubtless frustrated that its imperial ambitions could take it no further than Asia, and it was not for want of desire, ambition, and enterprise that its empire could only extend to those portions of Asia which it in any case considered to be within its proper orbit. Once one accounts for Dutch rule in Indonesia, the Belgian domination of Congo, the various outposts of the former Spanish and Portuguese empires, the Italian presence in Abyssinia, the American occupation of the Philippines and Puerto Rico, and other similar scenarios, the picture begins to become fully rounded out.

The acquisition of empire was sometimes a drawn-out affair, nowhere more so than in India, but the European powers were compelled to relinquish their territorial possessions largely over a period of two decades. Even a very cursory overview hints at the larger picture. In less than five years after the conclusion of World War II, the entire Indian subcontinent was free of British rule, though Britain's departure from India took place in tandem with the carving out of Pakistan from India; the Philippines was rid of American rule in 1946. The Dutch were likewise forced out of Indonesia, and Palestine was abandoned. Partition was one favored strategy of imperial powers, though to admit that is not to decry the presence of competing ideologies in the political territories that they relinquished and the power of indigenous politics to shape the hand of imperial policy-making. Between 1959 and 1965, a number of British colonies acquired independence: Cameroon, 1960; Sierra Leone, 1961; Uganda, 1962; Kenya, 1963; Tanganyika, 1961, though it merged with Zanzibar to form Tanzania in 1963; Zambia, formerly Northern Rhodesia, 1964; Gambia, 1965, and so on. These were not always transparent exercises in the mere transference of power: new lines demarcating states from each other were drawn, previously existing states were dismembered, and mergers of existing states were effected. The newly carved nation-state of Cameroon was comprised of portions previously under French and British mandate, but the northern portion of British-mandated Cameroon merged into Nigeria, which acquired independence in 1960; British Somaliland merged with Somaliland to form Somalia; and in Asia, East Pakistan and West Pakistan were divided by 2,000 miles of Indian territory.

Thus the reality of political decolonization was palpable to the colonized subjects, who witnessed the flag of the imperial power being lowered and the flag of the new nation-state being raised to the accompaniment of wild cheers of nationalist sentiment, and it is still visibly present in such institutions as the General Assembly of the United Nations, where all states – large or small, powerful or powerless, constitutional monarchies or one-party regimes – are entitled to a single vote. However, the principle of parity contained in the idea of decolonization was clipped at the very moment of inception, and has been relentlessly savaged in the United Nations, not to mention in the foreign policy relations of the great powers, ever since.[29] On the one hand, the formation of the Security Council did not merely contradict the idea of parity; it fostered, as the recent activities of the United Nations so amply demonstrate, a form of recolonization. Once the permanent members of the Security Council were invested with absolute powers, such as in the provision which authorizes them and the ten temporary members of the Security Council to install a punitive course of sanctions against offending states, the principle of inequality was enshrined as an ineradicable feature of international politics, more particularly since the power to veto the Council's proceedings is conferred only on the five permanent members. If China had to pay a price for its occupation of Tibet similar to what has been exacted from Iraq for its invasion of Kuwait, one could have taken a more benign view of the Security Council. On the other hand, the General Assembly was gradually stripped of any substantive power, since its resolutions were generally not only not binding, but were construed as having only some symbolic resonance. *The United Nations paradoxically embodied within itself the principles of decolonization and recolonization.*

Against this backdrop of the reality of formal political decolonization, the reasons for the absence of decolonization in modern political commentary take on added significance. As I have earlier argued, behind nationalism stood the modular form of the nation-state, and in every colonized domain the advocates of freedom aspired to rule over a nation-state. With a few exceptions, such as Gandhi and Tagore in India, or perhaps Fanon in Martinique and Algeria, nationalists took it as axiomatic that the nation-state was the only viable form of political community in modernity. They understood that the accoutrements of a nation-state, extending from a common language, common shared histories, and a national culture, to a national flag, anthem, and currency were calculated to unite the people. They viewed the strength of European powers in their ability to unite their respective subjects, and if the condition of such unity was violence – the imposition of a common language, for example, was almost always a bloody affair, and it is not always realized that much of France was not French-speaking until later in the nineteenth century[30] – they were prepared to tolerate, undertake, and promulgate such violence as the necessary price to be paid for political coherence and political respect in the modern world. Every desire to find political fulfillment in the form of a nation-state was, if only unselfconsciously, an invitation for recolonization.

From the standpoint of European powers, the language of decolonization posed at least two principal problems. First, they recognized nationalism as their own creation, but true decolonization would have entailed the repudiation of the nation-state model, or certainly – if the nation-state is to be viewed as a *fait accompli* of politics – its xenophobic, exclusionary, and violent aspects. But this was seen as quite inconceivable, since the nation-state became the repository for all legitimate political ambitions and desires; it was envisioned as the logical culmination of human history. The French Revolution had no other purpose, according to one of its leading historians, than to "complete the nation which became one and indivisible."[31] The British in India, to take another instance, claimed as one of their most enduring triumphs the welding together of hundreds of "native states," and the merging together of millions of people belonging to an extraordinarily diverse array of ethnic, linguistic, and religious communities, or otherwise fragmented by the institution of caste and other indigenous markers, into a single entity that would be known as India. Such a political entity could survive and flourish only as a nation-state; and perforce, as a nation-state, it would need those institutional features, such as a national language and representative democracy, which were calculated to sustain it and earn it a place in the community of nations.

Second, the idea of decolonization stood as an open and immensely unwelcome invitation to European powers to decolonize themselves. Before Europe colonized the rest of the world, it colonized itself in myriad ways,[32] though it seldom recognized, and almost never admitted, the fact of its brutalization of its own minorities, malcontents, and misfits. Large segments of the population of European nations, including women, religious minorities, the lower classes, peasants, and gypsies, existed in a state of subservience and serfdom to the male elites who dominated political, social, and religious institutions. One expedient available to Europe as the New World opened up, and transoceanic navigation led European explorers, conquistadors, traders, and self-aggrandizing adventurers to other parts of the world, was to transplant its religious dissenters, political rebels, and even common criminals to the settler territories and later other colonies. Indeed, the disaffected and the impoverished had a chance to make good outside Europe, and colonies such as India furnish ample stories of lowly British subalterns lording it over the natives.[33] But this was scarcely the only mode in which dissent was stifled and contained, and a copious amount of modern scholarship has alerted us to the ways in which modern states became hegemonic, persuading their subjects – who were serfs and subjects long before they became citizens – to signal their assent to the imperatives of state formation. After all, the agreement of at least 90 percent of Americans, as every poll taken showed, to the war unleashed upon Iraq in early 1991, when in fact much fewer than 50 percent of Americans would have been able to identify Iraq – or even the broader area of the modern Middle East –

on a map, suggests how modern states colonize their own subjects.[34] With the emergence of some of the instruments of the mass media, such as daily newspapers and the radio, in the nineteenth and early part of the twentieth centuries, European nations set out on the task, in which they were extraordinarily successful, of winning over their own subjects to the cause of empire.

The unattractiveness of decolonization as an idea demanding enactment stemmed as well from the entire course of the intellectual history of the modern West. One of the principal dogmas in the self-understanding of the West is the claim that the Euro-American world has, since at least the time of the Renaissance, though frequently this narrative is stretched back to the ancient Greeks, uniquely valued the spirit of open inquiry, intellectual combativeness, and the necessity of tolerance for dissenting frameworks of knowledge. The very idea of science, so runs the argument, is predicated on the assumption that one can postulate any number of hypotheses, and the most compelling ideas, subject wherever possible to the principles of verifiability, will triumph. On the contrary, as the work of many scholars is beginning to suggest, the intellectual frameworks that dominate Western learning and the various academic disciplines are extraordinarily homogeneous.[35]

The examples of Newton and Goethe are instructive. By far the greater part of Newton's existing body of work is in the area of alchemy, a subject in which he continued to have an abiding interest long after he had formulated the scientific laws for which he will doubtless always be remembered; and yet this history, and Newton's deep conviction in the promise of alchemy, would be obscured, by Newton and the community of scientists, as an embarrassment to science.[36] Goethe, one of the supreme figures of Western humanism, also discovered the intermaxillary bone and was a careful student of botany, geology, and zoology; he produced a huge body of work on color, light, plants, animals, fossils, rocks, and weather, among many other subjects to which he devoted his scientific labors. Goethe himself hoped that his scientific work, "rather than his literary work, would someday be recognized as his greatest contribution to mankind."[37] But the regime of positivist science, whose leading figures – Bacon, Newton, Descartes – were so memorably ridiculed by Blake, entirely sucked Goethe the scientist into oblivion. When we recall that Goethe described it as his life's ambition to show the veracity and desirability of "another method, one which would not tackle nature by merely dissecting and particularizing, but show her at work and alive, manifesting herself in her wholeness in every single part of her being,"[38] we can begin to comprehend why he could not be tolerated by the scientific community. Modern science thrives on vivisection: that is its very heart; and it has also, historically speaking, been energized by the idea that man rightfully exercises dominion over nature.[39] Goethe entirely repudiated the structure of positivist science.

It is scarcely my intention to suggest that alchemy and modern science are alike, or that we should resuscitate alchemy, or that alchemy has any promise, whether as a mode of knowledge or as an avenue to long life. Nor do I wish to convey the impression that all of Goethe's scientific work can be validated. If it is imperative to reject the constructivist view of science at its most extreme, which appears to suggest that there is nothing which can rightfully go by the name of science, or that there is nothing much scientific about science, it is just as important that we recognize that there are many kinds of science, and that modern science rejects any kind of science which does not speak in its own idiom. The practitioners and historians of science may well have succeeded in perpetuating the lovely story of how modern science rose to supreme eminence on account of its own merits, its stock of verifiable and universal truths, but the hegemony of modern science owes everything to violence, to its success in eradicating competing narratives of science, and to its ravenous appetite for colonization.

The success of modern Western or allopathic medicine, to take one example, owed much less to the clinical and pharmaceutical advancements that are constantly trumpeted in the celebratory accounts, and far more to the machinations of the American Medical Association (AMA) and similar organizations in Britain and other European countries.[40] Indeed, even in the early part of the twentieth century, homeopathy was at least as popular as allopathy; but sustained lobbying by the American and British Medical Associations drove the bulk of homeopaths out of business. It was alleged that the same notion of expertise did not attach itself to homeopathic medicine, and that the practice of homeopathy was not based on rigorous scientific research; and yet it was palpably evident that homeopathy could not be transformed into a gigantic money machine. Various medical specialists, pharmaceutical industries, chemists, and hospitals all vigorously opposed homeopathy. The immense fraud that is perpetrated in the name of cancer research, a "holy cause" on which trillions of dollars have been expended with few gains, could not have been carried out under the aegis of homeopathy.[41]

Allopathy would henceforth colonize the world of medicine. To speak of colonization is to return to its primal meanings – the drive not merely to dominate, but to initiate a different account of origins and prevent the flourishing of competing narratives. To speak of decolonization, on the other hand, is to conjoin two narratives which are seldom yoked together: that, too, is a consequence of the modern addiction to compartmentalization, and of the failure to weld the political task of decolonization of the nation to the intellectual enterprise of the decolonization of knowledge. As I have endeavored to suggest, even the proponents of decolonization have been reluctant to speak in that idiom, opting instead for the framework of nationalism, since genuine decolonization would demand the jettisoning of the categories of knowledge that are viewed as axiomatic. Yet a good part of the world was formally decolonized in the second half of the twentieth century, and the European powers were dispatched back to their own doorsteps; and, around the same time, the edifice of modern European learning began to face the first concerted onslaughts by formerly colonized people.

HUMAN RIGHTS

The notion of human rights is deeply embedded in contemporary legal and political thought and, by some measure, can reasonably be considered one of the most significant achievements of twentieth-century culture. Certain classes of people in all societies have from the beginning of time been endowed with "rights" or, to take recourse to less anachronistic language, privileges which others could not claim. The immunity that emissaries from one state to another have always received constitutes one of the norms of conduct that has guided interstate relations, and similarly there were always intricate rules, which were admittedly observed more often in the breach, governing the conduct of warfare. Civilians were not to be taken hostage as a military strategy; a soldier was not to be shot as he was surrendering; wounded men were not to be killed; and so on. Some of these customary modes of conduct, as it were, are now enshrined in the law, transmuted into rights: thus a soldier taken as prisoner of war has the right to be treated with decency and be given proper food, clothing, and shelter. There are rights that the citizen can claim against the state; on the other hand, rights should be understood as emanating from restraints placed on the state's agenda to produce conformity and contain dissent. The individual has been given a great many more rights, and what is unique to modern times, never before have such rights been placed under the systematic protection of the law.

In the twentieth century, as the popular franchise came to be extended in most countries, human rights were also seen as having application to a broader class of people. States were increasingly bound in their relations to their subjects by myriad international agreements and laws, including the Geneva Conventions, the International Covenant on Civil and Political Rights, the United Nations Charter, and the Universal Declaration of Human Rights. Moreover, it is only in our times that the international community, on which I shall have more to say elsewhere, seems prepared to enforce sanctions against a state for alleged violations of such rights. With the demise of communism, the principal foes of human rights were perceived to have been crushed, and the very notion of human rights was declared to be sovereign. Should we, then, unreservedly endorse the culture of human rights as it has developed in the liberal-democratic framework of the modern West, indeed as a signifier of the "end of history" and of the emergence of a new global order and what Naipaul termed "our universal civilization"?[42] I would, on the contrary, like to suggest several compelling reasons why, far from acquiescing in the suggestion that the notion of human rights is the most promising avenue to a new era in human relations, we should consider the discourse of human rights, not in its ideal representations but as a political practice, as the most evolved form of Western imperialism, the latest masquerade of the West – and particularly the United States, the torchbearer since the end of World War II of Western values – to appear to the rest of the world as the epitome of civilization and as the only legitimate arbiter of human values.

In the European tradition, the notion of "rights of man," promulgated in the French Declaration of the Rights of Man and Citizen (1789), was preceded by "natural rights" and "natural law." Jefferson's invocation in the Declaration of Independence (1776) of the inalienable rights of man endowed by the Creator was presaged by his earlier claim, advanced in the *Summary View of the Rights of British America* (1774), that his countrymen were possessed of "rights as derived from the laws of nature and not as the gift of their Chief Magistrate."[43] However, to understand the roots of the modern discourse of human rights, we need to isolate the two central notions from which it is derived, namely the individual and the rule of law. It is difficult to read a modern sociologist of the West without encountering the suggestion that individualism has been one of the defining characteristics of European history. Similarly, it has been a staple of Western thought since at least the Renaissance that while the West recognizes the individual as the true unit of being, the building block of society, non-Western cultures have been built around collectivities, conceived as religious, linguistic, ethnic, tribal or racial groups. As *The Economist* was to declare boldly in its issue of February 27th 1909, "whatever may be the political atom in India, it is certainly not the individual of Western democratic theory, but the community of some sort."

The lofty pronouncements of a legion of Western commentators and experts – Max Weber, Eric Jones, David Landes, Robert Kaplan, Bernard Lewis, Ernest Gellner, Samuel Huntington, Jared Diamond, Michael Mann, among many others who are distinguished at least by their unswerving commitment to naked Eurocentrism – all tend in the same direction, and the argument is usually associated with a complex of other factors alleged to be uniquely instrumental in the development of Western societies, such as the respect for private property, the absence of large states, the emphasis on autonomy, and the cold climate which energized individuals to action. In the West the individual stands in singular and splendid isolation, the promise of the inherent perfectibility of man; in the non-West, the individual is nothing, always a part of a collectivity in relation to which his or her existence is defined, never a being unto himself or herself. Where the individual does not exist, one cannot speak of his or her rights; and where there are no rights, it is perfectly absurd to speak of their denial or abrogation.

On the Western view, moreover, if the atomistic conception of the individual is a prerequisite for a concern with human rights, so is the rule of law under which alone can such rights be respected. In a society which lives by the "rule of law," such laws as the government might formulate are done so in accordance with certain normative criteria – for example, they shall be non-discriminatory, generally blind to considerations of race, gender, class, and linguistic background, except when legal equality can only be assured by granting well-defined privileges to certain groups, or exempting certain groups from the obligations imposed upon everyone else, such as allowing confirmed pacifists exemption from military service. In a society governed by the rule of law, laws are made public, so that no person might plead ignorance of the law; and the judicial process under which a person is charged for the infringement of a particular law must hold out the promise of being fair and equitable.

As in the case of the individual, the rule of law is held to be a uniquely Western contribution to civilization, on the twofold assumption that democracy is an idea and institution of purely Western origins, and that the only form of government known to non-Western societies was absolutism. Indeed, according to the evolutionary biologist Jared Diamond, the "proximate factors behind Europe's rise" include "its failure to develop absolute despots and crushing taxation."[44] In conditions of Oriental Despotism, the only law was the law of the despot, and the life and limb of each of his subjects was hostage to the tyranny of his pleasures and whims. As David Landes asks, after having characterized all civilizations of the East as Oriental Despotisms, "What did ordinary people exist for, except to enhance the pleasure of their rulers?"[45] In the despotic state, there was perhaps only one "individual," the absolute ruler; under him were the masses, particles of dust on the distant horizon. What rights were there to speak of then?

Having briefly outlined how the notions of the individual and the rule of law came to intersect in the formulation of the discourse of human rights, we can proceed to unravel some of the more disturbing aspects and unsavory implications of this discourse. Where once the language of liberation was religion, today the language of emancipation is law. The caretakers of the soul have not been driven out of work, but freedom, which should have been the site of an engaging philosophical and ethical discussion, has been largely reduced to a set of questions focused around a person's rights, access to the courts, recourse to lawyers, and so on. The very notion of human rights, as it is commonly understood in the international forum today, is legalistic; any innovation in human rights is sealed with a treaty, signatories of which are commanded to observe its terms, or face the opprobrium of other nations. The abrogation of international treaties has often had no legal consequences for offending states, but the framework in which one points to their dereliction of duty is legal. No one doubts that when one speaks, for instance, of the rights of a convicted prisoner, an ethical dimension is at once implied, such as the consideration that even those who have committed offences cannot be stripped of minimal entitlements, or that the prisoner on death row have the opportunity to receive spiritual counsel; and yet it is transparent that behind the ethical dimension lies the force of law, in the absence of which we may well be tempted to set aside the ethical considerations. If the most hated offenders, such as rapists, child molesters and serial killers did not have the right to be protected under the law from the harmful action of fellow inmates and prison wardens, it is doubtful that mere ethical thinking would be sufficient to save them from harm. The entitlements of women prisoners, such as the right to be free of sexual harassment or the threat of rape, have been procured only under the duress of law.

The transformation of human rights into rights enforceable under the law poses particular problems, since the operative assumption is that human rights can speak only in one language. That customs and traditional usages have in most Third World countries functioned for centuries in place of law, and that even without the rule of law in a formalistic sense there were conventions and traditions which bound one person to respect the rights of another, is not something that proponents of the rule of law, convinced of the uniqueness of the West, are prepared to concede. The rule of law and an elaborate legal system are generally taken as synonymous with justice, but this defies the experience of most societies that lived with complex notions of social, economic, and distributive justice. The right to freedom of religious worship, for example, was seldom if ever explicitly recognized in premodern societies, but is enshrined as a fundamental right in the constitution of virtually every secular modern nation-state. But is it a reasonable inference that the freedom of religious worship did not as a consequence exist in premodern societies, and by what extraordinary sleight of hand does the experience of Europe, where religious warfare was endemic, come to serve as a template for the history of India, Africa, or anywhere else?

Not a single instance of anti-semitism has ever been recorded from the Indian past; indeed the available evidence suggests that the Jewish community had every privilege accorded to other communities,[46] and yet one scholar, whose limited conception of world history is distressingly evident, can with utter ease write, apropos of the rights of citizenship conferred upon Jews by the French Revolution, that "nowhere else in the world, not even in the new United States, did Jews have full civil and political rights."[47] (Why "even" the United States? What standards did the US set for the world? Did not the US Constitution implicitly reduce a black man to three-fifths of a person?[48]) The Zoroastrians fled from Iran to India, and it is India, to rehearse well-trod ground, that gave birth to

Hinduism, Buddhism, Jainism, and Sikhism. The ground reality in India was always one of heterodoxy in religious worship, which is scarcely to say that religious persecution never took place. India was, in other words, a multi-religious society long before the right to freedom of religious worship was conferred in the United States and European countries. The only tenable assumption, solidly grounded in the historical experience of Europe, is that the right to freedom of religious expression was necessary precisely because Europe had a demonstrable history of extreme intolerance in matters of religious belief and worship. Though the human rights community in the West will be loath to admit it, the contemporary discourse of human rights is illustrative of a fundamental tendency in the West, namely to legalize various aspects of human experience and install the legal standard as the most desirable universal norm, and from there to suggest that societies lacking this standard, though the lived, historical experience of their people might have been far richer, are grossly deficient.

The anomalies in imposing a standard of "rule of law," and then tying it to a conception of human rights, are much too obvious, though the states which most vigorously push for human rights have seldom allowed any introspection to derail them from their missionary zeal. We now expect rights to be protected under the law and the conformity of states to the rule of law. But by what right, with what authority, and with what consequences do certain states brand other states as outlaw or renegade states, living outside the pale of the rule of law, allegedly oblivious to the rights of their subjects, and therefore subject to sanctions from the international community? There is one rule of law for the powerful, and an altogether different one for those states that do not speak the "rational," "diplomatic," and "sane" language that the West has decreed is the universal form of linguistic exchange.[49] It is not only the case that when the US and its allies retaliate against their foes, they are engaged in "just war," purely "defensive" measures in the interest of national security, or acts of "humanitarian intervention," but that when Libyans, Syrians, or Palestinians do so, they are transformed into "terrorists" or ruthless and self-aggrandizing despots in the pursuit of international dominance. There is the familiar problem, which in its various permutations I address at greater length in the following chapter: who is to police the police? The United States claims adherence to international law, but summarily rejected the authority of the World Court when it condemned the

United States for waging undeclared war against Nicaragua. Less than a decade ago, the United States Supreme Court, in an astounding judgment barely noticed in the American press, upheld the constitutionality of a decision of a circuit court in Texas which, by allowing American law enforcement officers to kidnap nationals of a foreign state for alleged offences under American law for the purpose of bringing them to trial in an American court, effectively proclaimed the global jurisdiction of American law. In earlier times, such lawlessness was rightly known as piracy.[50]

There are, however, less obvious and more significant problems with the legalistic conception of a world order where human rights will be safeguarded. The present conception of human rights rests largely on a distinction between state and civil society, a distinction here fraught with hazardous consequences. The rights which are claimed are rights held against the state or, to put it another way, with the blessing of the state: the right to freedom of speech and expression, the right to gather in public, the right to express one's grievances within the limits of the constitution, and so forth. The state becomes the guarantor of these rights, when in fact it is everywhere the state which is the most flagrant violator of human rights. Not only does the discourse of human rights privilege the state, but the very conception of "rights" must of necessity remain circumscribed. The right to a fair hearing upon arrest, or to take part in the government of one's country, is acknowledged as an unqualified political and civil right, but the right to housing, food, clean air, an ecologically sound environment, free primary and secondary education, public transportation, a high standard of health, the preservation of one's ethnic identity and culture, and security in the event of unemployment or impairment due to disease and old age, is not accorded parity. This division is reflected in the deeply ambivalent deliberations of the United Nations ever since its inception: though the economic and social charter of the United Nations speaks to the larger concerns which I have here adumbrated, the Universal Declaration of Human Rights is really a manifesto on political and civil rights. If the intention was to give the Declaration more visibility, and slight the more complex matter of socioeconomic rights, the Western democracies were remarkably successful. It requires no elaborate theory of conspiracy to understand that the United States, where entire communities – African-Americans, Native Americans, Puerto Ricans, and Asian-Americans – were laboring under systematic discrimination and severe deprivation, was not keen on the more expansive conception of human rights which would have called into question its treatment of its own minorities.

We should be emphatically clear, on the other hand, that the newly developed, developing and underdeveloped countries should not be allowed the luxury, much less the right, of taking recourse to the argument that the present conception of human rights is violative of "Asian values" or the indigenous cultural and political norms of other people. Political leaders who have been prone to advance this argument, such as Malaysia's Mahathir Mohamad, have embraced the developmental agenda of the West with vengeance, and are enthusiastic proponents of free market reforms, technological prowess, and the information superhighway. Apparently all of this can be happily reconciled with "Asian values," but human rights cannot be, judging from the persecution of Mahathir's political adversary, the former Deputy Prime Minister and Finance Minister, Anwar Ibrahim,[51] who is now serving a long prison term on what are almost certainly fabricated charges of homosexual conduct and sodomy. Mahathir and his like present us with a parody of the ludicrous evolutionary model where non-Western nations are destined – let us not forget the "end of history" vision – to become progressively free and democratic, just so long as they can ruthlessly forge ahead with development and progress in the wake of which human rights will doubtless follow. If this model has not met with as much criticism as one might reasonably have expected, it is because it is in conformity both to the historical experience of European powers, which brutalized the rest of the world before they conferred rights on their own subjects, and to the prevailing wisdom that adherence to a free market ideology will bring all the other good things in life in due course.

The seldom-noticed irony in the Asian values mode of argument is that the first and most ardent proponents of human rights in the twentieth century were largely nationalists and political leaders from the former colonies.[52] Gandhi's insistence on the struggle for economic and social equality as an inescapable part of the quest for "human rights," movingly captured in his directions to the Indian National Congress party on the eve of his assassination on January 30th 1948, where he suggested that its leaders and members endeavor to ensure full social, economic, cultural, and political rights for all Indians, was dismissed as so much utopian thinking.[53] When Nehru, Nasser, or Sukarno spoke of human rights,[54] with a view not only to the rights of individuals but to the immense global disparities, they were in turn advised that they should keep their objectives confined to realizable goals and admonished that the talk of human rights within the wider context of global exploitation and inequality was only a way of giving succor to the enemy. Against the backdrop of the Cold War, the United States adopted the view that the former colonies were to be prevailed upon to think not so much of their rights as of their duty to assist the free world in the containment of communism.

The idea of human rights, one can agree, is noble and its denial an effrontery to humankind. It is understandable that the most commonly expressed objection to "human rights" should reinforce the idea that, as an ideological and political tool of the West, and particularly of the only remaining superpower, human rights is contaminated. Perhaps, before human rights is flaunted by the United States, which imagines itself as the leader of the human rights movement, as what most of the rest of the world must learn to respect, the movement for human rights should first come home to roost. The barbarous record of European imperial powers and of the United States, which has the singular distinction of having engaged in mass slaughter of its real and imagined adversaries in as many diverse ways as history can furnish evidence of, from the deliberate infliction of disease and scalping to chemical warfare, napalm bombing, nuclear incineration, and terror bombing, stands forth as testimony to the human capacity for hypocrisy. It staggers the imagination to think that inscribed on the marble wall of the main lobby at no place other than the CIA headquarters in Langley, Virginia is this biblical quotation "And Ye Shall Know the Truth / And the Truth Shall Make You Free" (John 8: 32).

Invocations to hypocrisy, however, can only get us so far, even when the authoritative voice of Noam Chomsky is there to state that people in the Third World "have never understood the deep totalitarian strain in Western culture, nor have they ever understood the savagery and cynicism of Western culture."[55] It is even prudent to be self-reflective about summoning Chomsky as a witness, for in the last analysis his very presence, and that of like-minded critics, is adduced as an instance of the West's unique capacity for self-criticism and tolerance of dissent. A similar strand of thought, I have argued elsewhere,[56] is to be witnessed in the epidemic of apologies lately engulfing Europe and the US: now that the Western nations have tendered some apologies for previous atrocities, for instance those perpetrated against Native Americans (in the US and Canada), the argument frequently encountered is that such conduct points to Western culture's capacity for atonement, its willingness to seek forgiveness, and its generosity of spirit. The more substantive concern about contemporary human rights discourse and its principal location in the West is that it now appears to posit universal standards of human morality. This universalism, like all others which have constituted the fabric of modernity, is rooted in the specific cultural and political histories of Western civilization; it is also a universalism that stands for the "end of history," and its defiance is no longer possible in principle, though as long as political systems remain imperfect, and the trappings of power remain irresistible for political leaders, the quest for human rights will continue. Human rights, of all the ideas generated in contemporary culture, remains the most totalizing in its philosophical presuppositions, ideological fervor, and reach. The NATO bombing of Serbia and Kosovo gave us only the slightest hint of the terror of human rights discourses that we are yet to witness.

3 Governance in the Twenty-First Century

The United States is the world's sole superpower. One cannot be certain whether those nations which have been terrorized by the United States, or those which live in constant apprehension of American intervention, are more aware of the new reality; or whether, indeed, the United States itself is most awed by its own overlordship of contemporary world politics. Not more than two or three years ago, Madeleine Albright, the then Secretary of State, characterized the United States as "the world's indispensable nation";[1] and an even more widely circulating story, set in the time of her ascendancy to high political office, describes her as in turn stunned when a summary account of American military might was offered to her, and disturbed that this well-oiled machine was not being put to adequate use. Albright, one imagines, was suitably pleased by the outcome of the latter sentiment: her tenure at the State Department saw the United States initiate raids over Afghanistan and Sudan, the nearly daily bombing of Iraq in conjunction with crippling (and ongoing) sanctions[2] and the carpet bombing of Serbia over a period lasting into several weeks.

Let us be certain that Albright had no monopoly among highly placed American officials on the practice of evil and the display of callousness. The sheen of arrogance did not sit well on her frame, but it is everywhere to be seen in America's disposition towards the world, extending from George Bush Jr.'s declaration that the rest of the world is ill-informed about the global impact of greenhouse gases to "scholarly" studies, which the United States uniquely generates, purporting to show that more guns leads to less crime.[3] The execution of Timothy McVeigh, the convicted killer of 168 Americans in what without a trace of irony was invariably referred to as the worst act of terrorism on American soil, as though Native Americans and African-Africans were not terrorized for several hundred years, should have put a damper on the American notion that its mission is to show the way to the rest of the world. The European Union does not permit capital punishment, and recent reports by Human Rights Watch and Amnesty International have placed the US in the "same shameful death penalty league as China, Iran and Saudi Arabia."[4] Like gravitates towards like: the United States is also one of only five countries that execute mentally retarded people, as well as convicts who were juveniles at the time when the offending act was committed,[5] and in all these respects it finds itself in the company of countries that it likes to characterize as "rogue states," dictatorships, or totalitarian states. Amnesty International's most recent report says of the United States that it "is as frequently an impediment to human rights as it is an advocate."[6] Consequently, one would have thought that the United States would have been chastened by the searing criticism attendant upon McVeigh's execution, but instead we find one former US Ambassador to NATO stating that "perhaps the last thing that many Americans want, especially proponents of the death penalty, is interference from abroad, and especially from Europeans" – and why especially Europeans, if not for the obvious reason that Europeans clearly lack "'clean hands' after a century of mass barbarism from which, in fact, the U.S. on more than one occasion played a major role of deliverance."[7]

The United States, whatever the political affiliations of its leadership, constitutes one element of a tripartite regime of global governance that is the subject of the present chapter. In recent years, particularly after the fall of the Soviet Union, when it became possible to advance the fiction that the world would henceforth be able to move to the orchestration of a single purposeful end, the United States began to invoke the international community in defense or rationalization of many of its policies. The supposition, not in the least unwarranted as circumstances would reveal, was that the Soviet Union would no longer obstruct the United States in the Security Council, and that the United Nations could now be counted upon to reflect the global interests of the US (and its allies, if that should prove to be desirable). If the United States could be seen as acting justifiably in the name of the international community, it would rebound to its credit in numerous ways. It would show that in the moment of its triumph, the United States was prepared to be generous, charitable, supremely democratic; where circumstances had conspired to render it the only remaining superpower, it was nonetheless prepared to act in concert with other nations. Following Saddam Hussein's invasion of Kuwait, the United States chose to utilize the United Nations as the vehicle for its response: sanctions against Iraq were imposed by the UN, and a multilateral force, or at least the appearance of one, was gathered to offer resistance to Iraq and drive it out of Kuwait. There were some detractors, but the international community was nebulous enough as a category that some nations could opt out of the political arrangement without putting into doubt the legitimacy of the proposed enterprise. Indeed, unlike other blocs, such as NATO, the Warsaw Pact, OPEC (Oil Producing and Exporting Coutries), or the OAU (Organization of African Unity), the international community conjured the image of a non-ideological festival of humanity gathered to enhance world peace. Everything was to be gained, including diminished chances for the loss of American lives, and nothing lost by acting on behalf of the international community.

There can be no doubt that the United Nations has become, over the course of the last decade, increasingly visible – though visibility has no necessary correlation with importance – in the enterprise of global governance. It suffices to note for the present that, contrary to the conventional political interpretations of the seeming evolution of the United Nations into an international forum, it has become an increasingly less representative body of world opinion. There is, conceivably, an argument to be made to the effect that many of the ideas which are widely prevalent in social science literature, such as sustainable development and human rights, received a particular salience under the aegis of the United Nations. Similarly, the increasing importance of non-governmental organizations (NGOs), which in some countries – Nepal and Bangladesh, for instance – exercise a disproportionate influence in policy-making, owes much to the United Nations' encouragement of development initiatives stemming from civil society and its willingness to grant such organizations consultative status. The United Nations has also been the instrumental force in the reportedly worldwide efforts to combat contagious diseases, such as cholera, polio, and tuberculosis. The successful campaign which led to the eradication of smallpox was conducted by the World Health Organization (WHO), one of the many specialized agencies operating under the UN banner.

While the greatly enhanced sphere of activities of the UN and its specialized agencies cannot be doubted, and the very office of the Secretary-General, held for the greater part of the last 55 years by diplomats from Africa, Asia, and South America, appears to convey the notion that the organization has a truly ecumenical aspect, in respect of both economic and political governance the UN as a whole can no longer be seen as a body which speaks to the truth, is sufficiently attentive to the concerns of nations which do not belong to the upper strata, or accepts the idea that human life should be viewed as having the same value everywhere. The inequities generated by the United Nations are most transparent, as is later discussed, in the expedient and indiscriminate recourse to sanctions; they are much less apparent, but nonetheless just as acute, in the peacekeeping operations of the United Nations, a comparatively less discussed aspect of UN humanitarian work.

Around the time that the United Nations was brought into existence, the Bretton Woods Conference (1944) also gave rise to two organizations – the World Bank and the International Monetary Fund (IMF, often just "the Fund") – which today, conjoined with the World Trade Organization (WTO), are chiefly responsible for global economic governance. Their mandate, especially over the last decade when liberalization and deregulation were vigorously promoted by the US, was to bring errant countries, in what I would describe as the economic analogue to the idea of "rogue states," back on course, by assisting them to achieve a rapid transition, for instance by the removal of subsidies and the elimination of import tariffs, to a free market economy.

The first Director-General of the World Trade Organization (WTO) was effusive in noting that the "world changed" and "a defining moment in modern history" had been reached when signatory countries to the General Agreement on Tariffs and Trade agreed upon the much more ambitious agenda contained in the agreements collected together under WTO. "Put simply," Peter Sutherland declared, "governments came to the conclusion that the notion of a new world order was not merely attractive but absolutely vital; that the reality of the global market ... required a level of multilateral co-operation never before attempted."[8] The proponents of the WTO, and more generally of regional free trade associations, speak in an idiom which puts an onerous burden upon those who might wish to dissent from the promising vision to which they appear to be beholden. When world order is invoked, just whose world is serving as the template for understanding? What does it mean to speak of order, and what languages – of discipline, chastisement, enforcement, pacification, and exclusion – are summoned by the idea of order?

DEMOCRATIC TOTALITARIANISM: REQUIEM FOR THE US

The United States presents an altogether novel phenomenon in world history, but not for the reasons trumpeted by its supporters, lovers, and self-aggrandizing politicians. Periodically we are reminded by its presidents and leading politicians that it is the "greatest country on earth." There are also the thunderous cliches that proliferate in the American language. One hears of the "land of the free and the brave," of the "huddled masses" who found refuge from persecution, of "rugged individualism" and, the perennial favorite, of "the American dream."

It is not only the most astute observers who must have wondered why Americans are prone to think of the United States and the world as largely identical categories. The United States' umbrage at its recent exclusion from two UN bodies, the Human Rights Commission and the International Narcotics Control Board,[9] points unequivocally to its feeling that these organizations can no longer be viewed as "world" bodies. One has the inescapable feeling, upon reading American commentators when the country is confronted with even a modicum of adversity, that the world is diminished when the United States is diminished. But now is the time to recognize, to admit at least of the possibility, that in the diminishment of the United States lies the best hope for the future of humankind.

The trajectory of American exceptionalism generally goes back to the Declaration of Independence and the war for the emancipation of the colonies from British rule, though an earlier generation of scholars recognized that the seeds of American self-perception lay, in the phrase of Perry Miller, in the puritans' "errand into the wilderness" and the inheritance of some English characteristics.[10] The English in the nineteenth century doubtless thought of themselves as a people who were hardy, intrepid, quick of mind, entrepreneurial, and ambitious, and the spread of empire certainly convinced some of them that they had a distinct role to play in world history. At a time when the national character industry was beginning to emerge, it was customary to think of the English as especially predisposed towards the "spirit of democracy," though commentators recognized that aristocratic influence was required to open democracy to the masses. The contrast – the only contrast that the English could be bothered to make, before German militarism became the new benchmark for considerations of Englishness – with the curious despotism of the French was a firmly established trait of

English writing: in the words of Edward Lytton Bulwer, writing in 1833, "The vanity of the Frenchman consists (as I have somewhere read) in belonging to so great a country: but the vanity of the Englishman exults in the thought that so great a country belongs to himself."[11] Yet one seldom encounters in English writings the invocations to divine providence or special dispensation that are so characteristically, down to the present day, the bedrock of American exceptionalism and which have inspired not only the Shakers, the Mormons, the Seventh Day Adventists, and other like groups, but even ordinary Americans into thinking that no country has so favorably received the visitations of the Divine.[12] On the other hand, with the evident appeal in the opening lines of the American Declaration of Independence to "the people," it became customary to think of the United States as a place that was uniquely sensitive to the aspirations of ordinary people, a place that did not mark boundaries between aristocrats and commoners.

It is the conjoining of these two strands of thought, namely the self-representation of Americans as inheritors of God's special blessings and as originators of the democratic traditions of the modern world, which has turned the United States into the most dangerous political formation the world has ever known. An article published in 2001, and there are dozens more in a similar vein, states with evident approval that the prevailing consensus which drives American foreign policy is that the United States brings to culmination the manifest purpose of history, namely "freedom, achieved through the spread of democratic capitalism, and embodied in the American Way of Life."[13] Each generation's politicians capture this sentiment in a particular phrase, and Clinton referred to the US as the nation on "the right side of history."[14] Far more so than in other nations, when American politicians speak, they usually do so in the name of "the American people." Herein lies not merely the assurance that common people have not been forgotten, but that actions undertaken by the United States are done in the name of its people, with their consent, and ultimately for their good. That is one way of foreclosing dissent: no one wishes to be critical of political practices which appear to take the people as their constituencies. Again, self-righteousness is a vice on which the Americans scarcely exercise a monopoly, but politics elsewhere in the world has not been so suffused with the thought that the US and God are engaged in perpetual and privileged conversation. In the last presidential elections in the United States, which prides itself on setting the world standard for elections but suffered the embarrassment of the "stolen" votes farce, the world was witness to the ascendancy of a mass executioner who without a trace of irony described Jesus as his philosopher. The politician who ends his or her speech with the usual invocation, "God bless America," appears to take it as axiomatic that there is a special place for the US in God's heart; there is also the offensive presumption that the world can fairly be divided between those whom God chooses to bless and those not so chosen. Among the industrialized nations of the West, the United States remains distinct in having a majority of its population declare themselves religious-minded and church-goers; it is also distinct in that abortion providers are hunted down and killed because they are held responsible for spoiling the handiwork of God.

On closer examination, the United States turns out to embody what might be described as democratic totalitarianism. Its pathetic idea of exporting democracy, for instance to Latin America, is captured in Woodrow Wilson's declared intention, "I am going to teach the South American republics to elect good men."[15] The US has long pushed the idea that fair and open elections are the litmus test of a democracy, but that singularly dubious contribution to world politics rests on the same principle that informs market choice. The phenomenon of a communist party repeatedly being elected to power by a fully literate electorate, such as in the south Indian state of Kerala, is entirely unthinkable in the United States. "Choice" may be meaningful when genuine dissenters can make themselves heard. For all the exposés – by William Appleman Williams, Noam Chomsky, Michael Parenti, Edward Said, Gore Vidal, and Seymour Hersch, among others – of American foreign policy and its brutalities, it has not made one iota of difference. Indeed, their presence is publicly lauded by their critics as a standing testimony to the American appetite for debate, its tolerance of dissenting visions, and its enthronement of the idea of free speech. As the spectacle of Milosevic being dragged to The Hague began to loom large, the rare cry arose that Henry Kissinger and Robert McNamara, whose war crimes make Milosevic appear to be a common street criminal, be subjected to the same standards.[16] But the veneration of Kissinger as a grand strategist and elder statesman extends so far that his "expert opinion" was being solicited on *Le'Affair Milosevic*.

The United States furnishes, then, the most spectacular example in history of a nation-state which has succeeded in persuading the world that it sits atop the space of freedom – and it does so while it remains singularly catholic and ecumenical in its oppressive reach, beginning with some segments of its own population. This is one of the many ironic aspects of American freedom and its political system that justify the oxymoron "democratic totalitarianism." The Unites States now has the largest prison population in the world, and its incarceration rate of 690 prisoners per 100,000 people exceeds that of every other country, including Russia and South Africa.[17] While the US attempts to cajole the unfree world – the Freedom House, an institution that could have come straight out of Huxley's *Brave New World*, ranks nations according to the degree of freedom they tolerate – into an acceptance of democracy, a very considerable portion of its own African-American population, who won the right to vote in 1964 after a protracted struggle, has again been disenfranchised for life. All but two states deny prisoners the right to vote, but eight states disenfranchise all felons for life, and another five disenfranchise most felons for life. Since felony convictions fall disproportionately upon black men, in seven states one in four black men is unable to vote for the remainder of his lifetime. Of all African-American men, 13 percent are presently disenfranchised, a rate seven times the national average.[18] Behind bars, these men are not only robbed of their life, but are swindled by telephone companies, which charge prisoners a rate for calls several times higher than what is charged residential customers. Big business can be conducted profitably in jails.[19]

African-Americans are perhaps only the most unfortunate, since the heavy hand of American justice falls in their own backyard; those not dispatched to prisons are recruited to harness the fruits of oppression in other lands, if their disproportionately massive numbers in the US Army are any indication. Peasants in Vietnam and Laos, fruit growers in Central America, rice farmers in the Philippines, anti-imperialists, socialists and communists around the world – all have felt the crushing weight of American military boots upon them. This history is reasonably well-documented,[20] and though it has moved African-Americans, Native Americans, and others to the visible expression of rejection of dominant histories, America's imperious conduct of foreign policy has not been impaired. The United States as a whole has scarcely paused to reflect upon its grave misfortune in being the only country to have used nuclear weapons, and the predominant argument in defense of this action remains that it saved many lives. The veracity or falsehood of this argument apart, it is striking that "lives" always translates into American lives – that is the measure of worthwhile human existence. Perhaps in the atomic bombings of Hiroshima and Nagasaki lie the leitmotifs of two categories that in the 1990s became acutely expressive of American hegemony: non-nuclear nuclearism and rogue states.

Non-Nuclear Nuclearism

Though nuclear weapons have been used only twice, within days of each other, the threat of nuclear war loomed large during the Cold War. The United States alone is estimated (in 1996 dollars) to have spent $5.5 trillion on developing, building, and maintaining its nuclear arsenal since 1945.[21] Preparation for nuclear war gave rise to its own warped vocabulary, including "nuclear deterrence," "nuclear shelters," and "mutually assured destruction" (MAD). That same mentality has been imbibed by India and Pakistan, which many experts, in the US and some in the Indian subcontinent itself, consider to be the world's most likely zone of nuclear conflict. In recent years, the experts have also been given to speaking of nuclear terrorism at the hands of fanatics (usually Muslims in this discourse) and untethered political adventurists, though often certain states, notably Iraq and Iran, are construed as potential sponsors of "nuclear terrorism." The break-up of the Soviet Union, which unexpectedly turned Ukraine, Belarus, and Kazakhstan into nuclear states, gave rise to numerous alarmist scenarios in the minds of American policy-makers about the proliferation and sale of nuclear weapons to despots and "rogue states." In the United States, the unstated assumption has always been that nuclear terrorism would be directed at itself or its friends, especially Israel. But, once again, it is imperative to recall that it is the United States which terrorized Japan into submission with the nuclear incineration of Hiroshima and Nagasaki; that it is the United States which, on the documentary record, contemplated dropping nuclear bombs during the Korean and Vietnam Wars, and that the United States offers a standing threat to any adversary with the largest stockpile of the most advanced nuclear weapons in the world. The obscene happiness with which Truman received the news of Hiroshima's devastation, "This is the greatest thing in history," tells its own tale of the United States's enchantment with the atom.[22] Who terrorizes whom?

Such is the opprobrium now attached to nuclear war, however, that it is not prudent to think of nuclearism only in relation to the use, deployment, and threat of nuclear weapons. The bombing of

Japan with "conventional" weapons in the weeks and months preceding the attacks upon Hiroshima and Nagasaki offers an instructive and overlooked prologue to the emergence of non-nuclear nuclearism in the 1990s. Though the British had deliberately carried out the terror bombing of the civilian German population in retaliation for Hitler's relentless air assault on Britain in World War II, the Americans explicitly and repeatedly disavowed the aerial bombardment of urban areas, and as late as February 1945, Secretary of War Henry Stimson reaffirmed at a press conference that "our policy has never been to inflict terror bombing on civilian populations."[23] Yet this policy was abandoned when it came to war with Japan – and during three hours of the bombing of Tokyo on March 10th 1945, 125,000 civilians were killed and 40 percent of the city was destroyed. Neither Hiroshima nor Nagasaki left so many dead after the nuclear explosions: indeed, in three continuous days of bombing, the dead in Tokyo and other cities, numbered at far more than 300,000, was nearly twice the immediate casualties in Hiroshima and Nagasaki put together.[24] The American strategist who masterminded the incendiary attacks upon Tokyo, which created raging firestorms, described the victims as "scorched and boiled and baked to death" – so intense was the heat that "canals boiled, metal melted, and buildings and human beings burst spontaneously into flames."[25]

An altogether different kind of transgression was doubtless committed with the fatal decision to "nuke" Hiroshima and Nagasaki: both the scale and the manner of death, a compound of instant obliteration and, for the victims of radiation, suffering and death by inches over years, would distinguish the two kinds of bombings. Nor can one doubt that an immense psychological and moral barrier was crossed with nuclear weapons. However, many contemporary American observers, and even the statesmen entrusted with carrying out the war, failed to grasp the difference between the nuclear bomb and the largest or most lethal conventional bomb. "Most Americans supposed, like Stalin," write the authors of Total War, "that it was simply a bigger and more lethal weapon."[26] Perhaps, viewed from a different perspective, there is something to be said for not making that distinction. Both the carpet bombing of Tokyo and the nuclear incineration of Hiroshima stemmed from the perception that the Japanese had no claim on life, but at no moment of the war with Germany can such a view be discerned; the evil of German militarism was there to be seen, but the Germans did not

thereby cease to be human. No one ever called for the extermination of the Germans, or for the wholesale, systematic, and
overwhelming obliteration of German civilians; yet the Chairman
of the War Manpower Commission, Paul McNutt, stated publicly
that he "favored the extermination of the Japanese *in toto*."[27]
Moreover, and here the recent American-led aerial campaigns of the
1990s begin to take on a more ominous note, abstention from
nuclear warfare could serve as a license to permit no constraints on
the conduct of "conventional" bombing.

Critically, as I have already suggested, the barrier that prevents
further use of nuclear weapons is not so far recognized to exist in
the case of non-nuclear nuclearism, which may be termed a
worldview propounding total extinction without the fear of retaliation. The atomic bombing of Hiroshima and Nagasaki would not
have taken place, one can be sure, had the United States thought
Japan capable of retaliation, and the bombings of Iraq and
Yugoslavia were also similarly marked by cowardly sentiments. That
is what humanitarian warfare, most particularly against rogue states,
has come down to in our times.

Rogue States

Ronald Reagan made the expression "evil empire" famous, but the
1990s was the decade when "rogue states" firmly inserted itself into
the political lexicon. One scholar who has studied the emergence of
the Rogue Doctrine points to its origins in a speech made by Reagan
in 1985, when he referred to the financing and political support of
terrorist attacks against the United States and its citizens abroad by
a "confederation" of "outlaw states."[28] In the administration of his
successor, George Bush Sr., this language was deployed more
frequently, and the disintegration of the Soviet Union would become
cause for further alarm about the proliferation of nuclear weapons:
as Secretary of State-designate James Baker had informed the Senate
Foreign Relations Committee in 1989, "Chemical warheads and
ballistic missiles have fallen into the hands of governments and
groups with proven records of aggression and terror."[29] The United
States had for some time been predisposed towards viewing certain
hostile countries as rogue states, but the "evil empire" was the greater
adversary and the more tangible threat, and Saddam Hussein's
invasion of Kuwait, occurring in the context of the dissolution of
the Soviet Union, furnished just the pretext needed to give the
concept of rogue states legitimacy and a human face. Speaking to

reporters a few days after Saddam Hussein had occupied Kuwait, Bush described him and his ilk as "international outlaws and renegades."[30] Clinton's national security adviser, Anthony Lake, would shortly thereafter refer to "backlash states."[31] Here was a set of related terms to describe a family of states that bore malice towards the rest of the world.

It is sometimes suggested that far too much has been made of the designation "rogue states," and that the US itself might have had more to lose by this term than any state so designated by the term.[32] The rogue state designation prevents open engagement with a regime, such as Iran, that is changing. This mode of interpretation only presumes, however, that one-time rogue states might reform themselves, but it does not question the politics of nomination, or the power that some nations arrogate to themselves to name others and their power to have such nomination accepted by others. Naming is not innocuous: to name is to shape, exclude, include, form and deform identity; it is to confer or deny privilege. Numerous countries have frequently been tempted to designate the United States as the rogue state *par excellence*, considering its innumerable instances of violation of international law and its undeclared wars on civilian populations. But their influence in the international media, itself largely dominated by US-owned cartels, is negligible. Nor is it an accident, to hint further at the necessity of considering "rogue state" a critical category of hierarchy and domination, that rogue states became the successors to the Soviet Union and the Eastern bloc countries in the political imaginary of the Anglo-American world. Speaking on the fiftieth anniversary of Churchill's famous "Iron Curtain" speech, Baroness Thatcher warned the West (and the rest of the world) that the rogue states, many "led by megalomaniacs and strongmen of proven inhumanity or by weak, unstable, or illegitimate governments," had once been contained by their patron, the Soviet Union, but were now likely to seek "weapons of mass destruction" with the intention of destroying "major western capitals."[33]

If people and nations alike are known partly by the company they keep, then the United States is the pre-eminent rogue state of our times. Many of the wicked "strongmen" were proteges, friends, and allies of the Americans before it was discovered that they were expendable. Manual Noriega was catapulted into power by the CIA; Saddam Hussein was welcomed as a secular leader who would provide a critical counterweight to the Islamic fundamentalism of

Khomeini, and for some years the Americans and the Iraqis even traded intelligence reports; the Taliban, when they were merely Mujahideen, were feted as "freedom fighters" whose own hardy spirit seemed somewhat reminiscent of Yankee individualism, and so on. There are other reasons why the rogue state designation fits its creator snugly.[34] We are reminded by the etymology of the word "rogue" that it is a characterization not only of the vagabond and the knave, but also of those fatally marred by arrogance. The United States has taken the view that it need not be bound by many of the world's most important treaties and agreements. Its unwillingness to abide by the Kyoto Protocol on global warming is a matter of public knowledge, as is the failure of the US Congress to ratify the Comprehensive Test Ban Treaty (CTBT). But the roguish failure extends well beyond these treaties, where the US is not spectacularly isolated – India, Pakistan, and Israel have failed to sign the CTBT as well. Similarly in its opposition to an international criminal court the US was joined by China, Syria, and Iraq. The Unites States shares distinction with rogue states or countries supportive of reprehensible political systems in many of its other abnegations of international obligations:

- Law of the Sea Treaty
- Convention on the Elimination of All Forms of Discrimination Against Women
- Convention on the Rights of the Child
- Anti-Personnel Landmines Ban [Ottawa] Treaty

The argument generally proffered by American critics of these agreements is that they are an affirmation of the sovereignty of the United Nations, or that American law would be superseded by international law, or that American interests would be ill-served. Another spurious argument commonly advanced is that such universal treaties have their origins in the Universal Declaration of Human Rights, and that this document goes much too far in that it stipulates the entitlements which governments must provide, while the US Constitution is far more prudent in prescribing limits to what governments can do. The Universal Declaration of Human Rights, we are told, is condemned by the fact that one of its signatories was Joseph Stalin; but this argument is never advanced to its logical conclusion, namely that since rogues and tyrants also signed countless other international agreements, the United States should opt out of those as well.[35] One is tempted to conclude that there remains in American thinking the inescapable tension between the desire for isolationism and the attractions for the United States of unprecedented engagement with the world's affairs as the only remaining superpower ... but perhaps more enticing is the thought that rogues all find each other in the end.

NATIONS, BUT FAR FROM UNITED: NEANDERTHAL POLITICS

The history of the inception of the United Nations commonly begins with its predecessor organization, the League of Nations. It is understandable that the prevention of war should have been foremost in the minds of the founders of the League, which was established in the immediate aftermath of World War I. Member states of the League agreed to respect each other's sovereignty, to resort to various dispute settlement mechanisms, and to enter into an agreement for collective security. In these respects, and in many others, such as the power invested in the League to impose sanctions in an effort to enforce settlement, the League anticipated the provisions of the UN Charter. In the standard narrative, the League's early years were not without some successes: it conducted a plebiscite in Silesia, and settled territorial disputes between Bulgaria and Greece, and between Lithuania and Poland. But its viability as a political force is said to have been vitiated by the League's failure to respond to Ethiopian pleas for protection against the aggression of Mussolini, and its weakness in acting to forestall or even condemn the Japanese occupation of Manchuria. Much has been written about the "weakness" of the League, and it is suggested that the founders of the United Nations, which grew out of the Atlantic Charter, a joint declaration by Churchill and Roosevelt in August 1941 to enhance cooperation on economic and security issues, were determined that the new organization would not be similarly emasculated.

The United Nations Charter, drafted in 1944, stated that membership of the United Nations would be confined to "peace-loving" countries (Chapter II, Article 4.1). The principle of sovereignty, inherited from the Westphalian state system, was enshrined as the basis of the United Nations system, and the General Assembly, as I have earlier observed, was conceived as the organization which would embody the principle of one state, one vote. The Charter states unequivocally that "the Organization is based on the principle of the sovereign equality of all its Members" (Chapter I, Article 2.1), but it is instructive that the principle of sovereignty is implied as being sovereign with respect to the United Nations as a whole, rather than to any particular portion or body of the UN. Chapter V of the Charter, however, conferred permanent membership of the Security Council, which alone has enforcement powers, upon the US, UK, China, France, and the then Soviet Union; and the stipulation, in Article 27.1, that "each member of the Security Council shall have one vote," is entirely misleading, since it obscures the critical fact that the power of veto conferred upon the five permanent members means that not all votes are equal. During the Cold War, the Soviet Union exercised its veto power 121 times, the United States 72 times: the American involvement in Nicaragua and El Salvador, the Soviet occupation of Afghanistan, and China's invasion of Tibet could not be the subject of enforceable Security Council Resolutions.[36]

Thus from the outset the United Nations came to embody, in two vital respects, neanderthal politics. First, the supposition was that the nation-state is the most representative form of political community, and that it stands at the apex of political achievement. The Peace of Westphalia (1648), which brought to termination the Thirty Years War, and which has since proved to be inimical to peace everywhere else, furnished legitimacy to those ideas, such as embodying sovereignty in the nation-state, which still dominate modern politics. Religious terror had gripped Europe, and around the same time the "new science" was beginning to impose its own fundamentalism: the nation-state became the ground of the desperate quest for certainty. The nation-state was viewed as the natural fulfillment of human aspirations, the proper channel for the expression of territoriality and the cultural and social life of a well-defined people. Political leadership would no longer be derived from an external source, such as the Pope or an imperial authority headquartered outside the nation-state. The nation-state contained within it the idea, central to the principle of sovereignty, that other states would not be allowed to meddle with its internal affairs. Though the Dutch legal scholar Hugo Grotius had already formulated elementary principles of international law, it is no surprise that the nation-state then incorporated a principle of absolute sovereignty. As is quite evident, however, from the history of European imperialism, the nation-state system was not generally envisaged as having any applicability beyond Europe's borders, and European rulers consistently failed to recognize the sovereignty of rulers in Asia, Africa, and elsewhere. What is striking is that when the UN Charter was drawn up, it rendered an explicit homage to the Westphalian tradition by conceding that the Charter did not "authorize the United Nations to intervene in matters which are essentially within the domestic jurisdiction of any state" (Chapter I, Article 2.7).

In its conception of, and reliance upon, the nation-state as the modular form of political life, the United Nations became the expression of the poverty of political thinking. Systemic inequality was structured into the very organization of the United Nations: on the one hand, the nation-state was assumed to be the *sine qua non* of modern political life, but on the other hand it was assumed that the nation-state would, in most of the non-Western world, remain largely unrealized as the fulfillment of a people's political aspirations. This could be interpreted, whenever circumstances warranted, as a license to set an errant nation-state on the right course. Sovereignty of states was assumed as being inviolable, but since "domestic juris-diction" was not defined, that left open the possibility for such innovations as were exemplified by NATO's bombing of Kosovo, which was defended as humanitarian intervention, or by the regime of disciplinary surveillance unleashed upon Iraq since its defeat in the Gulf War. China has consistently refused to countenance any interference from Western powers or the United Nations in the matter of its occupation of Tibet on the plea that Tibet falls entirely within its domestic jurisdiction, but it is useful to recall that Iraq, utilizing a similar argument, and with perhaps far more justification insofar as colonial powers had acquired a habit of arbitrarily parti-tioning colonized provinces, claimed – with some reason – that Kuwait was historically a province of Iraq. Indonesia's claim of domestic jurisdiction over East Timor, with the attendant implica-tion that the sanctity of Indonesia would be put into question if the case of East Timor was dragged before the court of world opinion, was accepted merely because Suharto was a loyal and zealous ally in the worldwide anti-communist designs of the United States.

At the heart of neanderthal politics lies the exceedingly old view, which no generation has ever been able to relinquish, that might determines right. The first interpreter of *realpolitik* in the West, Thucydides, suggested that the fate which befell the Melians, who unsuccessfully pleaded for their lives before the Athenians, could have been avoided had they been wise enough to understand that "right, as the world goes, is only in question between equals in power, while the strong do what they can and the weak suffer what they must."[37] The United Nations appeared to offer an advance, in its apparent advocacy of the complete equality of all nations, upon the previous history of humankind, and certainly upon the League of Nations's obsessive concern with the future of Europe. The UN "reflected a sharp awareness," one scholar has written, "of the developing significance of non-European peoples as full representatives in world affairs ... the new system was directed towards the problems of a world in which Europe would appear in drastically shrunken, and Asia and Africa in greatly enlarged, proportions."[38] And yet, as I have previously remarked, *realpolitik* was immediately embraced, not only by instituting a hierarchy of permanent and rotating membership in the Security Council, and conferring veto powers on its permanent members, but by institutionally awarding proportionately greater influence to countries which contributed the most to the World Bank, the IMF, and other important organizations affiliated to the UN system. Moreover, not to speak of the present, when the General Assembly has been all but reduced to a ceremonial speech-making body (its power in determining the UN budget aside), even in the early days of the United Nations it was manipulated by Western powers. In the critical period which saw the outbreak of the Korean War and a debate over Chinese representation in the UN, the Western powers were able to command a majority in the General Assembly. They engineered, under the Acheson Plan, the transference of the powers of the Security Council, where the Soviet Union could block resolutions with a veto, to the General Assembly; but when, as anti-colonial struggles gathered momentum, and the non-aligned movement came to occupy a significant third space, Western powers lost much of their support in the General Assembly, they insisted on reviving the Security Council as the only organization which could claim exclusive jurisdiction over matters pertaining to peace, security, and enforcement measures.[39]

No one who has been a student of geopolitics would have failed to observe that the ebb and flow of the Security Council's influence over world politics has a decisive relation to the degree to which the United States and its allies can rely upon the Council to advance unequivocally their interests. After the disintegration of the Soviet Union, when Russia and the Eastern bloc became acutely dependent on the West for financial credits and investment, the Security Council became a party to political actions that would have been previously unthinkable. The multilateral force pitted against Iraq, and put together, as has been amply documented, by a multitude of coercive and unethical actions undertaken by the United States

extending from bribery to the threat of military and economic reper-
cussions,[40] is the most well-known example of action authorized by
the Security Council in the post-Cold War period. The sanctions
regime in place against Iraq since before the commencement of the
Gulf War is similarly mandated by the Security Council, and the
Council's Resolution 687 also created UNSCOM, the United Nations
Special Commission, to monitor the destruction of Iraq's biological,
chemical, and nuclear weapons and facilities as part of the ceasefire
agreement of 6 April 1991. However, for all of their declared intent
to transform the United Nations, and in particular the Security
Council, into the supreme body of global political governance,
Western powers chose to bypass the UN when they decided that a
campaign of aerial bombardment was called for to render Yugoslavia
– a founding member of the UN and of the non-aligned movement,
and a major force of resistance against Nazism and fascism in the
dark days of World War II – compliant to the wishes of the international community.

The Security Council is seen by some critics, not without some
reason, as a law unto itself, despotic in its reach and the very
harbinger of evil for those who have been at its mercy. A number of
UN personnel charged with the responsibility for overseeing the Oil-
for-Food Program, designed to offer some relief to Iraq without
relieving it of its responsibility to comply with UN resolutions, have
resigned in recent years in protest against what is increasingly
described as the genocidal policy of the US and the UK towards
Iraq.[41] UNSCOM itself became embroiled in allegations, which its
previous head, Richard Butler, has scarcely been able to dislodge,
that it had far exceeded its mandate and was spying on the Iraqis on
behalf of the CIA. Against all this, the United Nations is invoked for
all the good it has done, most particularly in the areas of women's
development, the worldwide improvement of health and the elimination of disease, its monitoring and settlement of refugees, and in
its sponsorship of various global summits – on climate change, biodiversity, food security, women's empowerment, child labor, energy,
water, environmental policies, drug trafficking, among other
pressing subjects. But the greater part of the UN's visibility in the
political domain is derived from two sets of political operations,
which though subjected to much criticism, are also generally viewed
as the UN's greatest contribution to world peace and stability. The
UN peacekeeping forces were very much in the news in the 1990s, a
decade that saw a fourfold increase in their operations, and in the

same decade sanctions began to be deployed widely against rogue states or otherwise recalcitrant regimes. But perhaps a closer scrutiny of these recently revived categories of international politics might give some reason to doubt their supposed efficacy and morality.

Peacekeeping

The United States is often described as a merchant of death; it is much less frequently recognized as a merchant of peace, an appellation that will doubtless be mistaken by the uninitiated as an encomium. The US has been the world leader in the lucrative arms trade for several decades, and from 1994 to 1998, its share of the trade, at $53.9 billion, exceeded that of its 15 closest competitors put together.[42] In the same period, Russia earned $12.3 billion, France $10.6 billion, Britain $8.9 billion, and China $2.8 billion from arms trafficking: these are the five permanent members of the Security Council to whom the world has entrusted its security and well-being. The two largest buyers in the same period were Taiwan, which need only mention China to elicit the sympathy of American law-makers, and Saudi Arabia, a monarchial dictatorship which swims in oil and is the world's leading oil-producing country. Other pretexts have been found to justify arms sales on this magnitude, but nothing can disguise the fact that the United States remains the principal force for aggression and violence in the world, and that its government acts at the behest of corporations for whom the arms trade is the most lucrative part of their business.

It is apposite that the United States should also be the largest financial contributor to UN peacekeeping operations, which began in 1948 as an initiative of the Secretary-General and his Secretariat. There is provision for the pacific settlement of disputes, but not for peacekeeping forces, in the UN Charter: neither the US nor the Soviet Union would have permitted meddling by armed troops against their allies or within their spheres of influence, and so evolved the idea of deploying non-combatant forces with the consent of the parties to the conflict. The United Nations was entirely sidelined in many of the most important crises and conflicts of the second half of the twentieth century, and 36 of the 54 peace-keeping operations in the UN's history were established after 1991. Three years after the fall of the Soviet Union, the number of operations had risen from eight to eighteen, apparently another indication that the end of the Cold War had made possible the attempted resolution of violent conflict.[43]

In 1991, the budget allocated for peacekeeping operations amounted to $400 million; two years later, at nearly the height of such operations, when UNOSOM II (UN Operations in Somalia) and UNPROFOR (UN Protection Force in the Former Yugoslavia) were both at their peak strength, the budget had increased to $3.6 billion. However, the United States, Russia, France, Japan, and China, among other countries, all owed arrears; none more so than the United States, which in October 2000 was $1.14 billion dollars in debt for peacekeeping operations alone. That the country which has been the most assiduous in peddling arms to the entire world – democracies, real and alleged; authoritarian regimes; dictatorships; monarchies: all have been fed by the country that is sworn to the elimination of discrimination – should have been hesitant to support peacekeeping operations comes as no surprise. An "authoritative report on UN finances" in 1993 stated that for every $1,000 spent on their armed forces, member states spent only $1.40 on peace-keeping;[44] moreover, the United States has failed even to make its assessed payments. In the fiscal year 1997, Congress apportioned only $352.4 million of the $425 million assessed by the United Nations, and the constant endeavor of Congress has been to lower US contributions. With the demise of the Soviet Union, and the reassessment of Russia's contributions, the peacekeeping assessment for the US and other countries increased marginally: a consequence of the "Fall" which the US found deplorable.[45] UN peacekeeping is one growth industry that the United States disowns.

Some commentators have traced the recent disenchantment with UN peacekeeping operations among Western powers to the experience in Somalia. One can imagine that the death of 18 American peacekeeping soldiers in Mogadishu, the pictures of whose dead bodies being dragged around were flashed across the world, strengthened the American resolve that their own troops would no longer be sent to the field. However, it is commonly forgotten that 23 Pakistani peacekeepers were killed by warlord Mohamed Farah Aidid's militia before the assault on the Americans, and that in 1993 fatalities were exceptionally high (over 250). Americans were not the only ones to suffer losses: indeed, in most years UN peacekeeping forces have suffered an average of 50 fatalities, almost none of them Americans. UNOSOM was handicapped not only by an immense rift between its own field commander and the Secretary-General, and by the US insistence that its own troops not be placed under UN command, but also by the public knowledge that the US was keen on winding up the operation and that it would not tolerate casualties among its own soldiers. Aidid construed this as an open challenge and wisely calculated that an attack on American soldiers would induce their departure.[46] The common interpretation of the death of American soldiers in Somalia, namely that it was an immensely chastening experience, occludes the fact that the participation of American troops in UN peacekeeping operations is restricted by the UN Participation Act (1945, amended by Public Law 79–264) to a total of 1,000 troops in a noncombatant capacity, and that American forces have never been sent for peacekeeping operations in strength.

In 2000, when the US was the single largest monetary contributor to UN peacekeeping operations, it was *not* among the top 20 contributors of military personnel. That honor belonged overwhelmingly to India, which contributed 3,233 troops, and Nigeria, which contributed 2,931 troops. Even countries with relatively miniscule populations, such as Fiji, Guinea, Ireland, New Zealand, and Finland contributed between 550 and 800 men each.[47] The cynical will doubtless suggest that poor countries are emboldened in dispatching their military personnel with the knowledge that they will receive comparatively large salaries, and that such operations are, on the whole, an easy way to acquire "cultural capital." But such speculations aside, it cannot be doubted that the US and the other great powers, who have been similarly slack in contributing manpower to peacekeeping, have adopted the chilling view that not all lives have an equal value. This is the true mercenary spirit, an unhesitating endorsement of Malthusian worldviews in the era of late modernity. One has to recall that Senator Phil Gramm, then a presidential candidate, let it be known on the campaign trail in 1995, in response to a query about whether he would support sending US troops to Bosnia as part of UN peacekeeping operations, that all of Bosnia was not worth the life of a single American soldier.[48] It is this principle, as I have previously alluded, which guided US and NATO operations in Kosovo. If this is what peacekeeping amounts to, one shudders to think what might be accomplished with warmaking.

Sanctions

The 1990s was supremely the decade when the various elements of the "new world order" began to be put into place: the international community was apparently aroused to an awareness of the threat from rogue states, and the Security Council took heavy recourse to both peacekeeping operations and the imposition of sanctions in its aspirations to provide some global governance. When the UN was founded, it was understood that sanctions, which the League of Nations had occasionally imposed, would remain in the arsenal of both the UN and other regional political organizations as a measure for enforcing compliance. In 1962, the General Assembly, which had been repeatedly petitioned by the African National Congress (ANC), voted overwhelmingly in favor of the economic boycott of South Africa. Owing to the opposition of Britain, the United States, West Germany, and Japan, which between them accounted for by far the greater portion of South Africa's exports and imports, sanctions against South Africa could not come into force. The General Assembly insisted that action under Chapter VII of the UN Charter was "essential in order to solve the problem of apartheid and that universally applied economic sanctions were the only means of achieving a peaceful solution."[49] Under the terms of Articles 41–2 of this chapter, only the Security Council has the power to impose mandatory sanctions, but its three permanent members from the West torpedoed every attempt to render South Africa compliant. However, the tide of international opinion could not altogether be resisted, and even in the US the anti-apartheid movement and dis-investment campaigns gained strength. Eventually the Comprehensive Anti-Apartheid Act was passed, over President Reagan's veto, by the US Congress. Ironically, in 1993, the ANC, which had at one time pleaded with the world to isolate South Africa, but was now almost on the verge of officially acquiring power, had once again to plead to have sanctions removed.

The case of South Africa might well have remained the most well-known instance of the force of sanctions in international politics, but for the fact that from mid-1990, the most rigorous sanctions ever known to have been inflicted on one nation have been in place against Iraq. The Security Council moved quickly to show its disapproval of Saddam Hussein's irredentism, which had led to the occupation of Kuwait, by enforcing comprehensive sanctions against Iraq. Resolution 661, which urged all member states to adhere to a strict embargo on all trade with Iraq, exempted "supplies intended strictly for medical purposes, and in humanitarian circumstances, foodstuffs."[50] Even before the commencement of hostilities between Iraq and the American-led international force in early 1991, the sanctions had nearly crippled Iraq's economy. Proponents of sanctions, who opposed armed intervention, argued that Iraq had already been greatly debilitated, and that the rigorous maintenance of sanctions was bound to produce Iraq's submission; on the other hand, the United States and its allies, less persuaded that sanctions would render Iraq compliant, successfully pushed for a decisive military engagement with Iraq to compel its withdrawal from Kuwait. When, as in the last few years, the rest of the world called for an end to the sanctions, the United States and its compliant ally, Great Britain, insisted on the opposite course of action.

Ten years later, sanctions tell a woesome tale about Iraq. Before sanctions were first enforced in the late summer of 1990, Iraq unquestionably had among the highest standards of living in the Arab world, a flourishing and prosperous middle class, and a formidable social welfare system that provided considerable material security to ordinary citizens. The economists Jean Dreze and Haris Gazdar noted in 1992 that the

> government of Iraq has a long record of active involvement in health care, education, food distribution, social security and related fields. Notable achievements in these fields include free public health care for all, free education at all levels, food distribution at highly subsidized prices, and income support to "destitute" households ...[51]

A campaign of sustained bombing was to relegate Iraq, in the words of an official UN fact-finding team, to the pre-industrial age.[52] Iraq has now joined the ranks of the underdeveloped nations and become economically regressive: it has among the highest rates in the world of maternal and infant morality, and correspondingly the fewest number of hospital beds; an astronomical increase in diseases and mental illnesses has been documented, and there have been numerous outbreaks of cholera and typhoid.[53] More than one observer has noted an "alarming reappearance of malnutrition."[54] A report released in 1997 by UNICEF described 1 million children in Iraq under the age of five as being chronically malnourished; the same organization in 1999 published another report which stated that under-five mortality had increased from 56 deaths per 1,000 live births in 1984–89 to 131 deaths per 1,000 live births during 1994–99. A Human Rights Watch report in January 2000 described Iraq's "civilian infrastructure and social services" as "dangerously degraded."[55]

The evidence is unimpeachable: though the war itself led to the deaths of perhaps as many as 200,000 Iraqis,[56] the number of fatalities since the war far exceeds this number, and the vast majority of Iraqis are experiencing poverty on a scale that would have been considered inconceivable before 1990. Many American foreign policy "experts," the bulk of whom have never been accustomed to independent thinking, and whose working lives have been devoted to the service of so-called think tanks that have always deemed the country's national interest to be paramount, maintain that UN figures are contaminated by reliance upon Iraqi data, and one such expert was merely content to note in 1999 that there were "problems with malnutrition, infant mortality, and medical services."[57] What is critical is that, severe as the sanctions have been, they have scarcely made a dent in the public imagination in the US; about the only concern is whether sanctions are harmful to American business interests. On the rare occasions that the American media has pondered over the long-term consequences and moral efficaciousness of sanctions, the "experts," following the lead of their politicians, have quickly come to the agreement that Saddam Hussein is to be held responsible for holding the children of Iraq hostage to his whims. Speaking at the Pentagon in February 1998, as he prepared the United States and the world for an American military strike against Iraq, President Clinton repeatedly declared that if Saddam evaded his obligations, "he and he alone will be to blame for the consequences."[58]

How did sanctions, then, become so pervasive as a "collective security" measure, and what conclusions are we permitted to draw about global governance from the sanctions presently in place? Though the United States has made a concerted endeavor to represent the present regime of sanctions in force against Iraq and a number of other alleged outlaw states, such as Iran, Sudan, and Afghanistan, as the outcome of the will of the "international community," the history and increased use of sanctions is demonstrably associated with the dominance of the United States over the preceding 50 years. With the exception of measures taken against Rhodesia and South Africa, in 1966 and 1977, respectively, sanctions before 1990 were imposed unilaterally, mainly by the United States. The halo of multilateralism that is spun around sanctions can barely disguise the fact that between 1945 and 1990, when sanctions were imposed more than a hundred times, the United States had to act with little or no support from any other nation on two-thirds of those occasions.[59] In the aftermath of the fall of the Soviet Union and the removal of the last obstacles to the unimpeded exercise of American hegemony, what the UN itself describes as "sanctions regimes imposed by the Security Council" were to show a dramatic increase. As of January 31st 1988, Security Council-mandated sanctions were in place only against South Africa; exactly four years later, the number of countries against which sanctions were in force had risen to two, and at the end of December 1994, this number had jumped to seven.

Some scholars, while recognizing that multilateralism is scarcely more than a charade, take the view that the sanctions policy of the United States cannot be impugned, since it is conducted under the rubric of the Security Council, but this argument is vitiated by the unfortunate assumption that the Security Council is incapable of terrorizing the world, or acting as a law unto itself.[60] Rather poignantly, the General Assembly itself has drawn attention to the "Security Council's greatly increased use of this instrument," and "a number of [consequent] difficulties, relating especially to the objectives of sanctions, the monitoring of their application and impact, and their unintended effects." The General Assembly was to recall the "legal basis [of] sanctions," which are described in Article 41 of the UN Charter, as "measures not involving the use of armed force in order to maintain or restore international peace and security," in order to "underline that the purpose of sanctions is to modify the behavior of a party that is threatening the international peace and security and not to punish or otherwise exact retributions."[61] Can sanctions against Iraq possibly be conceived as intended merely to "modify the behavior" of Iraq's political leadership, when Saddam Hussein has been declared beyond redemption?[62] Britain relied on the "punitive expedition," the United States takes recourse to sanctions: this is the *politics of chastisement* in the Anglo-American world order for the last 100 years.

The enormous margin by which the United States in 1991 vanquished the so-called elite Iraqi Republican Guards paved the way for a ceasefire agreement that required Saddam Hussein to consent to conditions for the termination of the sanctions that no sovereign country could reasonably be expected to adhere to, extending well beyond the destruction of all chemical, biological, and nuclear weapons and missile production facilities, to include the payment of impossibly large sums of money as reparations to Kuwait and stipulations about the future of Iraq's internal political arrangements.

Significantly, unlike the widespread boycotts of corporations doing
business with South Africa, it is not clear that the much wider and
indiscriminate sanctions against Iraq have the same legal and moral
mandate to serve as their foundation; moreover, the sanctions
imposed on South Africa were supported by its majority black
population, and even those inadvertently impacted by sanctions
were agreed on retaining them. In Iraq, notwithstanding Saddam
Hussein's immense unpopularity, sanctions have no support among
any Iraqis other than Saddam's political opponents who are largely
funded by the United States. Though the sanctions are retained by
order of the Security Council, they might well constitute an infringement of other international laws and agreements: thus sanctions
against Iraqis, one Austrian jurist maintains, constitute an infringement of Section 1.2 of the International Covenant on Economic,
Social and Cultural Rights, which says: "In no case may a people be
deprived of its own means of subsistence."[63] In making a representation before the UN Commission on Human Rights in 1991, the
NGO International Progress Organization made the more forceful
point that "the continuation of the sanctions policy implemented
through the United Nations Security Council" constituted a "grave
and systematic violation of human rights and fundamental
freedoms" of the entire population of Iraq, who were being denied
even the most basic right, the right to life. As such sanctions constituted a grave violation of Articles 3, 22, and 23 of the Universal
Declaration of Human Rights; they were tantamount, it was
suggested, to genocide as defined by the Convention on the
Prevention and Punishment of the Crime of Genocide.[64]

To offer a critique of sanctions by no means compels one to the
espousal of the view that sanctions in themselves can never be
defended. But, in the present circumstances, they seriously call into
question the very idea of the United Nations as a fully representative,
or even ethical, organization. Article 2 of the UN Charter loftily
declares that "the Organization is based on the principle of the
sovereign equality of all its Members," but everything in the recent
history of the UN suggests its complicity in having "principle"
transmuted – with obvious reference to the "indispensable power" –
into "principal." We cannot contemplate the day when nations may
be able to enforce sanctions against the United States for its defiance
of civilized opinion, whether with respect to its sanctimonious
display of public executions, its criminal levels of consumption, its

sponsorship of dictatorships, or its deliberate disenfranchisement of its African-American population. It is a further problem that, far from making the world a more just place, or opening targeted societies to international pressure, sanctions appear to exacerbate political repression within targeted nations and increase inequities between nations. The recent destruction of precious Buddha statues at Bamiyan by the Taliban, which was shortly before burdened with a new set of crippling sanctions, suggests that some nations may even be provoked into outrageous conduct by sanctions.

Sanctions conjure a macabre dance of death: they are being applied against Iraq in order to compel it to demolish its weapons of mass destruction, but sanctions have become that very thing, a weapon of mass destruction, which they are designed to save us from. The prospects for the international rule of law can be nothing but appalling, as the American scholar John Quigley has noted, if the United States continues to act on the presumption that multilateralism is a worthwhile enterprise only if it "can control the outcome."[65] That is obvious enough. By far the greater consideration, from the standpoint of the politics of knowledge which sanctions conceal, is that they are generally represented as a non-violent and least objectionable way of chastising recalcitrant states. As the former United States ambassador to the UN, Thomas Pickering, put it in a Security Council debate, "sanctions are measured, precise and limited. They are a multilateral, non-violent and peaceful response to violent and brutal acts."[66] In reality, sanctions constitute a form of invisible death, and ought to alert us to the fact that in late modernity even our genocides can appear as benign interventions. We associate war with death and violence, but sanctions with non-violence and human rights. Non-violence, however, is not only, or even, a doctrine of abstention from force: it requires us to take active measures for peace and the well-being of all, and it is obscene to suppose that the denial of basic amenities to people, including the right to life, might be construed as a respect for human rights. We have to consider that sanctions, particularly on the scale we are now witnessing, constitute a new technology of governance, and that they induce a living death; and as before vast numbers of people were enjoined to lay down their lives in the name of a greater good described as development, so citizens of a country crippled by mandatory sanctions are now sought to be consoled with the thought that the denial of human rights to them constitutes the only means of enforcing a yet higher conception of human rights that purportedly prevails in the West. Depravity knows no end.

THE ECONOMIC IMPERIUM: THE ERA OF THE WTO

A financial crisis engulfed many of the Asian tigers a few years ago, and the IMF was once again in the news, its mandarins dispensing advice (and much more) to countries that suddenly witnessed the dramatic decline of their currencies, soaring unemployment rates, and the flight of capital. It is, of course, both a mark of the insularity of the United States, as much of its prowess, that the IMF and the World Bank mean almost nothing to most Americans, who measure the strength of the economy by the rise and fall of the Dow Jones and NASDAQ indices. It has become habitual in the United States to think of the stock market *as* the economy, and every change in the stock market is closely watched, not only by Alan Greenspan, the Chairman of the Federal Reserve who is sometimes referred to as "the most powerful man in the world," but by tens of millions of devout stockholders.

Most of the world's population inhabits a space different from the world conjured up by the stock market. They are animated not by stock ownership but rather by those very considerations of security – of food, water, employment, housing, to name only some among the most obvious – for which the grand economic restructuring of the world has little time. Their lives can be impacted as well by the mandarins flown in from the World Bank and the IMF, and lately by rulings issued by the WTO and GATT. As the countries of Asia and Africa acquired their independence, the World Bank stepped in with the financing of specific long-term development projects and creation or improvement of infrastructural facilities. The World Bank's policies were aimed at increasing supply-side efficiency and stimulating productive investments; the Fund, on the other hand, was created to furnish short-term loans to countries with small foreign exchange reserves and to support macroeconomic reform. In his draft plan for the two organizations, Harry White described the Fund as

designed chiefly to prevent the disruption of foreign exchange and to strengthen monetary and credit systems and help in the restoration of foreign trade, whereas the Bank is designed chiefly to supply the volume of capital to the United States and Associated

Nations that will be needed for reconstruction, for relief, and for economic recovery.[67]

Over the years, these distinctions have become considerably blurred, and the Bank and the Fund are beginning to look quite alike: they are the Democrats and the Republicans of the international monetary system, partners in the same enterprise, and both are *de facto* under American jurisdiction.[68] This, too, is one of the mechanisms of power: the splintering of the unitary self into its purported other, all the more so that the exercise of power might seem democratic, equitable, even reluctant. Lately, however, the Bank and the Fund, until recently the twin towers of economic terrorism, have in the public eye been superseded by the WTO, which is far, far more than the successor regime to GATT, as is commonly described. Coming into existence in 1995 upon the completion of the Uruguay Round of talks (1994), the WTO obligates member countries – nearly 150, following the admission of China and Taiwan in September 2001 – to accept all of the agreements and treaties under its jurisdiction. GATT had, by way of contrast, permitted free-riders: members could opt out of some of the agreements encapsulated under GATT, and agree to be bound by the others. Among the score of agreements presently bundled into the WTO, the more significant ones include GATT, which in turn includes the broadest principles governing world trade, such as the related notions of the Most-Favored Nation and National Treatment, whereby governments, organizations, and individuals are prevented from legally favoring goods produced locally or under environmentally more sound conditions; Trade-Related Intellectual Property Rights (TRIPS); the Agreement on Trade-Related Investment Measures (TRIMS); the Agreement on Agriculture (AOA), and the Agreement on Textiles and Clothing (ATC). Together the agreements cover virtually every facet of economic exchange and activity with economic potential, from trade in agricultural products, goods and services and the regulations governing utilities and industries to taxation policies, insurance, licenses, investment, patents, and copyrights.

It would be difficult to envision a global institutional arrangement more encompassing and totalizing in its sweep than the WTO. Its fundamental premise is that the integration of human societies is best achieved by free trade, and that the unhampered access to goods, services, and markets across international borders is only possible when local and even national governments cede their autonomy and decision-making powers to an organization which can be entrusted with the fair enforcement of rules and regulations calculated to maximize economic activity. Borders are no longer to be viewed as inviolable, except in the matter of the transference of human populations: in this domain, the WTO forswears any juris-dictional authority, for the obvious reason that this traffic is almost exclusively one-way, with skilled and unskilled laborers in the developing world seeking to find their way to greener pastures in the more affluent West. Here the ingress of migrants is entirely at the sufferance of the receiving countries, who hold out incentives and rewards – the green card in the US, and its equivalent in Canada and Australia – for the most talented professionals, and reserve the right to deal with other immigrants in whatever manner they deem fit.

The WTO might be understood as incorporating the ideology of economism, or the principles that free or unregulated economic activities should be viewed as constituting the basis of modern democratic life, and that the concerns of communities in the various domains of human, social, and cultural rights – the right to dignity of labor; clean food, air, and water; safe and inexpensive housing; cultural sovereignty; local expressions of self-governance, among hundreds of others – must not be allowed to impede the activities of markets. That the principal beneficiaries of the global trade agreements now comprising the WTO are the more affluent nations, not to mention the transnational corporations which dominate the global economy, is something which the advocates of the WTO are not prepared to concede. Quite to the contrary, they argue that the WTO uniquely enables smaller and larger nations, developing and developed countries, to compete as equals under the law, and they point to the mechanism for the resolution of disputes available under the WTO as in instantiation of how the law is designed to remove the disadvantages under which the poorer countries have labored so far.

The Dispute Settlement Mechanism

Since the WTO is something of a world government with vast juris-diction over numerous areas of trade, as well as investment, insurance, and finance, it is but natural that it would have some mechanism for resolving disputes between member states. Such disputes may break out, for example, when one member country believes that it is being denied unhampered access to the markets of another country, or that the actions of one or more countries claimed to be at fault are putting its goods or services at a deliberate disadvantage. In the famous banana case brought against the European Union (Case WT/DS31), the United States, acting on behalf of the US-based Chiquita corporation (formerly United Fruit[69]), claimed that the EU was privileging suppliers based in its former colonies in the Caribbean. The EU countries have been inclined to buy bananas from small-scale farmers in the Caribbean rather than from large producers in Latin America, who employ laborers at exploitative wages and use farming techniques that are environmentally unsound. The WTO panel ruled in favor of the US.[70]

In another dispute, the mere threat of US action was enough to bring what was construed as the offending party to its senses. Acting in accordance with guidelines issued by the United Nations Children's Fund (UNICEF) and the WHO, Guatemala banned claims on Gerber baby food packages on the grounds that these claims conveyed the misleading message that such food could substitute for breast milk. Speaking for Gerber Products Company, the US State Department threatened Guatemala with action under the WTO-TRIPS and advanced the argument that Gerber had an intellectual property right under the TRIPS agreement. It was argued by the US that the exceptions to free trade allowed under WTO rules did not apply in this case. Guatemala succumbed to the American threat, with the consequence that the country's law was altered to allow such labeling, even though it contradicted WHO/UNICEF guidelines.[71] Complaints brought before the WTO, or merely proposed to be taken to the WTO, may thus refer to any one of the twenty-odd agreements now encapsulated under the WTO.

Proponents of the WTO claim that one of its greatest strengths, and the source of its attractiveness to all nations, is the improved Dispute Settlement Mechanism (DSM) to which any party that feels itself aggrieved may take recourse. Under GATT, disputes between parties were resolved according to the measures mentioned in Articles XXII and XXIII, the latter of which allowed the dispute to be brought to the attention of the GATT Council and a panel appointed to examine the issue. The GATT Council could take a decision to accept the report of a panel, but only if the vote to do so was unanimous – which is to say, the party against whom a judgment had been delivered would have to vote against itself, a very unlikely outcome.[72] This was not the only stipulation which, in the pre-Uruguay Round (1986–94) days, hindered the smooth operation of the dispute mechanism under GATT: in one scholarly estimate, its other undesirable, certainly inefficient, features included: "overly long delays from the establishment to the conclusion of panel proceedings; the ability of disputants to block the consensus needed to approve panel findings and authorize retaliations; and the difficulty in securing compliance with panel rulings."[73] It remained for the party whose position had been vindicated by the panel to chastise the offending party, whether by the threat of economic sanctions, the imposition of tariffs, or the withdrawal of trade benefits. But, not unexpectedly, only the United States, the European Union, Japan, Australia, Canada, and a handful of other countries were able to take unilateral measures.

The Dispute Settlement Mechanism (DSM) under the WTO is described by its votaries as a vast improvement over GATT's dispute settlement procedure. Panel reports now automatically come into effect after 60 days, unless there is a consensus to reject the report – again an implausible outcome, since this would require the party that has been vindicated to reject the judgment in its favor. It is suggested, consequently, that the DSM under WTO places the smaller and less powerful nations on a parity with the larger ones. However, such an apolitical reading rests on the obvious assumption that once legal parity has been given to states – if indeed it has been, which itself is questionable – that is tantamount to substantive equality. One of the most respected advocates of the rights of developing countries, Bhagirath Lal Das, has noted that the work of the panels before which disputes are brought is intensely technical, and that many countries do not have the intellectual resources to deploy large teams of specialists, advocates, and researchers who can go into the fine points of law. Although developing countries are entitled to the services of one legal specialist from the WTO, scholars agree that the burden placed on developing countries in prosecuting their claims is tremendous. "In the case of very poor developing countries," Das has written, "the cost of taking a case to the panels may be totally prohibitive."[74] Unlike GATT, WTO rules allow the finding of a panel to be taken before an appellate body, but the findings of this body are decisive, and if rejected by the offending party can lead to the imposition of sanctions by the WTO. The loopholes that were once available to the poorer countries under GATT now stand closed; but who would enforce sanctions against the US or Japan? The ultimate sanction envisioned under the DSM is retaliation, but how exactly would

Nicaragua or Guatemala retaliate against the United States if the panel ruled in their favor? The remedies available to the poorer countries under WTO rules are, howsoever reluctantly this might be conceded, "next to meaningless."[75]

If the DSM is as equitable as its proponents claim, it is a telling fact that as of October 1999, 50 of the 117 cases brought before panels convened under the DSM were initiated by the United States.[76] Once one accounts for complaints made by the EU, Japan, and Canada, it is transparent that the stranglehold of the rich countries upon the WTO's judicial process remains nearly complete. And yet the former Director-General of the WTO described the dispute settlement body as the WTO's "best achievement," and stated, inexplicably, that "the system is being used by developed countries, not just developing countries."[77] Though Article 23 of the Dispute Settlement Understanding (DSU) requires members to settle differences within its framework, and was clearly intended to prevent countries from taking unilateral actions under their own legislation, the United States has on numerous occasions in the last few years invoked Section 301 of the US Trade and Competitiveness Act of 1988, known ominously as Super-301 around the developing world, and threatened countries with punitive actions under its provisions. Not only this: when the EU reluctantly decided to pursue a complaint against the United States with respect to the extraterritorial reach of the Helms-Burton law, under which foreign companies can "be sued by private parties in U.S. courts for 'trafficking' in those assets confiscated by the Cuban government from them," the US announced that it was unable to accept the jurisdiction of the WTO panel and that the WTO has "no competence to proceed in an issue of American national security."[78]

Fewer commentators have paid attention to the constitution of the panels, whose members "rarely have any training or expertise in the subject areas about which they are ruling: environment, patents, agriculture, or finance." NGOs are excluded from the deliberations; only representatives of governments, "often aided by lobbyists from affected industries," are permitted to present legal briefs and the proceedings are strictly confidential.[79] One can reasonably expect that, as is customary with such institutions, a WTO panel convened under the DSM will on a rare occasion hand down a ruling which will serve to demonstrate the sensitivity of the WTO to environmental or social concerns, or suggest that the poorer countries need not be apprehensive about being ill-served by the WTO. But this mask of equality cannot disguise the systemic inequality which is structured into the very constitution of the WTO; nor should we forget the operation of power, which is more effectively exercised when it can be seen as working impartially for the common good.

4   Modern Knowledge and its Categories

For several years, my wife and I have been driving to work at the University of California, Los Angeles (UCLA) from our residence in Woodland Hills in the San Fernando Valley. This trip generally involves negotiating Los Angeles' (in)famous freeways for most of 15 miles, though it is possible to undertake the trip entirely on surface streets. The latter half of the trip brings one to the 405 Freeway, an interstate highway which in any other state would have been known as the I-405. During rush hours the average speed on the 405 is between ten and twelve miles an hour, though long-time residents, and even newcomers, have noticed that rush hour no longer resonates with the distinct meaning it once had. The 405 can be clogged at almost any hour of the day, barring a few hours past midnight, and a drive along the 405, and from there to the 10 Freeway on to the famous beaches of Venice and Santa Monica, on a Saturday or Sunday morning can take as long, or even longer, than a rush-hour trip to work. The rush hour itself, which in the urban centers of the US has generally been understood to mean 7–9 a.m. and 3–6 p.m., has over the years become longer, and in Los Angeles it is more accurately conveyed by these two blocks of time: 6–11 a.m. and 3–7 p.m. Since that four-hour stretch between 11 a.m. and 3 p.m. is not part of the vocabulary of the rush hour, an increasingly large number of people have taken to the freeways at this time, with the predictable consequence that non-rush-hour trips occasionally take longer than rush-hour trips.

Sepulveda Boulevard, a surface street, runs roughly parallel to the 405. No one in Los Angeles appears to know who this Sepulveda might have been, and for some time I was filled with rage to think – incorrectly, as the works of the California State Librarian reveal – that it had been named after Juan Sepulveda, the notorious defender of the rights of the conquistadors who advocated placing the Indians in slavery.[1] Too many places, buildings, and people have been named after scoundrels: that is the way of the world, free and unfree. But perhaps the more interesting observation about Sepulveda

Boulevard is that, having ventured on it when we first started commuting between our residence and UCLA, we found the street relatively barren of traffic. On most days the hour-long commute on the 405 could be cut down to 30 minutes along Sepulveda, but surely this was no secret. From various points on the 405, as one is incarcerated in grindingly slow traffic, one can look down upon the cars that seem to be racing along Sepulveda. Yet the commuters on the 405 showed no interest in taking Sepulveda, and we puzzled over this for some time: this is the culture where the slogan "time is money" was reborn, but nonetheless thousands of people appeared to have no misgivings over squandering their time. Should we have been relieved that even in Los Angeles, with its disdain for the more leisured lifestyles of other times and other places, the irrational is (reluctantly) allowed a place?

Perhaps the mystery is easily decoded. The Southern Californian is famously attached to his or her car and, more than anywhere else, Los Angeles is where the car is one's second (and occasionally only or primary) home. Who, unless it be the pubescent teenager, does not want to be at home? But I wish to suggest that the mystery runs much deeper. We are confronted here with the *imperialism of categories*, and any interpretation must begin with the reflection that only in California, and most particularly in Southern California, are highways called freeways. Southern California has no toll roads; that is the most obvious, though scarcely the most interesting, signification of freeways. As the west came to open up, and California was absorbed into the union, the state came to exemplify the American Dream. The gold rush brought thousands of fortune seekers; the vast expanses beckoned all those who saw the frontier closing in on them. Here, with "space to spare and where history is scarce,"[2] the American could remain unencumbered. Much later, as the highway system developed around the country, given an immense boost by World War II, the freeways of Los Angeles promised a different emancipation from the toll roads of the east. Architectural writer Reyner Banham marvelously summed up the Angeleno's utopia by calling it "Autopia." The "freeway is where the Angelenos live a large part of their lives," "the place where they spend the two calmest and most rewarding hours of their daily lives;" and, not surprisingly, even Paris is not as famous for its Metro as Los Angeles is "as the home of the Freeway."[3]

Writing in 1965, another enthusiast declared that "the essence of Los Angeles, its true identifying characteristic, is mobility." There is something ironic in this observation: less than a month later, the Watts riots broke out and the center of gravity shifted to those parts of the city grid which the freeways hide and obscure. Moreover, a good many people, especially those unaccustomed to having constraints placed on their movements, found themselves immobile in their homes, waiting for the fires to burn out. But let us continue with this writer: "Freedom of movement has long given life a special flavour there [on the freeways], liberated the individual to enjoy the sun and space that his environment so abundantly offered, put the manifold advantage of a great metropolitan area within his grasp."[4] We begin to understand why the freeways are just that, freeways, while the other roads are surface streets. Freeways exact no toll – not only those dreaded taxes which led the colonies to revolt in the first place, but the toll on the foot and the soul. Unlike city streets, where one has to constantly stop and go, freeways allow the foot to remain on the accelerator; they are the space of freedom, of soaring – Angelenos are after all named after angels – dreams, though once in a while these dreams are brought to a braking halt. In Los Angeles, those who drive on the surface streets are condemned to remain on the surface: they have renounced the advantages of freedom, movement, speed – they are the colonized people.

Los Angeles, one expects, gave rise to the expression "life in the fast lane." Though there is no longer any "fast lane," the commuters on 405 have resolutely stuck to the idea that the freeway is the very space that the word captures and that they have always imagined. Since the 405 is a freeway, it must be faster, easier to navigate, and more expressive of the human spirit. Everything in their experience contradicts their idea of the freeway, and every nationwide study of congestion on American highways is an affirmation of the fact that the Los Angeles freeway system is the most heavily trafficked and slow-moving one in the country. What the English weather is proverbially to English chit-chat, the Los Angeles freeways are to the discussions frequently encountered in the metropolis; they monopolize most idle conversations, putting in jeopardy another space of freedom. Moving along the 405, bit by bit, the freeway commuters have the choice to move over to Sepulveda (particularly that scenic stretch along which we drive), but, as in most matters, Americans are enthralled by the idea of choice in the abstract but know little about creating the conditions for its substantive exercise.

Los Angeles freeways are illustrative of the fundamental problem of modernity, namely knowledge and the categories it has created.

They point, as much as the loftier ideas of development, history, consumption, terrorism, and the nation-state, on some of which I shall largely be focused in this chapter, to the largely unrecognized power of categories and the imperialistic sway they hold over us. Ashis Nandy has suggested that in the twenty-first century, domination will no longer be exercised predominantly through "familiar organized interests – class relations, colonialism, military-industrial complexes, and so on. Dominance is now exercised mainly through categories."[5] This may seem somewhat overstated, and no one imagines that class oppression will disappear, or that class hierarchies will cease to be meaningful. Even as apparently trifling a matter as the books one lays out on one's coffee table, as Paul Fussell reminds us in his witty study,[6] is laden with class distinctions. The military-industrial complex also appears to have remarkable longevity, though, as the previous discussion on sanctions should have suggested, governance knows many other forms. But the central import of Nandy's observation should not be lost on us. Categories dictate whether forms of medicine are authentic or quackery, whether societies are developed or underdeveloped, whether despotisms are authoritarian or totalitarian (a distinction lost to everyone except Jeanne Kirkpatrick and her cohorts in the American foreign policy establishment during the Reagan years), and whether the wanton destruction of lives is murder or "collateral damage."

It was these same categories of modern knowledge systems that throughout the 1980s enabled politicians to describe 30,000 homicides in the United States annually as street crime, but fewer than 70 deaths a year in Northern Ireland as terrorism, though a sociologist might find, on closer examination, that both street crime and terrorism are deeply rooted in class inequities, unemployment, and the anomie associated with massive structural shifts in local and global economies. The CIA has itself estimated that during the period 1969–80, international terrorists claimed 3,368 lives, but in just two years, 1965–66, Suharto's armed forces massacred not less than 500,000 communists.[7] Suharto's forces then went on a killing spree in East Timor, where conservative estimates place the number of those murdered at about 200,000. Yet Indonesia, a bulwark in the anti-communist defense shield, was *never* described as a terrorist state by the United States. Or ponder this: why is it that the United States describes itself as producing counter-terrorism experts, rather than terrorists, even though the country's foreign policy and defense establishments engaged in the illegal bombing of Laos and

Cambodia and sponsored, ironically under the aegis of an anti-terrorist law, deaths squads in El Salvador and Guatemala? These distinctions have their consequences. As I sought to show in the previous chapter, the charge of terrorism leads to the designation of some nations as rogue states, and to their ostracism from something called the international community, an expression that, given its self-referentiality, American politicians have become enamored of in the extreme.

Though categories, without which professional social science would be inconceivable, should enable communication and furnish illumination, they can be uniquely disempowering: indeed, no category is meaningful if it does not exclude as much as it includes. It is these same categories of knowledge that turn the American into an icon of freedom and individuality, an Arab into the sign of terror and irrationality – consider the haste with which the Oklahoma City bombing was attributed to Islamic terrorists, a Chinese into an emblem of Oriental deceit, an Indian into a representation of excess and irresponsible fecundity – but an Indian in America into a "model minority." The conventional and still largely dominant history of immigration into America, which eventually produces the category of the "American" who could never be successful in the home country, obfuscates the almost inevitable transformation of the "successful American" into an "ugly American," a prolific consumer with membership in a collectivity that is criminally responsible for depleting the earth's finite resources. This successful American, whose very success erases "minority," is no "model" either of ecological thinking or ecological plurality.

No one, then, ought to view the oppression caused by knowledge systems with indifference, since in the name of development alone, millions of underdeveloped people around the world, not all of whom desired higher standards of living or more access to consumer goods, have been killed, maimed, pauperized, displaced, culturally cauterized, and museumized. The nineteenth century originated the culture of museumizing people; the twentieth century greatly expanded on the ambition, extending its reach to portions of the world that even the long arm of colonialism could not reach and finding corporate sponsors to celebrate diversity; and it appears that the twenty-first century will offer the fulfillment of the desire to have a complete fossil record of diversity. As the underdeveloped are introduced to development, their museumization begins.

Other categories of modernity, the nation-state for instance, tell a similarly sordid tale. We have lost the capacity to envision any other form of political organization but the nation-state, as if that is the telos of human activity and aspirations, and notwithstanding the advent of multiculturalism and identity politics, the nation-state itself appears unable to recognize that people have always lived comfortably, until relatively recent times, with multiple identities. Though the Sikh secessionism that troubled India in the 1980s and early 1990s appears to convey the impression that Sikhs and Hindus have always been sworn enemies, much less than one generation ago it was common in many households in the Punjab to raise some children as Sikhs and others as Hindus.[8] Identities were seldom exclusive in the past, and even the events in Bosnia and Rwanda allow for no other interpretation. From being a truly cosmopolitan city, where synagogues, Catholic and Orthodox churches, and mosques occupied a space on the same street, Sarajevo has now become emblematic of that particularly modern phenomenon of ethnic cleansing – a phenomenon that is as much about supposed racial purity and the hierarchies of culture as it is about the elimination of fuzziness and the repudiation of the compositeness of common cultures.

Modernity is sworn to nothing as much as it is sworn to enumeration, categorization, classification, and the strict maintenance of boundaries. This explains, in part, why a people like the gypsies have suffered persecution in every European state where they are to be found: a constantly itinerant people, being neither here nor there, they defy easy classification and enumeration, and are a nightmare for the bureaucrat. The genocide against the gypsies under the Nazis is frequently commented on, but the assault upon their identity from 1945 to 1989, when a policy of assimilationism nearly achieved the end – namely their disappearance – that the fascists had always desired, and the continuing policies of systematic discrimination against them pursued by post-communist regimes in Eastern Europe, suggest that the profound anxieties generated by gypsies have not disappeared. Their subversion of the dogmas – the work ethic, profit, the factory mode, surplus – of organized economic life under private and state capitalism alike is enough to earn them the animus of the modern nation-state.[9] Similarly, though premodern India does not appear to have had any acute difficulties with the *hijras*, described by anthropologists as the "third sex,"[10] and appears even to have bestowed on them various forms of livelihood,[11] modern India is uncomfortable with, and unable to account for, those who are neither males nor females, even neither non-males nor non-females. Numbered in the several hundred thousands, *hijras* – castrated men, transvestites, hermaphrodites, androgynes, gynemimetics, eunuchs, none of that and far more than what any of these terms might convey, the defiers of all categories – have not even entered into the categories of fashionable queer discourse. Can we imagine anywhere a census that, in the box for sex, offered a person the choice of the following designations: female, male, neither, both?[12]

In our era of globalism, then, when the same icons of popular culture are to be found throughout the world, trade disputes come under the jurisdiction of the WTO, and financial markets are inextricably linked, nothing is more global than modern knowledge and its categories. The problem of knowledge – the manner in which it is embedded in systems of thought that have monopolized our capacity to comprehend the world, narrowed our options of resistance, assaulted the dignity of particular histories and cultures, demeaned the faculties of the imagination, and compromised the futures of people around the world – will haunt us in the twenty-first century. In the previous chapter, I endeavored to show that the creation of world bodies such as the United Nations, and even of a "new world order," has not made the problem of governance any easier or more promising. In the famous aphorism of Carl von Clausewitz, diplomacy is merely war by other means; and though one might well resist that level of cynicism, it is critical to recognize that violence in our times is practised in myriad ways, from the enforcement of sanctions to the forcible imposition of development and even the celebratory deification of that mode of knowledge which goes by the name of history. The modern academic disciplines, especially the social sciences, are now replicated in universities around the world, and in the closing section of this chapter, the disciplinary structure of modern knowledge will be examined in closer detail to see what epistemic and political assumptions inform the aspirations of academic practitioners of knowledge.

THE VIOLENCE OF DEVELOPMENT

If we understood the Holocaust, following the work of Bauman and many others, as a form of social engineering, the violence perpetrated upon people in the name of development and progress would more readily be seen as belonging to a similar strand of phenomena. Staggering as is the number of soldiers and civilians – in the neighborhood of 54 million – killed during the course of World War II, it comes as an acute shock to realize that greater still is the number of lives lost in the name of development. The saga of Soviet terror originated in the brutal collectivization of Russian agriculture and in the impulse to industrialize rapidly, and consequently increase productivity, by the use of forced labor. Millions of deaths were achieved, not by superior forms of armament, but by coolly and rationally conceiving of these deaths as the necessary price to pay for development. Human lives have always been expendable, but never with so much detachment as in the twentieth century, which we are also accustomed to thinking of as a time of rapid and enlightened progress. I have already alluded to the Chinese Communist Party's heartless embrace of ruinous economic policies, the attempt by political functionaries to make the subjects of the state partake in the Great Leap Forward, and the consequence of this extreme folly: 25–30 million people dead from starvation. Yet these starvation deaths are not routinely thought of as constituting a holocaust, and neither have they impacted our memory and sensibility with the same force and effect; indeed, other than certain scholars, such as demographers and specialists in Chinese history and politics, the world has never been very much bothered by this history. We are likely to see starvation deaths and the killings in concentration camps as discrete forms of violence, when in fact they are equally derived from the categories – development, nation-state, bureaucracy, progress, instrumental rationality – of modernity. The victims of social engineering will surely not care to choose between different forms of death, but some victims are assured at least of monuments in their name. The victims of development remain singularly underdeveloped even as a public warning of the genocidal impulses of modernity.

The idea of development remains the clearest example of the violence perpetrated by modern knowledge systems upon the integrity of human communities. The very word "development" perpetually unsings its own grave, so to speak: every parent is rightfully persuaded, for instance, that nothing should obstruct the development – growth and well-being – of his or her child. A battery of experts in most modern cultures provides the optimum conditions under which the development of children might take place, and no reasonable person considers the objective as less than laudable, though we are all aware that many of the "experts" are entirely dispensable. What passes as common-sense impedes the placement of development alongside the Holocaust, genocide, wanton killing, destruction, and dispossession. That is one obstacle to the construction of a political archaeology of the idea of development; the second is the supposition that development is, apart from its early use by Lenin in his 1899 work, *The Development of Capitalism in Russia*, which proposed the creation of an indigenous market for large-scale industrialization,[13] entirely a twentieth-century construct. The expression "colonial development" had no reference to the development or welfare of the colonies; quite to the contrary, to develop the colonies meant little more than to mine them for their wealth and to engage in extraction of taxes as well as their natural resources. Colonial development was a form of underdeveloping the colony. The strict association of development with welfare, or something that could be adduced as positive, dates to the period after the conclusion of World War II.[14]

Nonetheless, by the second half of the nineteenth century, if not earlier, social thinkers in the West had largely come to accept the idea that civilizations were to be placed alongside a scale. Whether a civilization deserved to be placed at the top, or whether it fell to the bottom, depended on a number of criteria. One such widely used criterion was the treatment meted out by that civilization to its women. Not surprisingly, if we take the example of one colonized people, India was relegated to the bottom, since British travelers, administrators, and members of the governing elite could point to such phenomena as the burning of widows, female infanticide, the prohibition among upper-caste Hindus against widow-remarriage, and the wide, almost universal, illiteracy of women and female children as indicative of the deplorable status of the Indian female. Indian social reformers readily accepted this form of evaluating civilizations, though in truth all criteria offered by colonial knowledge for such judgments were entirely redundant. By virtue of the fact that Britain governed India and numerous other colonies, and the same could be said of other European powers in relation to their colonies, it was quite self-evident, as far as Europe was concerned, that the colonized and colonizers belonged at different ends of the scale. The hierarchy was unmistakably clear; and when occasionally it appeared that the social and cultural practices of the colonizers and the colonized might have far too much in common, thus blurring the boundaries, colonial administrators fixated on some native practice, real or alleged, for which no analog could be found in European culture. An Englishman in India complaining that women in Britain were treated with scant respect, and deprived of access to education, could be reminded that English society was free of the hideous practice of *sati*, or widow-immolation; similarly cannibalism, whether in Fiji or Borneo, could be used to underscore the idea that Europeans were clearly incapable of descending to such levels of barbarism. Perpetrators of cannibalism, human sacrifice and head-hunting were clearly at the bottom end of the scale of civilization. This mode of what Stephen Greenblatt characterizes as "epistemic blockage" was critical to colonial discourses of evaluation;[15] the empirical fact of cannibalism, or lack of it, mattered much less.[16]

A similar form of evaluative scale still survives, indeed thrives, in the idea of development. For this idea to be at all meaningful, it must presuppose that there are nations which are developed, others which are developing, and yet others which doggedly persist in remaining underdeveloped, a testament to Oriental laziness or the savagery of a dark continent. Frequently these terms are substituted by others, though each set has its own particular resonance: most commonly, there is the First World, and the Third World, with the eclipse of the Second World, or the former Eastern European bloc, ominously pointing to a worldwide trend whereby the middle is being squeezed out. Elsewhere, the developed nations are characterized as post-industrial societies (already somewhat archaic), or as nations in the throes of "advanced" or "flexible" capitalism, an information revolution, and cyberspace democracy, while countries in Africa and the Indian subcontinent, when not outright "backward," are merely "industrializing." The countries of sub-Saharan Africa are sometimes called failed states, and we know what remedies lie in wait for those who fail; at the other extreme, the proponents of the development lexicon are reluctant to use the word "overdeveloped" to describe some of the developed states, though that description seems apt for countries where obesity afflicts more than 20 percent of the population. Some of these terms have other insidious histories: flexible capitalism is a short-hand for the corporate strategies that have led to downsizing, increase in part-time labor, the reduction of the permanent work force, and the emasculation of labor unions.

In the near aftermath of World War II, the underdeveloped areas of the world were invited to open themselves to intervention by the more developed countries, though perhaps no one had quite reflected on Gandhi's observation that if a small island required a good deal of the world to satisfy its wants and vanity, one shuddered to think what the consequences would be for the world if a large country such as India resolved to imitate England. A document prepared by the Department of Social and Economic Affairs at the United Nations in 1951, adverting to the shortage of food, the spread of disease, hunger, and malnutrition, and the "primitive" and "stagnant" economic life of people in underdeveloped countries, proposed a plan to rescue them from their poverty. The report states:

> There is a sense in which rapid economic progress is impossible without painful adjustments. Ancient philosophies have to be scrapped; old social institutions have to disintegrate; bonds of caste, creed and race have to burst; and large numbers of persons who cannot keep up with progress have to have their expectations of a comfortable life frustrated. Very few communities are willing to pay the full price of economic progress.[17]

This price might entail the abandonment of unproductive human relations, the untethered exploitation of natural resources, the rejection of religious values and spiritual sensibilities, the loss of traditional livelihoods, the displacement from ancient homelands, the diminishment of the moral economy: yet people were enjoined to contemplate this with utter equanimity, for as one well-known UN official put it,

> I still think that human progress depends on the development and application of the greatest possible extent of scientific research ... The development of a country depends primarily on a material factor: first, the knowledge, and then the exploitation of all its natural resources.[18]

By the mid-1950s, the idea of development had achieved the status of certainty, global in its reach and totalizing in its capacity to order and evaluate human relations. This was unequivocally the way to the future, and all who dared to reject development as an ill-thought panacea were condemned to become pariahs, the burnt carcasses and rejects of history. Yet the violence perpetrated under the name of development was never recognized as violence, and not merely because it makes for poor media coverage or non-sensational journalism. A single enterprise, the Three Gorges Project in China, which entails the construction of the world's largest hydroelectric dam, will upon completion have displaced 1.2 million people.[19] In India, between 12 and 33 million people have been displaced by large dams alone since 1949, but nothing more was contemplated beyond compensating (and that always infrequently and inadequately) them for their land and, on occasion, livelihood. In the interest of national development, displaced people, who are preponderantly from the ranks of tribals and the lower castes, have perforce had to surrender their claims and natural prerogatives. It was considered of no importance that tribal people, in particular, have associations with their land to which monetary value cannot be ascribed. It is through their land that they speak across generations and communicate with their ancestors; it is the land that fills them with a sense of their own fertility and mortality, and from which they derive their myths; it is the land that teaches them the principles of veneration: and so what is barren to an outsider is fecund to them, and what is ignorance to the outsider is a storehouse of wisdom and knowledge to the inhabitants. All over the world, according to the recent comprehensive report by the World Commission of Dams, between 40 and 80 million people have been displaced by dams; then there are other similar stories of dislocations, whether occasioned by the creation of national parks, the establishment of industries, or by the government and its armed forces in the name of national interest. That these dislocations induce despair, unemployment, the loss of ancestral land, forcible migration, and loss of belief in the sacred means nothing to policy planners and technological visionaries.[20] Developmental violence on this scale has every characteristic of ethnic cleansing – the open targeting of a particular group, in this case the poor and the underdeveloped, drawn largely from the ranks of ethnic minorities or indigenous peoples, and their subsequent eviction – but it is not recognized as such. Practitioners of ethnic cleansing are increasingly being hauled before courts, but exponents of large-scale development, when they are not recipients of awards for humanitarian service, still receive "attractive compensation packages" from governments and international organizations.

Though the idea of development purports to capture and transform reality, describing societies at different stages of social growth and political evolution (the ascent to electoral democracy being merchandised as the moment of arrival), the more insidious part of the notion of development is its colonization of our notions of time and space. The present of the developing world is none other than the past, sometimes the very remote and mist-shrouded past, of the developed world; and indeed in this lies one of the greatest uses of the developing world, which preserves in its institutions and social practices the memory of an European past that is lost or of which there are only very dim traces. The "barbarism" of the developing world is always a reminder to the developed world of the past it left so long ago, and of the profound blessings of Christianity, reason, and Western science. The future of the developing world – well, there is no future, since its future is already known to Europe and America; indeed, the developed world already lives the distant future of the developing world. As the future of the developing world as a whole is none other than the present of the developed world, so the future of the tribal or the peasant is only to live the planner's limited conception of life. In this respect, at least, oppression must show itself as consistent from the macro to the micro. The developing world can only arrive at the point from which the developed world makes its departures. It arrives to find that the world which it sought to emulate is no longer desirable, that many aspects of the industrialization and development which it so avidly sought are now derided as wasteful, environmentally destructive, and socially unsound – dams being a case in point.

In the matter of spatial geopolitics as well, the developing world has no autonomy. As the lodestar shines in the West, the Orient must orient itself towards the Occident: it must forget that it is the Orient, or – a rather more germane consideration – it must forget it enough to allow the Occident to transgress its borders. National borders are sacrosanct, except in the developing and underdeveloped worlds – here, in the interest of inducing a more open society, wisdom demands the toleration of multinational corporations, various imperial formations such as the World Bank, the United Nations, and the International Monetary Fund and transnational forms of pop culture. Recalcitrance on any of these counts unequivocally condemns developing countries: they appear to have regressed to the stage of being the "least" (not merely "lesser") developed, open themselves to the charge of being parochial and backward, and face the risk of being pushed further back on the evaluative scale of civilizations. Even a refusal to accept the hazardous wastes of the West is viewed as a violation of free trade. Having first characterized their colonized territories as waste lands,[21] and having then proceeded to waste away the land and its people, Western powers have now discovered in these places the perfect repositories for their own garbage – literally and metaphorically.[22] No one who has read the memo written by Laurence Summers, the then Chief Economist at the World Bank, is likely to forget soon that he thought that sub-Saharan Africa could be more effectively integrated into the global economy if only it could be persuaded to ship its natural resources to the developed world and in return accept frequent shipments of asbestos, leaded gasoline, nuclear wastes, and other toxins. In his own words, "I have always thought that underpopulated countries in Africa are vastly underpolluted; their air quality is probably vastly inefficiently low in pollutants compared to Los Angeles or Mexico." When Summers wrote of "world welfare enhancing trade in air pollution and waste," we can imagine whose welfare was being enhanced.[23] In so creatively designing an agenda of development for the largely "failed" continent, Summers won promotion to the office of Secretary of the Treasury under Clinton, and has now been elevated to the presidency of Harvard University. The non-Western world, one sadly concludes, must become what it has always been in the Western imagination: a self-fulfilling destructive prophecy.

THE FORGETFULNESS OF HISTORY

History as a discipline is eminently familiar; as a category of knowledge, we seldom give it much thought. The eminent American anthropologist, Marshall Sahlins, observed that the word "culture," or "some local equivalent, is on everyone's lips. Tibetans and Hawaiians, Ojibway, Kwakutl, and Eskimo, Kazakhs and Mongols, native Australians, Balinese, Kashmiris, and New Zealand Maori: all discover they have a 'culture.'"[24] Had Sahlins substituted "history" for "culture," he would not have been any less accurate; but perhaps he may have been more prescient, more discerning in understanding what forms of knowledge have monopolized our thinking in late modernity. No one today can be told that they are a people without history, and lately a discipline that is seldom energized by the theoretical impulse has found itself enormously refurbished by the immense interest in various forms of minority histories. A great many people have discovered that historians of earlier generations were oblivious to the interests and life experiences of those who stood at the margins of society, and generally offered a rather seamless account of the achievements of the white man. Minority activists and scholars have been rightly determined to redress this injustice, and consequently we have seen the flourishing of identity-based histories – most particularly in the United States.

What in truth were profoundly interesting questions have, however, been trivialized, and just when the practitioners of identity-based histories thought that they had inserted politics into the study of history, posing difficult queries about history and its exclusions, as well as its practices of representations, they have again taken the politics of knowledge out of history. Personal identity has been rendered into a monstrously boring subject that is pursued with extraordinarily self-indulgent passion; at the same time, the critique of historical practices has refused to engage in any thoroughgoing epistemological critique of history, or paused to consider the claims of voices that have spoken in the language of ahistoricity, prophecy, and myth. The professional study of history in the West made its first appearance in the eighteenth century, but the taste for history among the middle classes goes back further; in the nineteenth century, the study of history began to acquire the paraphernalia of a discipline. By the middle part of the twentieth century, history had become ascendant: indeed, it is no exaggeration to suggest that it is now poised to be the universal narrative of our times, having an appeal greater than any that positivist science had at its peak. How history came to acquire such resonance is a story that cannot be narrated here, but the two world wars, the fetish for military history, the attractions of nationalism and the imbrication of the nation in the narrative of history, the continuing appeal of the "great man theory of history," the notion of "the lessons of history," the immense valorization of personal and collective identity, and the idea of history as an unavoidable tool of citizenship have all played a critical part in making history the pre-eminent mode of accessing the past, and indeed of modern knowledge.

To be sure, there are disputes about history, perhaps more so about whose history is most authentic than about any other subject. People are still agitated by how the past is represented, whether in exhibitions, history textbooks, memorial commemorations, or the media. There were always competing narratives on the past, and historiography has always been centrally concerned with both the traditions of history writing and the criteria used to determine which accounts are more compelling than others. Nonetheless, the recent drift towards multiculturalism and identity-based history, and at another level of sophistication, the inspiration derived from poststructuralism and postcolonial theory, have put on offer a more diverse array of perspectives on the past, and contemporary scholarship has made us more attentive to various considerations. Who writes history? In what voice and with what authority? What constitutes history? When do people become the subjects of history? Almost everywhere, history textbooks have become the site of protracted debate on the nature of the past and the politics of representation. In Japan, the demand has surfaced that history textbooks should be more forthright in admitting to Japanese atrocities committed during the war, and the matter has gone not only to the courts, but well beyond the borders to neighboring states who remain agitated by Japan's apparent unwillingness to express remorse over wartime behavior.[25] In the United States, the revised National History Standards released in 1996 aroused some controversy, and the conservatives – a peculiar word in the American context, where the political spectrum effectively ranges from the radical right to the moderately right, and occasionally to the faintly liberal – who claimed that the standards had gone too far in minimizing the role of the Founding Fathers, the distinct character of American freedom, and white men, were drawn into battle with the multiculturalists, whose claims predictably hovered around the argument that the standards were inadequately revisionist.[26] In India, meanwhile, there is mounting evidence of official interference in the management of various important institutions, including the National Council for Educational Research and Training (NCERT), an organization charged with producing textbooks for schools, and the Indian Council for Historical Research (ICHR), a body which sponsors scholarly research. History textbooks have doubtless been doctored to reflect the views of Hindu nationalists.[27] Such disputes, and they are found elsewhere in the world, have become commonplace.

It is no part of my endeavor to suggest, then, that history remains an uncontested terrain, and yet it is transparent that important as are the passions which people bring to the study and interpretation of history, which will also have the effect of making history a more representative, sensitive, ecumenical, and democratic discipline, the various disputes are all family quarrels. They are largely about how to improve history – becoming sensitive to sources previously neglected, such as diaries of women and the working classes, oral histories, and even contraband histories – or how to make it ethically acceptable, which generally entails more inclusivity, the acceptance of the idea that imperialism and racism are inextricably a part of the history of the West, and an earnest endeavor to fill the gaps of conventional histories. The ease with which history, after some initial rumblings of discontent, incorporated minority pasts into its master framework is a striking testimony equally to its capacity for generating an illusory pluralism, its elimination of other modes of comprehending the past, and its mesmerizing attraction for all possible dissenters. Indeed, now that women, oppressed minorities, colonized subjects, the working classes, and various kinds of outcasts have found that history can be accommodative enough to include them in its universe, the last objections to historical discourses have nearly disappeared. History no longer furnishes substantial onto-logical or even epistemological problems for its former critics, since it is widely believed that dominant historical narratives can increas-ingly be manipulated, without much offense to their practitioners or wider segments of society, to make room for minority and oppressed histories. History now appears to be liberated – by the drift not only towards multiculturalism and minority histories, but as much by the increasingly frequent gestures made towards interdis-ciplinarity and world history – from the older modalities in which it is described as having been trapped in the past – as the history of elites, the history of the white race, the history of European powers civilizing the savages and barbarians, and the positivist history of Ranke and other worshippers of facts.

Thus the noose of history has tightened around us even as it has become wider. The enterprise of these newer minority and world histories is to facilitate conversations, especially between hitherto dominant and suppressed narratives, but it is my submission that in the present iniquitous state of world relations, with the North dominating both the economic and knowledge sectors, conversa-tion will result in the further erosion of plurality and lead to increased homogenization, though undoubtedly the more sensitive of the cultural theorists will defend such conversations as harbingers of liberating hybridities. (Like much else that is supposed to emancipate us, and be the succor to good thought, hybridity is for the West: in much of the rest of the world, the ground realities were such that there was always mixing, a term that has attracted none of the pompous posturing that cultural theorists have attached to hybridity. Mixing is characteristically unselfconscious; hybridity is always a stance, a postmodern form of self-performativity.[28]) World history as a pedagogic tool and field of study seems entirely unob-jectionable, even laudable: considering the notorious provincialism of American students, who are likely to know little of their own history and even less of what transpired outside the borders of the United States, it seems churlish to suppose that world history can do anything but some good. Practitioners of world history themselves admit to some shortcomings, such as the difficulty of specializing in world history, the extraordinarily heavy demands – linguistic and historiographic, to name two – it makes upon those who teach and write it, the dangers of falling into superficial generalizations, and the like. There is also considerable disagreement about whether world history is ever truly what it claims to be, or merely window-dressing for more sophisticated versions of Eurocentric history. But by far the most substantive criticism of world history, almost never entertained in the literature, is that world history has every potential of deepening the present inequities: it further opens up the world to the West, brings those who are unable to make themselves heard under the orbit of alien spokespersons, and is in every respect polit-ically disempowering for those who have repudiated the language of history. World history appears in the guise of disinterested learning and even kindness, but the experience with development, the Security Council, and sanctions should introduce at least a cautionary note.

History is inescapably the sign of the modern. Moreover, the reference point for all histories, even those of India or Africa, remains the West – not only Europe, but the West within the non-West.[29] The software engineers of Bangalore and the developers of India's nuclear bomb make history: they are the historically minded among an ahistorical people. Even the study of comparative history has generally meant little more than the study of India and Europe, or China and Europe, or "the Muslim world" and Europe: one nodal point is almost invariably Europe, and the other is determined by the historian's nationality or other principal field of interest. On the infrequent occasion that the historian dares to venture beyond this comparative framework, the interpretation is mediated by the categories derived from the West, including the nation-state, devel-opment, secular time, the autonomous individual, and history itself. But the historical sensibility has not everywhere been predominant, and though there have been various attempts to suggest that historical thinking resonated deeply with Indians, a brazen indiffer-ence to both historical thought and the production of historical knowledge appears to be far more characteristic of India.[30] The ascendancy of history in India is remarkably recent and has every relation to the thinking which has made the idea of the nation-state so fatally attractive to its elites. One of the most striking aspects of the dispute over the Babri Masjid – a sixteenth-century mosque in the north Indian town of Ayodhya which ideologues of Hindu militancy claimed was the original site of a Hindu temple that was supposedly built to mark the exact place at which Lord Rama was born – is how it brought to prominence historians who were called upon to render their expert testimony.[31] The historians took the charge seriously; but few, it can safely be averred, pondered to ask whether the historical veracity of one or other account struck most people as a truly meaningful intervention, and whether Indians care to speak at all in the idiom of history. It is odd that fundamentalism should always be described as generating myths, since fundamentalism and secularism are generally united in their unabashed enthusiasm for the historical mode and disdain for myths. The history of fundamentalists is decidedly bad history, but no one should mistake it for the world of myth.

History commends itself to our attention with the claim that it is the most powerful tool in our endeavor to keep alive the memory of the past and the links to human experience over time. But a critical interrogation of the received view of history calls for a hermeneutics which would bring us to the awareness that some forms of remembrance are but forms of forgetfulness. It is all too often argued, for instance, that the public acknowledgement and public memory of wartime atrocities and crimes against humanity is much stronger in Germany than it is in Japan, and various commentators have pointed to Japan's alleged inability to come to terms with its past. Yet there is no ready reason to believe that those who are inclined towards historical thinking are better equipped to live in the present, or that they have a more ecumenical notion of the future, or even that their actions are laced with nobler intent. If history were a guide to moral action – a notion firmly inscribed in the dominant commonplace view, where the "lessons of history" are fondly enumerated – then we might suppose that nations with more finely attuned historical sensibilities should be setting moral examples for humankind.

But we should stay with the strongest argument yet: judging from the case of India, it is possible to make a philosophical – and, shall we say, historical – argument for the disavowal of history as a mode of knowing. Indians, as I have said, were never much interested in the production of historical knowledge, but this can in no way be attributed, as the British were wont to do, to a lack of analytical abilities or critical skills, since Indians produced a huge corpus of learned texts in mathematics, astronomy, aesthetics, linguistics, law, philosophical disputation, metaphysics, and theology. The ahistoricism of the Indian sensibility remains one of the most attractive and enduring features of Indian civilization, and most Indians would have agreed with Gandhi when he declared that "the Mahabharata is not to me a historical record. It is hopeless as a history." We cannot be surprised that all shades of nationalists and modernists have wanted to massacre Gandhi, when we hear him adding: "I believe in the saying that a nation is happy that has no history."[32] Gandhi has been buried by India's history-minded elites, for history has no way of describing ahistoricity except as a form of primitivism, backwardness, and myth.

THE DISCIPLINARY STRUCTURE OF MODERN KNOWLEDGE

It has been my argument that some of the most intense battles in the twenty-first century will be fought over the shape of knowledge, and in consequence a more politically informed ethnography of the disciplinary structure of modern knowledge will be required. The academic disciplines are disciplines in more than the commonly accepted sense of the term, for they also perform the work of disciplining recalcitrant elements of society, endorsing and justifying inequality, creating new forms of oppression, and stifling dissent. We have all heard of chemists and doctors who accept commissions from the pharmaceutical industry to promote various drugs, of various specialists working for the tobacco industry who have offered testimony to the effect that there is no verifiable link between smoking and the incidence of cancer, and of the serious compromising of standards at the US Federal Drug Administration (FDA), reportedly the most reputable organization of its kind in the world.[33] These are only the most egregious and publicly known examples of how the corporate world has rendered research compliant to its own will, but recent studies suggest that the links of the scientific and academic communities to the corporate world are extremely widespread,[34] extending well beyond the known connections with the defense establishment and the national security state.[35]

The problem of disciplinary knowledge, however, runs much deeper. Academic disciplines have so disciplined the world that any intellectual, social, cultural, or economic intervention outside the framework of modern knowledge appears to be regressive, a species of indigenism, the mark of obdurate primitives, and certainly futile. One has only to think of the extraordinary legitimacy granted to economic science and the role of economists as the pundits of our times: their very word, when dispensed through such conduits of the imperial financial architecture as the World Bank and the IMF, is law to beleaguered developing countries. While scholars recognize national traditions of inquiry – such that, to take a simple instance, the analytical tradition of philosophy is more distinct to the Anglo-American world, while structuralism found its most ardent advocates in France – they would find it unintelligible to speak of Japanese physics or Islamic economics.[36] Japanese physics can only mean physics as it is conducted in Japan, or even the culture of physics in Japan, as contrasted with the culture of physics in the United States;[37] but it can never be taken to suggest, according to the prevailing wisdom, that there may be more than one kind of physics.

Though globalization has spawned a prodigious literature, scarcely a faint note of recognition exists that nothing is more spectacularly global than the formal frameworks of knowledge which have bequeathed to every corner of the globe a universal and supposedly tested and verifiable recipe for development, technological progress, successful management, and democracy. Certain historically rooted differences distinguish the practices of the social sciences in Europe and the United States, as evidenced, for example, by the absence of a separate social science faculty in French universities.[38] Nonetheless, the social sciences are nearly everywhere the same, and the most one can admit to is that they are practiced more or less successfully in any one country: economists in Nigeria, Zimbabwe, Bangladesh, France, and Chile understand their counterparts in the United States and Britain.

When, a few years ago, Kentucky Fried Chicken sought to open its first restaurants in India, it faced determined opposition from opponents of liberalization and neo-imperialism in India, and the showdown in Delhi was widely reported in the press. Similarly, attempts by the gigantic agrobusiness Monsanto to introduce genetically modified foods, and especially the terminator seed, which self-destructs after the first harvest, continue to be vociferously contested everywhere and have received wide media coverage.[39] The protests in Seattle, Quebec City, and Davos against free trade agreements are a matter of public record. These gestures against globalization are captured in popular memory, but it is useful to recall that American-style management schools are being embraced around the world, that the American MBA is one of the most dramatic examples of globalization, and that for well over a generation the economics textbooks of Paul Samuelson – who stated in 1986, 'I dislike being wrong' – have reigned dominant around much of the world.[40] No one protested when social science in the

American or British idiom began to prevail in the developing and underdeveloped world. Indeed, the very ideas of development and poverty with which economists, social planners, sociologists, and politicians in the non-Euro-American world work, are sanctified by several generations of Western experts. Far more so than Coca-Cola or Disney, it is the frameworks of knowledge, encapsulated in the academic disciplines, which have become universalized. Every traveler has been struck by the ubiquitous presence, in the remotest parts of the globe, of Nike shoes, Nintendo, Levi's jeans, and (in the 1990s, Chicago Bulls T-shirts), but no commentator on globalization has noted the yet greater reach of formal modeling and other mathematized forms of social science.

The story of the development of the social sciences begins with the transformation of such fields of study as geography, history, sociology, and anthropology into academic disciplines. This story has a particular American valence: since Americans, in the words of Burton Bledstein, "lacked tradition as a source of authority," they were particularly keen to demonstrate that they did "not lack science."[41] Indeed, being free of the blessings of the tradition of authority, as well as the authority of tradition, they could be expected to be superlative scientists. The "expert" had to be born in America. Professionalization of the disciplines necessitated their location in the university, the creation of new standards for certifying a professorate, a prescribed course of study, the formation of scholarly societies, the founding of specialized journals, the publication of monographs, and often their eventual fragmentation – whether into other disciplines, or into numerous subfields and subdisciplines. The disciplines grew incrementally, and the heroic narrative of modern knowledge bursting the dam of medieval ignorance has encouraged the belief that the practitioners of any discipline, relentlessly committed to the pursuit of truth, discarded falsehoods along the way. One could argue, for instance, that the vast majority of contemporary sociologists, evolutionary biologists, and historians have rejected the claims of eugenics and racially motivated science that their predecessors in the nineteenth and earlier part of the twentieth century were so widely predisposed towards accepting. However, it is not commonly realized that the nineteenth-century discourse of race and eugenics was transformed into a twentieth-century discourse of development, which, as the preceding discussion argues, deploys a similarly evolutionist framework – dividing people and nations into the categories of underdeveloped, developing and developed – and has been much more insidious in its effects, reach, and acceptability, since no one wishes to be considered anything but developed. Once one begins to launch into an exercise of this kind, it soon becomes transparent that many of the most conventional and cherished assumptions about the various disciplines – the story of their increased sophistication, their supposedly clear line of demarcation from each other, their claim to represent different areas of human expertise and knowledge – are often little more than embellished fairytales.

The most productive way of understanding the epistemological shortcomings and political conservatism of the structures of knowledge in the social sciences lies in understanding those categories generated by the disciplines which have become sacrosanct in the social sciences. Scarcity, poverty, and literacy furnish three such instances of categories. The contemporary discourse of poverty hovers around the economist's notion of a poverty line below which someone might fall, thereby excising from memory the earlier and richer history of this concept. Historically speaking, many people have chosen to embrace poverty, and it is only an assumption of the moderns that the poor have always been a problem.[42] If at all they were a problem, it is not clear that the problem was to be shunned: "Give me your poor, your homeless, your huddled masses," state Emma Lazarus' lines on the imposing Statue of Liberty, though America is now fenced to keep out precisely these undesirables. The traditional diversity of ideas surrounding poverty is expressed in the fact that Persian has more than 30 words to describe those who are perceived as poor, while in Latin there were 40 words to cover the range of conditions embraced by the conception of the poor.[43] The saying of Christ, "It is easier for a camel to go through the eye of a needle, than for a rich man to enter into the Kingdom of Heaven" (Matthew 19: 24), must appear as something of a joke and embarrassment to social planners, economists, and development specialists, since their expertise has no purpose but to raise the poor into the ranks of the consuming classes with the hope that some will become wealthy – that is, members of the obscenely consuming class.

The poor that social science speaks of are largely a construct of modernity, and of the gap, which all indices show is increasing, between socially induced wants and the resources required to fulfill those wants. Social science pretends that a consumer class only emerges when people are lifted out of poverty; it refuses to register the political observation that consumerism itself aggravates and creates poverty, and not only in the economic idiom. The only real problem with the poor, from the perspective of economists, politicians, businessmen, and policy experts, is that they are poor or negligible consumers: the goods and services that they need, such as low-cost and public housing, and subsistence meals, generate little or no profit. Those who fail to consume are themselves consumed: that is the draconian law of modern economic existence. So long as the dominant economic mode remained production, the poor could be summoned to do their bit; they had something to contribute. But now that consumption has replaced production as the leitmotif of human existence, the poor can only be seen as an immense drain on society, a palpable reminder of what might happen to the consuming subject if he or she becomes similarly disenchanted with work. The socially acceptable way of making this "cancerous sore" disappear from public view is to render the poor into a law and order problem. Thus the social science disciplines would find incomprehensible Thoreau's remark, "A man is rich in proportion to the number of things he can afford to let alone." Such observations have been banished to the realm of mysticism, or are seen as emanating from a class of people advocating New Age philosophies or, from the standpoint of personal salvation, an ethos of austerity. From the point of view of social scientists, it is a self-evident truth that poverty is an economic problem and results from lack of income or entitlements, and lack of income can, in turn, be traced to poor people's repudiation of the work ethic and their laziness.

It is similarly obvious to social scientists that literacy is one of the most important and indisputable criteria by which the progress made by a people or a nation-state ought to be judged. Literacy is one of the cornerstones of the Human Development Index (HDI), itself a notable improvement over the previous tendency to rank countries exclusively by gross domestic/national product. Yet the word "literacy" makes its first appearance in 1883, not surprisingly in the United States, which has been in the forefront of developing concepts that, sometimes in place of blatantly oppressive categories, might be used to suggest the higher evolution of some people in comparison to others. Literacy properly belongs within that cluster of terms which are used to measure, order, evaluate, hierarchize, and condemn. What, after all, is the meaning of measuring the literacy rates of countries, if not to suggest that in the scale of civilization some countries are better than others, and so to chastise those which have lower literacy rates? The political intent of literacy is to suggest that illiterates have – or should I say must have – no place in the world, no access to power and the social institutions through which it is exercised, indeed no substantive claim on the attentions of humanity. They exist only to be pitied, a reminder of the darkness, chaos, and poverty from which literates have been rescued. Literacy doubtless opens wide the doors of society to whose who enter its portal, but it shuts out many of the ways in which people customarily sought livelihoods and gained the respect of others. The late Mahbub ul Haq, the pioneer of the Human Development Index, described the HDI as having three key components, "longevity, knowledge and income," but the index itself measures "literacy."[44] If literacy can so effortlessly substitute for knowledge, then the preponderant share of human history and the labor of billions of largely illiterate people who have until now inhabited this earth should simply be viewed as wasted.

The disciplines, and the categories of knowledge they have generated, have doubtless failed us. It is a reasonable assumption, unfortunately belied at every turn, that the classificatory mechanisms of any knowledge exist to make the world better known to us, and have been designed to shut out the noise of the world and so enable us to meditate on a problem and its solution. One elementary way to understand the ominous failure I have spoken of is to examine the disciplinary contributions to the solution of human ills, and to measure the disciplines by their own preferred yardstick of practical success and utility. Someone might well be prepared to argue that the enormous growth in productivity, world trade, national incomes, and individual wealth since the late nineteenth century owes as much to economic theory as it does to material conditions, the exploitation of natural resources, and the enhancements in science and technology. But surely the massive increase in disparities between the nations of the North and the South, the increasing concentration of wealth in fewer hands, and the numerical increase in the number of poor should then also be attributed to economic theory? For all the massive investment in empirical inquiry, no one can say that economists have succeeded in furnishing a template for alleviating problems of poverty and deprivation; quite to the contrary, most economists would risk unemployment if they dared to suggest that economics might usefully have some relation to the ethically desirable objectives of alleviating inequality, reducing waste, interrogating received notions of growth and productivity, and advocating marked decreases in lifestyles in the overdeveloped countries. The tribe of economists, one suspects, has been more seriously devoted to aggravating social problems and creating new forms of inequity.

Similar arguments can be advanced about other disciplines; anthropology is a case in point. Anthropology originated under conditions of domination and imperialism, and its *raison d'être* was the study of the diverse customs and modes of living of people who shared little or none of the intellectual, social, cultural, and political histories of the Western world, so that Western scholars could form a more comprehensive picture of the diversity of humankind, or understand their own past by surveying the present lifestyles of those viewed as underdeveloped. Of course this was generally put in more sophisticated form. Marshall Sahlins described the question animating *Culture and Practical Reason* as "whether the materialist conception of history and culture, as Marx formulated it theoretically, could be translated without friction to the comprehension of tribal societies."[45] At the date of this writing (1976), Sahlins would have been unable to use the words that his predecessors had favored, "primitive" and "savages," without inviting some opprobrium, but one can already sense the family resemblances in each of the two sets of terms: tribal, savage, primitive, underdeveloped ... and anthropology (the study of primitives), eugenics (the science of racial hierarchies), economics (the study of the developed, or those with "money": one of Sahlins' favorite aphorisms was, "money is to the West what kinship is to the Rest"[46]), history (the study of those with developed notions of time), and so forth.

There can be little doubt that many societies that fell under the gaze of the anthropologists, or the scholar-administrator types who preceded them in the nineteenth century, suffered a precipitous decline and very often extinction. There was no greater misfortune for some people than to have become the objects of supposedly benign anthropological inquiry that some scholars still construe as a sign of the Western world's unique thirst for knowledge. For all its repudiation of its colonial past, its turn towards self-reflexivity, and its promise to be responsive to the people it studies, anthropology may not have gone very far towards becoming a humane discipline. Whatever the merits of the recent allegations, for example, made by the writer Patrick Tierney regarding the conduct of the American anthropologist Napoleon Chagnon and the geneticist James Neel, who were charged with deliberately introducing among the

Yanomami Indian tribe – apparently in the name of scientific advancement – a deadly measles virus to which they had no immunity, and encouraging the Yanomami to engage in violent behavior so that they might appear to the rest of the world as the very savages that anthropology has represented them as, it is not insignificant that such allegations are even possible in the first instance.[47] It cannot be a mere coincidence that the erosion of human social and cultural diversity, whether measured by genocide, the death of languages,[48] or the increased homogenization of lifestyles, has been in tandem with the growth of anthropology. Many anthropologists working among Native Americans generally endorsed official policies which led to the decimation and degradation of the very people whose life and culture had been placed in their charge.[49]

It has now become common for anthropologists to adopt the stance that they have far more to learn from their subjects than they had ever supposed, and to admit that their subjects may gain nothing from the encounter – barring some pecuniary advantages, perhaps. There is comparatively little talk of the "civilizing mission." Anthropologists are expected to approach their subjects with some humility, and the profession has elaborate guidelines about the treatment of subjects and the ethical conduct of the anthropologist. But it is a rare anthropologist – and much rarer are the apostates in economics – who has come away from his or her research with the distinct impression that "the focus of anthropological enquiry [should be turned] back onto ourselves." The quote is from Felix Padel's remarkable study of the Konds, a tribal people in the Orissa hills in eastern India, who practiced human sacrifice. The Konds came to the attention of British administrators, missionaries, and anthropologists, all inclined to view them as savages, and intent upon suppressing this abominable custom. However, as Padel points out, there is something ironic and even ominous in the manner in which British officialdom and Western scholarship has dealt with the Konds. For one thing, in seeking to extinguish the custom and impose civilization upon the Konds, the British probably sacrificed more human lives than were killed in the Konds' sacrifices. The British made an example of the Konds by publicly hanging their chiefs, burning their villages, and instigating the rape of their women: their behavior, in a word, was barbaric. Padel boldly suggests that the "enlightened treatment and strong hand of the British Government," to quote a British official charged with curing and obliterating the "plague" inflicting the Konds, "involved a greater, more insidious form of human sacrifice."[50]

The British, representatives of patriarchal Christianity, may have found unsettling the fact that the Konds' chief deity is the Earth Goddess, and that her human incarnation is also a woman. That may have been one of the main sources of their immense anxiety. In the worldview of the Konds, the Earth Goddess would be satisfied by nothing less than a human sacrifice every year, and failure to comply entailed risk both to crops and to the well-being of the people. In Padel's moving account, every sacrifice was followed by mourning, and he suggests that human sacrifice among the Konds should be interpreted as a profound affirmation of their value for human life. The British, in contrast, displayed little respect for the sanctity of life; as they torched villages and scorched the land, they also showed themselves utterly devoid of the ecological sensibility. If we had to extend Padel's account further, and ponder over the larger meaning of human sacrifice, it is reasonable to ask why anthropologists have not focused attention on capital punishment in the United States as late modernity's version of human sacrifice. Capital punishment is limited and highly ritualized – from the fulfillment of the prisoner's wish for a last meal to the manner of execution. We know almost nothing of the victims of the Konds, but those done to death in the United States are predominantly poor, disproportionately black, relatively less educated, occasionally retarded, and often (as in Texas) poorly served by legal counsel: they make for the perfect human sacrifice. It becomes clear why the disciplines have spectacularly failed us: no American anthropologist has cared to place capital punishment in juxtaposition to human sacrifice of the variety practiced by the Konds. The Konds, at least, practiced human sacrifice because it satisfied deeply felt beliefs and needs, and partook of the sacral order; American politicians support it so that they might appear to be tough on criminals.[51] Not only that, in the US there is no mourning; the families of the victim declare themselves satisfied, and the idiotic word "closure" closes all further discussion. Anthropology should find itself a new subject.

5   Ecology, Economy, Equality

A volume recently published in Hong Kong paints a grim picture of the impact of development on the environment in countries throughout Asia. Two of the four major rivers in South Korea that provide for the needs of 30 million people are so polluted by industrial waste and sewage that their water is no longer fit to drink. Two big dams in China, Banqiao and Shimantan, collapsed in 1975, killing no fewer than 86,000 people, and perhaps as many as 230,000, but state censorship kept this information from the public until a decade later. The damage to crops, forests, and buildings from acid rain in China, which records the highest acid rain precipitation in the world, was estimated recently at $2.8 billion. In Sri Lanka, forest cover had shrunk from 44 percent of the land area in 1956 to 20 percent in 1994, while in Peninsular Malaysia, forest cover declined from 70 percent in 1966 to 40 percent in 1984.[1] In 50 years since independence in 1947, the land under dense forests in India had shrunk from nearly 20 percent to slightly more than 11 percent, and as the well-known scholars of environmental history, Madhav Gadgil and Ramachandra Guha, remind us, more was "achieved" in these 50 years than in the preceding 100 years of colonial rule.[2] True, the population also trebled in the same period, but the inescapable feeling remains that the brutalization of the earth would have proceeded apace even without so dramatic an increase in the population. Everywhere the statistics tell the same gruesome tale of water, soil, and air pollution, of rapid deforestation and heavy logging, and of the disappearance of wildlife. The canvas for this epic tale extends much beyond Asia, of course, and its contours and details are available in pivotal texts, from Rachel Carson's *Silent Spring* and the reports of the Club of Rome to the annual *State of the World* reports as well as the publications of the Sierra Club, Greenpeace, and thousands of NGOs moved by the fate of the earth.

The same story can be told in other modes, in the anecdotal and poetic veins as much as in the language of the observant sociologist, though perhaps occasionally it may be hard to disaggregate the statistics. My wife, an avid birdwatcher before she moved to the United States from India in the mid-1980s, informs me that even a

131

densely populated city like Delhi had an abundance of bird life; she even speaks of electricity wires and branches of trees sagging under the weight of birds. Increasing urbanization, development, and the loss of trees have driven the birds out of the city. Both of us recall separate visits in the early 1980s to Manali, a famous hill-station which was the favorite summer retreat for hippies and college students before the Indian middle-class started descending on it. On our last visit, in 1995, the roads and hillsides were littered with polythene bags. This, too, had become a sign of "progress" in India, much like the traffic jams about which my neighbor in west Delhi had spoken to me with great pride, suggesting that the stalled or slowly moving vehicles were emblematic, more so than even in New York, of development, affluence, increased mobility, the fast tempo of modern life, and the fact that Indians like other developed peoples were now beginning to be busy: the "lazy native" was apparently an aspect of India's past. Even the vegetable vendors who moved from house to house were now packing the string beans, carrots, and onions in plastic bags, instead of emptying out the scales into the large bowl extended by the householder. The syrupy *gulab jamuns* that would be dished out in small clay pots were now being ladled into plastic bags, and what was diminished was not merely the taste of these delicacies, but the entire aesthetic experience; moreover, one had also to be prepared for the rejoinder that only those hopelessly consumed by nostalgia would overlook the convenience of modern arrangements.

Ziauddin Sardar has similarly written of Malaysia that people are aware of the pollution of rivers in which they swam and bathed with abandon as children.[3] The same is true of diverse bodies of water in virtually every developing country. The degradation of rivers is an empirical fact; but the loss cannot be captured only in the language of the environmentalist or sociologist. It is the plurality of experience that is eroded as well, a thought that is less often encountered in the growing accounts of pollution, loss of biological diversity, and contaminated water supplies: everyone is being forced into the Western-style bathroom, and our very conception of what constitutes a proper bath becomes homogenized. The supposition that elephants and humans might bathe together in rivers will in time no longer be part of our imaginary. There is the equally complex consideration that even empirical facts have a particular social grounding: thus, though the Ganga [or Ganges, in its anglicized form] at various places, such as Benares, is known to be dangerously contaminated, reeking with dead bodies, human and animal faeces, and the garbage emptied into it through the city's sewage pipes,[4] to the devout – and perhaps to those for whom the language of scientific authenticity has to compete with other forms of expression – its water remains the very embodiment of purity. The contemporary discourse of ecological degradation, compelling as it is, nonetheless has little place within it for the idea that among some cultures rivers may have sacred associations, and that contamination, far from diminishing the notion of the sacred, is its breeding ground. Pollution and purity may cohabit the same space.

The intertwined stories of ecological degradation, the decreased plurality of experience, the scarcity of resources, the emerging conflicts of the twenty-first century, and the increasing economic and cultural disparities between and within nations can be captured in immense nuance through the idiom of water. In its various aspects and incarnations – as the sustenance of life, the source of agriculture, the playing field for sportswomen and men, the marker of boundaries between nations, the site of notions of the holy, the passageway for goods and ideas, the index of lifestyles – water is increasingly becoming the subject of reflection and rumination.[5] Water is no longer simply *there*, filling up the bulk of the earth's surface, occupying a certain portion of every person's tummy. Increasingly, it isn't where it ought to be, or where one might reasonably expect it to be, in the homes and communities of many Third World nations and very occasionally even in First World communities. China has less than 7 percent of the globe's freshwater, but 21 percent of its population. However, China is not alone in facing this problem, since around the world over a billion people lack access to fresh drinking water.[6] As Jacques Leslie has suggested in a recent piece in *Harper's*, the world faces "an unassailable fact: we are running out of freshwater."[7] Indeed, freshwater comprises a miniscule portion of all the earth's water, less than 0.5 percent; its consumption has doubled in the last 20 years, and has vastly outpaced the growth of human population.[8]

Countries have been locked in battle over water, and as nations scramble to retain and protect limited water supplies, it seems that conflicts over water may rival those over oil. The Vice-President of the World Bank warned a few years ago that "the wars of the next century will be about water,"[9] and no one is describing this as an alarmist scenario. *Forbes* magazine noted that "water will be to [the] 21st century what oil was to the 20th," and a report presented to the

CIA by the National Intelligence Council predicts that water "will increasingly affect the national security of the United States."[10] Water is already coming under the purview of agencies and organizations charged with the task of global governance, and the commodification, trade, and privatization of water are increasingly becoming strident realities. In 1999, the Bolivian government, acting under pressure from the World Bank and IMF, privatized the water supply of the city of Cochabamba, and Aguas Del Tunari, a local subsidiary of the gigantic Bechtel Corporation, became the sole supplier. For some customers, water bills tripled; and even citizens who had relied upon older irrigation systems or family wells found themselves compelled to pay Aguas Del Tunari a royalty. Widespread resistance to the contractual agreement between the Bolivian government and Bechtel's local subsidiary led to violence on the streets of Cochabamba and, eventually, to the termination of the agreement in April 2000 – to the accompaniment, of course, of threats of legal action by Bechtel for losses in investments and profits.[11]

Water, under the present political and economic dispensation, is a commodity like any other, subject to the laws of free trade. The proponents of the privatization of water supply, who evidently are not constrained by sentimental or humane considerations, must think that the invisible hand, in a manner akin to the star guiding the traveler to the oasis, will apparently ensure that water reaches where it must. They are not bound by the idea that access to safe water is an intrinsic, non-negotiable right; much less would they be able to entertain the suggestion that even the language of rights, which is the inheritance of modern political thought, is grossly inadequate in capturing the idea of water as a gift. The free trade economy has no conceptual place for gifts: not only does the gift belong to an earlier phase of non-economic activity, but the gift ceases to be a gift as soon as it becomes the object of exchange, is given or received with the expectation of reciprocity, or otherwise lends itself to economic transactions. Water, then, has transmogrified into a marker of economic exchange and cultural capital, and we have stumbled upon it as an insoluble line dividing the haves from the have-nots, the Perrier drinking haves from the haves with less rarified tastes and slimmer pocketbooks.

Bottled mineral water has inserted itself into the story of water forcefully in recent times. To take one country, in 1995 revenues from the sale of mineral water in South Korea amounted to $117 million. The market for bottled water has grown astronomically in every part of the world; the market in some European countries exceeds $2 billion. In the cities of South Korea, we are told, "there are few people who drink tapwater directly; most people drink mineral water or water purified at home."[12] The ethnographer of mineral water is still awaited, and one is sorely needed: the often-told tale of globalization and upward mobility can be lavishly etched through bottled water. Some 25 years ago, mineral water in India could scarcely be found, except among the homes of diplomats from the affluent West and among the wares of vendors in only the most heavily trafficked tourist towns. Even 15 years ago, bottled water was relatively scarce, and a single litre bottle would have set a clerk in a government office back at least half a day's wages. The well-heeled might not have had to give much thought to the matter, but the professional middle-class, who had been offered the Brahminical solution of trading the necessary comforts of the material world for the dubious rewards of being "respected" and making do with small salaries, had perforce to resort to less expensive solutions than bottled water in an endeavor to procure clean drinking water. Though it isn't demonstrably clear that the quality of the water supplied by the Municipal Corporation of Delhi, and the same could be said for the municipal water supply in some other metropolises, had declined over the years, the taps were increasingly dry. At the best of times, in some neighborhoods the corporation supplied water for no more than an hour in the morning and evening each, and as neighborhoods expanded and consumption increased, some households resorted to illegal mechanisms, such as the installation of machines to the main pipe attached to the water meter to "drag" the water at an increased pace, to ensure that they were not without some water supply. Those who stayed within the confines of the law soon found that such machines were not only dragging water into homes where they were installed but preventing the supply from reaching their own homes. Others installed what in India came to be known as jet pumps, or machines that fetch water from deep down in the ground: 20 years ago it was enough to bore 20–30 feet into the ground, but over the years the water table receded precipitously, and by the mid-1990s one had to bore 50 feet or more into the ground to hit the water.

Though the acquisition of water after this heroic endeavor could be justly celebrated, such water was not fit to drink; this in turn necessitated the installation of home water filtration systems, a much cheaper option in the long run than the purchase of bottled water.

By the early 1990s, Aqua-Guard, a water filtration system operated by a company named Eureka Forbes, was becoming a familiar name in professional Indian middle-class homes; by the late 1990s, as a friend of mine informed me, almost all Indian politicians – the most crooked of the lot (some with felony records) and the highest of the land (the President and the Prime Minister) not excepted – had installed Aqua-Guard at their residence. This was doubtless the surest sign that Aqua-Guard had not only arrived, but that it was viewed as a reliable filter of water; if the two most closely guarded of the Indian political elites were predisposed towards Aqua-Guard, its reputation as a safe water delivery system could be assumed. Hospitals and restaurants followed suit: in fact, the good restaurants were known for serving Aqua-Guard filtered water as much for their cuisine, a not insignificant detail in a country where water-borne diseases are still common, and where the traveler's diarrhea still helps to keep the country's tourist traffic at levels far below those found in countries with scarcely anything resembling the rich attractions that India has to offer. Meanwhile, in the mid-1990s, as liberalization threw open the economy, multinationals came trooping into the country, and salaries leap-frogged, the price of bottled water declined rapidly. These bottles, known by the generic name of Bisleri after the Italian company that first began to popularize bottled water, began to make their way into solidly middle-class homes, and in the more affluent neighborhoods, even 5 gallon bottles, more appropriate to Indian households, could be found.

If these fragments of the story of water in Indian middle-class homes seem to belong to mundane histories of the domestic, that is only because the scholarship on the politics of water, enslaved to narrow conceptions of the political, is itself captivated by the stories of water in the "real" metropolis. It is extraordinary how many full-length accounts have been written of how water had to be diverted to Los Angeles from the distant Owens Valley, 250 miles away, and the manner in which the titanic project, to use the words of the *Los Angeles Times*, of bringing the river to the city was achieved.[13] True, this narrative has in it all the elements that could bring it to the attention of Hollywood: political intrigue, corruption, criminal activity, ambition and greed, billions of dollars, and the future of a megalopolis.[14] Hollywoodization is perhaps one of the criteria by which phenomena and events become the objects of scholarly inquiry and investigative journalism, and the water travails of a large Indian metropolis such as Delhi, which will surely lead in the very near future to further aggravation of hierarchies marked by relative degrees of accessibility to safe drinking water, make for (in journalistic parlance) poor copy. Astonishingly, the narrative of water in the Indian house, city, and community has attracted no anthropologist or sociologist, since evidently caste, Hindu ritual and religion, and communal violence are the only subjects worthy of inquiry. Yet all across the country, the elements of the story remain the same, and Indian houses, villages, and communities have generated their own gargantuan epic of water wars, complete with jet pumps, city water trucks, water tanks, buckets being hauled from door to door, taps left high and dry, hoses being passed from one roof top to another, and daily battles between neighbors.[15] Today's Mahabharatas are being fought over water – or its absence.

I began with an exploration of ecology, and in the meandering way of water have found myself at the door of inequality and the cultural and economic capital that water in its various dimensions conveys. The story of water is generally told through the framework of ecology; the custodians and nurturers of the world's water sources are those who are styled ecologists. Some might say that oceanographers have a story to tell as well; doubtless they do, but it is less a story of water and more of oceans. But the story of water is much less, inexplicably, told in the idiom of equality and inequality – and, even then, almost never as a story of households and communities drawn into political struggles over the entitlements to water. Thus have I endeavored to stretch the meaning and signification of ecology and equality; and indeed, as my probings of Gandhi's life in relation to ecology will suggest, that is how it should be.

The word "ecology," let us recall, is derived from "economy" [from Greek *oeconomy*] which itself has little to do, in its primal sense, with inquiries made by those now designated as economists; rather, economy was understood to pertain to the most efficient and least costly management of household affairs. It is largely an application of this meaning that Thoreau had in mind when, in entitling the opening chapter of *Walden* "Economy," he described the manner in which he reduced his needs as much as his wants to the bare minimum, and so lived life to the fullest. It is the same economy of lifestyle – and indeed of conduct, speech, and thought – that Gandhi ruthlessly put into practice in his various *ashrams*. From there, then, one can follow the trajectory from "economy" to "ecology." The *Oxford English Dictionary* defines ecology as the "science of the economy of animals and plants," and this implies the imperative to look after animals, plants, and the environment to which they bear a relation. Ecology consequently means, in the first instance, that we are commanded to economize, or render less wasteful, our use of the earth's resources. To do so, we have to use our own resources, howsoever narrowly conceived, with wisdom and with the utmost respect for economy. At the interstices of ecology and economy, Gandhi's life begins to unfold in unexpected ways.

THE ECOLOGY OF EQUALITY: THE ECOSYSTEM OF A LIFE

It is tempting to think that Gandhi may have been an "early environmentalist,"[16] and yet there appear to be insuperable problems in embracing this view. Though Gandhi was a vociferous critic of modern industrial civilization, he had relatively little to say about nature. His views on the exploitation of nature can be reasonably inferred from his famous pronouncement that the earth has enough to satisfy everyone's needs but not everyone's greed. Still, Gandhi appears to have been remarkably reticent on the relationship of humans to their external environment, and though his name is associated with countless political and social reform movements, it is striking that he never explicitly initiated an environmental movement, nor does the word "ecology" appear in his writings. The Indian environmental historian, Ramachandra Guha, has averred as well that "the wilderness had no attraction for Gandhi."[17] His writings are singularly devoid of any celebration of untamed nature or rejoicing at the chance sighting of a wondrous waterfall or an imposing Himalayan peak; and indeed his autobiography remains silent on his experience of the oceans, over which he took an unusually long number of journeys for an Indian of his time. The 50,000 pages of his published writings have barely anything to convey about trees, animals, vegetation, and landscapes, with the notable exception of pages devoted to the subject of cow-protection and the goat that Gandhi kept by his side.

No one would think of comparing Gandhi to John Muir or Aldo Leopold. He was no naturalist, not even a scientific conservationist, and it is also doubtful that he would have contemplated with equanimity the setting aside of tracts of land, forests, and woods as wilderness areas, though scarcely for the same reasons for which developers, industrialists, loggers, and financiers object to such altruism. Though an admirer of Thoreau's writings, such as the essay on "Civil Disobedience," Gandhi would not have thought much of the enterprise, rather familiar to him from the Indian tradition, of retreating into the woods. He was by no means averse to the idea of the retreat, but Gandhi spent an entire lifetime endeavoring to remain otherworldly while wholly enmeshed in the ugly affairs of the world. Gandhi acquired the ability of retreating into himself and listening to his "inner voice" at critical junctures when the noise outside became deafening. Similarly, the problems posed by the man-eating tigers of Kumaon, made famous by Jim Corbett, would have left less of a moral impression upon him than those problems which are the handiwork of men who let the brute within them triumph. It is reported that when the English historian Edward Thompson once remarked to Gandhi that wildlife was rapidly disappearing in India, Gandhi replied: "wildlife is decreasing in the jungles, but it is increasing in the towns."[18] If Gandhi was not predisposed towards lavishing much attention upon wildlife, Guha maintains that he also failed to recognize adequately the "distinctive social and environmental problems" of urban areas.

Thus neither "ecologist" nor "environmentalist" seem to sit on Gandhi's frame with ease. And, yet, few people acquainted with Gandhi's life, or with environmental movements in India, would cavil at the suggestion that Gandhi has been the inspirational force behind the ecological awareness of contemporary Indians. Gandhi's own immediate disciples, Mirabehn and Saralabehn, came to exercise an incalculable influence on Chandi Prasad Bhatt, Vimla and Sunderlal Bahuguna, and others who have been at the helm of the Chipko agitation, a movement to ensure, in the words of women activists, that Himalayan forests continue to bear "soil, water and pure air" for present and future generations.[19] Similarly, Baba Amte and Medha Patkar, the most well-known figures associated with the more recent Narmada Bachao Andolan, a movement aimed at preventing the construction of one of the world's largest dam projects and the consequent dislocation and uprooting of the lives of hundreds of thousands of rural and tribal people, have been equally generous in acknowledging that they derived their inspiration in great part from Gandhi. It may be mistaken to speak of these movements as "Gandhian," since any such reading perforce ignores the traditions of peasant resistance, the force of customary practices, and the appeal of localized systems of knowledge, but the spirit of Gandhi has undoubtedly moved Indian environmentalists. Not only that: far beyond the confines of Indian environmental movements, exponents of deep ecology have spoken glowingly of the impress of Gandhi's thought upon them.[20] Arne Naess, the Norwegian

philosopher with whose name deep ecology is inextricably intertwined, has testified that from Gandhi he learnt that the power of
non-violence could only be realized after the awareness of "the
essential oneness of all life."[21]

To comprehend the ecological dimensions of Gandhian thinking
and practice, we shall have to go well beyond the ordinary implications conveyed by the categories of ecology and environment;
indeed, we may not even find much in these words, as they are conventionally understood, to bring us close to Gandhi, unless we are
prepared to concede that ethics, ecology, and politics were all closely
and even indistinguishably interwoven into the fabric of his thought
and social practices. If, for instance, his practice of observing 24
hours of silence on a regular basis was a mode of conserving his
energy, entering into an introspective state, and listening to the still
voice within, it was also a way of signifying his dissent from ordinary
models of communication with the British and establishing the
discourse on his own terms. Similarly, Gandhi deployed fasting not
only to open negotiations with the British or (more frequently)
various Indian communities, but to cleanse his own body, free his
mind of impure thoughts, feminize the public realm, and even to
partake in the experience of deprivation from which countless
millions of Indians suffered. Gandhi deplored the idea of waste, and
fasting was a sure means of ascertaining the true needs of the body
and preserving its ecological equanimity. But to eat, or not to eat,
was for him a far more vital question than for many others, one that
anticipated the connection of the body to the body politic: no one
could have said of him what Edmund Burke imputed to Warren
Hastings, namely that when he opened his mouth at the dining
table, it caused a famine.[22]

The ecological vision of Gandhi's life opens itself before us in
myriad ways. First, as nature provides for the largest animals as much
as it provides for its smallest creations, so Gandhi allowed this
principle to guide him in his political and social relations with all
manner of women and men. Gandhi's close disciple and attendant,
Mirabehn, wrote that while he worked alongside everyone else in
the ashram, he would carry on his voluminous correspondence and
grant interviews. "Big people of all parties, and of many different
nations would come to see Bapu [the affectionately respectful term
for Gandhi], but he would give equal attention to the poorest
peasant who might come with a genuine problem."[23] In the midst
of important political negotiations with senior British officials, he

would take the time to tend to his goat. Gandhi remained supremely indifferent to considerations of power, prestige, and status in choosing his companions; similarly, he was as attentive to the minutest details as he was to matters of national importance. One of his associates has reported – and such stories proliferate – that when news reached Gandhi of the illness of the daughter of a friend, he wrote to her a long letter in the midst of an intense political struggle in Rajkot, detailing the medicines that she was to take, the food that she was to avoid, and the precautions she was to exercise. Though he was notoriously thrifty, writing even some of his letters on the back of envelopes addressed to him, he did not begrudge spending a large sum of money to send her a telegram.[24] His own grandniece, pointing to the meticulous care with which Gandhi tended to her personal needs, all the while that he was engaged in negotiations for Indian independence, perhaps showered him with the most unusual honor when, in writing a short book about him, she called it *Bapu – My Mother*.[25]

Second, without being an advocate of wilderness as it is commonly understood today, Gandhi was resolutely of the view that nature should be allowed to take its own course. Arne Naess has written that he "even prohibited people from having a stock of medicines against poisonous bites. He believed in the possibility of satisfactory co-existence and he proved right. There were no accidents ... "[26] His experiments in nature care are well-known, as is his advocacy of enemas and mud baths, but there is more to these narratives than his rejection of modern medicine. Gandhi scarcely required the verdict of the biologist, wildlife trainer, or zoologist to hold to the view that nature's creatures mind their own business, and that if humans were to do the same, we would not be required to legislate the health of all species. On occasion a cobra would come into Gandhi's room: there were clear instructions that it was not to be killed even if it bit Gandhi, though Gandhi did not prevent others from killing snakes. "I do not want to live," wrote Gandhi, "at the cost of the life even of a snake."[27] In some renderings of these stories, the cobra would often be described as rearing itself up before Gandhi and placing its hood above his head, as if in homage to the Emperor.[28] The hagiographic tone of these accounts does not, however, detract from the fact, for which there is ample evidence, that Gandhi was quite willing to share his universe with animals and reptiles, without rendering them into objects of pity, curiosity, or amusement. He described himself as wanting "to realise identity with even the crawling things upon earth, because we claim descent from the same God, and that being so, all life in whatever form it appears must essentially be so,"[29] but it is altogether improbable that he would have followed some deep ecologists in treating animals, insects, and plants as persons.

Third, Gandhi transformed the idea of waste and rendered it pregnant with meanings that were the inverse of those meanings invested in it by European representational regimes. As the complex scholarship around the practices of colonialism has now demonstrated, and as I have argued in the previous chapter, almost nothing was as much anathema to European colonizers as the idea that the vast lands lying before their gaze, whether in largely barren areas of Australia and Canada, or in the densely inhabited parts of India, were entirely or insufficiently unproductive. To render them fertile, Europeans had to first render them productive of meaning, as something other than realms of emptiness (and hence of nothingness), which was only possible by construing them as wastelands which required the brain, will, and energy of white men to effect their transformation. Gandhi, on the other hand, was inclined to the view that man was prone to transform whatever he touched, howsoever fertile, fecund, or productive, into waste. His close disciple and associate, Kaka Kalelkar, narrates that he was in the habit of breaking off an entire twig merely for four or five *neem* leaves he needed to rub on the fibers of the carding-bow to make its strings pliant and supple. When Gandhi saw that, he remarked: "This is violence. We should pluck the required number of leaves after offering an apology to the tree for doing so. But you broke off the whole twig, which is wasteful and wrong."[30] Gandhi also described himself as pained that people would "pluck masses of delicate blossoms" and fling them in his face or string them around his neck as a garland.[31]

Yet this alone was not wasteful: there was also human waste, around the disposal of which an entire and none too savory history of India can be written. While it was a matter of shame that Indian society had set apart a special class of people to deal with the disposal of human excrement, whose occupation made them the most despised members of society,[32] Gandhi found it imperative to bring this matter to the fore and make it as much a subject of national importance as the attainment of political independence and the reform of degraded institutions. Unlike the vast majority of caste Hindus, Gandhi did not allow anyone else to dispose of his waste.

His *ashrams* were repositories for endeavors to change human waste into organic fertilizer. Moreover, during the course of the last 20 years of his life, he was engaged in ceaseless experiments to invent toilets that would be less of a drain on scarce water resources. If Gandhi had done nothing else in his life, one suspects that he would still find a place in histories of sanitation engineering in India; he would also be remembered as one caste Hindu who did not hesitate to wield publicly the toilet broom.

Fourth, and this is a point that cannot be belabored enough, Gandhi did not make of his ecological sensitivities a cult or religion to which unquestioning fealty was demanded. One writer credits him with the saying, "I am a puritan myself but I am catholic towards others."[33] His attitude towards meat is illustrative of his catholicity in many respects: Gandhi was a strict vegetarian, some might say in the "unreflective" manner in which many Indians are vegetarians from birth. He was aware, as his writings amply demonstrate, of the cruelty to animals, but he may have been unaware of the argument, which is widely encountered in the ecological literature today,[34] about the extreme pressures upon the soil and water resources induced by the meat industry. In this matter, as in many others bearing upon critical elements of his thought and ethical practices, the anecdotal literature is more revealing, more suggestive of the extraordinary notion of largesse which informed every action of his life. Once, when he had a European visitor at his *ashram*, where only vegetarian meals were prepared, Gandhi had meat served to him. This surprised everyone, but Gandhi, who had come to understand that his visitor was habituated to meat at every meal, construed it as unacceptable coercion to inflict a new diet upon him.

Gandhi himself partook of milk and milk products, unlike those who style themselves vegans in the United States, and his reverence for life and respect for animals did not border on that fanaticism which is only another name for violence. Jehangir Patel, an associate of Gandhi, has written that one day Mirabehn came running to him in an agitated state of mind. "Bapu won't be able to eat his breakfast," she said. "Some one has put meat into the fridge where his food is. How could you allow such a thing?" The cook, Ali, explained that he had gotten the meat for the dogs, and offered to remove it at once. Jehangir asked him to let the meat remain there, and Gandhi himself was fetched. Jehangir then apologized to Gandhi: "I did not think of speaking to Ali. I did not realise that this might happen." Gandhi replied, "Don't apologise. You and Ali have done nothing wrong, so far as I can see." Gandhi took some grapes lying next to the meat, and popped them into his mouth; turning then to Mirabehn, he said: "We are guests in our friend's house, and it would not be right for us to impose our idea upon him or upon anyone. People whose custom it is to eat meat should not stop doing so simply because I am present." Similarly, though Gandhi championed prohibition, he would not prevent anyone from drinking alcohol, and he condemned altogether the principle of drinking on the sly; as he told Jehangir, "I would much rather you were a drinker, even a heavy drinker, than that there should be any deceit in the matter."[35]

Though Gandhi was, then, no philosopher of ecology, and can only be called an environmentalist with considerable difficulty, he strikes a remarkable chord with all those who have cared for the environment, loved flowers, practiced vegetarianism, cherished the principles of non-violence, been conserving of water, resisted the depredations of developers, recycled paper, or accorded animals the dignity of humans. He was a deep ecologist long before the term's theorists had arisen, and one suspects that even the broadest conception of deep ecology is not capacious enough to accommodate the radically ecumenical aspects of Gandhi's life. He wrote no ecological treatise, but made one of his life, and it is no exaggeration to suggest that he left us, in his life, with the last of the Upanishads, or forest books. This is one life in which every minute act, emotion, or thought was not without its place: the brevity of Gandhi's enormous writings, his small meals of nuts and fruits, his morning ablutions and everyday bodily practices, his periodic observances of silence, his morning walks, his cultivation of the small as much as of the big, his abhorrence of waste, his resort to fasting – all these point to the manner in which the symphony was orchestrated.

THE ECONOMICS OF INEQUALITY: POVERTY AND WEALTH

Gandhi was no theorist of ecology or equality, and yet his life is a striking testimony to his lifelong reflection on the dense patterns woven by these concepts. On the other hand, it is an abiding fact of modern civilization that equality is a subject of thoughtful and dedicated interest only to some political activists and fewer philosophers, though unarguably it is the subject of animated discussions at many dinner tables, mainly among right-thinking but not right-leaning people. With the demise of political theory, for example in

American political science departments, where rational choice theory and formal modeling have preempted any wider concerns with politics, philosophy, and continental traditions of inquiry, one can scarcely expect political scientists to take any interest in the subject. Even the most well-intentioned political scientists, who are demonstrably concerned with issues of equality and inequality, justice and injustice, labor so heavily under the burden of the mathematization of their discipline and its surrender to rampant modeling techniques that they are unable to write discursively or engage with what was once a rich philosophical and political literature on these subjects.[36] Economists, with few exceptions, have had little interest in equality, whether as a subject of inquiry or a principle to be striven for: their *raison d'être*, I have previously suggested, is to aggravate the conditions of inequality, though if that seems an unusually harsh view of the exponents of the aptly-named dismal science, it will suffice to represent economists as specialists who service the engine of growth. One of the icons (mainly American, and there too affiliated in disproportionately large numbers with the University of Chicago) of the discipline admits that "the concept of 'equality' has no place in positive economic theory," but disingenuously adds that welfare economics – whose exponents are viewed as the subalterns of the profession – has dedicated itself to exploring the ramifications of the "idea of equality of result[s]."[37] The mantras of the profession revolve around free trade, deregulation, liberalization, wealth: in a word, the market; in a phrase, the growth of markets.

The matter goes well beyond the economists' indifference to questions of equality and inequality. For the people who are evidently, and even uniquely, on "the right side of history," a phrase used by Clinton but embraced with relish by Colin Powell, Condoleeza Rice, and others in the new American administration,[38] it has always been enough to say that we were all created equal, and then to proceed with the business of creating wealth (or, what is much the same thing, inequality). Some people have imagined that the declaration of equality, by advocates of the French and American Revolutions, is about as far as one can sensibly go, and that positive prescriptions for equality are bound to lead to the nightmarish excesses that came to characterize communist regimes. The explicit recognition that in some grand scheme of things we are all equal is said to be a sufficient advance upon the thinking of the pre-Enlightenment world, and there are those who doubtless think that the mere iteration of the ideal of equality is tantamount to declaring it to be a fact of life. Polls taken over the decades have consistently shown that Americans by an extremely wide majority do not consider inequality objectionable, and equality strikes very few as a laudable, not to mention achievable, goal. To state that we are all equal in the eyes of the Creator has never appeared to most Americans as incommensurable with the observation that it is equally natural that some should be born into extreme wealth and others into poverty.

The extremely wealthy are held up as examples of men and women to be emulated, and sometimes arguments which seek to demonstrate widening gaps between the rich and the poor are sought to be struck down with the observation that the American Dream furnishes always vibrant examples of the extreme fluidity of social class in the United States and the ever present possibility that even those who are in the ranks of the poor can reasonably hope to attain the sublime heights of opulence. It would be idle to pretend that most Americans have not thought in the same idiom as Ronald Reagan, whose aspirations for the common person are summed up in this observation: "What I want to see above all is that this remains a country where someone can always get rich."[39] Two decades ago, the United States had 2.4 million millionaires, and in late 1999, the number had risen to 5 million; in 1982, there were 13 billionaires and this had swollen to 267 in 2000.[40] As incomes surged in the last few years, the number of people who might have despised, or merely remained indifferent to, the extremely wealthy declined precipitously. This phenomenon appeared in the most exaggerated form in the United States, which has generated the most immense mythology around the super-rich, but it was on display almost everywhere in the world, particularly in countries with heavy investments in computer-related technologies. Thus in India, which some middle-class people, delighted equally at the country's new-found nuclear prowess and its enviable software successes, began to fancy as a superpower, an inordinate amount of interest began to be taken in Indian "billionaires" – their wealth counted not in billions of rupees, which would be a rather trivial matter, but in billions of dollars.

The pages of *India Today*, still the country's most widely read English news-magazine, began to surge with accounts of the lives of Indian billionaires, among them Wipro's CEO Azim Premji, Infosys Technologies' Narayana Murthy, and Sycamore Networks' Gururaj Deshpande, and diasporic newspapers, such as *India Abroad* (New

York) and *India-West* (California), now routinely scan the pages of *Forbes* magazine to report on how many Indian billionaires have made it to the top 500. The mercurial rise of Premji was the leading story in the Indian media through much of 1999 and 2000, and when the *Sunday Times* placed him third in the world on its Rich List, estimating his net worth at £35 billion, the chest of nearly every middle-class Indian puffed up with pride. A country of 1 billion could take pride in at least one Indian – a billionaire to boot, and no "half-naked fakir"; but since the genius of Indian civilization is believed to reside in the uniquely spiritual disposition of its people, it became incumbent to add, in respectful tones, that Premji appeared to have absolutely no attachment to his wealth.

One interview after another with Premji purported to show that wealth could no more contaminate him, or diminish his uniquely democratic sensibilities, than a mother could ever cease to love her child. But as quick as Premji's rise was, he took something of a tumble, and lately one of India's leading English dailies, the *Hindustan Times*, pondered why in less than a year Premji had vanished from the ranks of the top 50.[41] Each ascent into the ranks of the exalted is triumphed as a sign of the self-confidence of Indian entrepreneurship and India's coming of age. No achievement, short of some other demonstration of India's manhood, seems more striking to the upwardly mobile and Westernizing class of Indians. In the midst of all this, no one ever reflected on how the category, the Indian billionaire, which was all but inconceivable until a few years ago, came to supplant the indigenous category, *crorepati*. The sum of 100,000 is represented by a *lakh*; the sum of 10 million is known as a *crore*. There has never been a term to signify a million, much less a billion; but, to gesture at the politics of knowledge entailed in the transformation of the Indian sensibility, *pati* which follows *crore* means husband. Thus a *crorepati* is one who husbands great wealth, and in the term reside the traces of the moral economy which once obliged men of immense wealth to husband their wealth for some higher end.[42]

As the number of millionaires and billionaires rose in the last few years, diminished only by the sluggishness which stock markets everywhere are displaying since mid-2000, an astonishing amount of popular political and social commentary came to be devoted to what was transparently the growing inequality *within* most nations. Though the reports of various international agencies, such as the UN's Development Program and the World Bank, and NGOs – Third

World Network (Penang), the International Forum on Globalization (San Francisco), and Worldwatch Institute (Washington, D.C.), among many others – also pointed to the widening gulf between the North and the South, popular commentary was fixated on the rapidly expanding ranks of the wealthy and the poor in most countries. In the United States, there is no dissent from the prevailing orthodoxy that gross inequality between nations (and individuals) is one of the unavoidable facts of history; nor does the plight of sub-Saharan Africa, where real incomes have been *declining* for the last decade,[43] attract any attention except when its genocides, child soldiers, droughts, and wars force themselves upon the world's conscience.[44]

The *Wall Street Journal*, resting its case upon research that purports to show a firm relationship between growth and entrepreneurship, predictably offered the conclusion that "entrepreneurial societies have and accept higher levels of income disparity."[45] Similarly, inequality between Africa and the United States or (say) the OECD (Organization for Economic Cooperation and Development) countries is construed as part of the natural order: in this domain, as in all others, the model of evolutionism facilitates the most unthinking acceptance of inequality.[46] Moreover, it is easier to gauge increasing inequality in one's own city or nation than in the world; to that extent, other nations still remain abstract entities to most people. The dog killed by an enraged driver makes the national headlines, and even the cat stuck in a tree elicits the attention of primetime local news crews, but any more expansive notion of justice is beyond the ken of most Americans. William James, a prescient student of more than individual psychology, remarked that "callousness to abstract justice is the sinister feature ... of our U.S. civilization."[47]

In the considerable hoopla over the rapid increase of millionaires and the rise of a new generation of billionaires, the wealth of Bill Gates has served as the template for evaluating the well-being and poverty of individuals and nations. One may be tempted to find Gates' predecessors in the Rockefellers and Carnegies of the *fin de siècle* nineteenth-century US and the sheikhs of Kuwait and Saudi Arabia in our times, but nothing can detract from the supremely iconic presence of Gates in the culture of late modernity. The "Bill Gates Personal Wealth Clock" is updated every time the price of Microsoft stock changes, and on August 25th 2001, when the price of a single share stood at $62.05, his wealth was estimated at $70.07 billion. As the author of the site reminds us, that sum represents a figure of $245.884 for every woman, man, and child in the United States, and a figure of $11.3586 for every person in the world.[48] Assuming that Bill Gates worked 14 hours every day for the last 25 years of his life, his hourly wage amounts to about $1 million, and *each second* he earns $300. The creator of another website, "Bill Gates Wealth Index," suggests that, were Gates to "see or drop a $1,000 bill on the ground, it's just not worth his time to bend over and pick it up. He would make more just heading off to work."[49] The "Bill Gates Net Worth Page" offers a yet more elaborate set of calculations, comparing his wealth to the GDP of numerous countries, the total assets and market capitalization value of the world's largest corporations, and the total deposits of the largest banks. Conservatively estimating Gates' wealth at a mere $40 billion, the author found that this still exceeded the GDP of numerous reasonably large countries, including Nigeria and the Ukraine.[50]

It is understandable that the internet should be particularly hospitable to speculation and number-mongering, but it is not the internet alone which has fueled recent political commentary on the gulf that separates Bill Gates, technological magnates, and CEOs from millions of slum-dwellers, "internally displaced persons," victims of war, genocide, and drought, and many of those leading lives of endemic poverty in the hinterlands of India, China, Africa, and South America. The print media has furnished its own share of scales to gauge the gargantuan gaps between the haves and have-nots. Jeff Gates – Jeff, not Bill – of the Shared Capitalism Institute, relying upon the frequently quoted estimates furnished by the economist Edward Wolff, who has been studying the place of wealth in American society, puts a different perspective on Bill's wealth: it exceeds the net worth of the bottom 45 percent of all Americans, though to heighten the profound implications of that statistic, he could well have added that the bottom 45 percent of Americans generally have more wealth than the middle classes of the developing or underdeveloped countries. The personal assets of Gates and his Microsoft co-founder, Paul Allen, combined with those of fellow billionaire Warren Buffet exceed the combined GDP of the world's 41 poorest countries.[51] Other figures, which extend well beyond a few individuals to embrace the American population as a whole, tell a similar story. Each of the 400 richest Americans saw their wealth increase by an average of $940 million each year over the period 1998–99, while the net wealth of the bottom 40 percent diminished by 80 percent between 1983 and 1995. Of the United

States' total assets, 1 percent of Americans own 95 percent, and 80 percent of households take home a proportionately smaller amount of the national wealth than they did 20 years ago.[52]

The story of rising global inequality is foretold, but only dimly so, in the statistics that point to the burgeoning margins of American society. Each year the *Human Development Report*, whose authors doubtless aspire to put on a brave face, and who manage to sprinkle some purportedly welcome news of social and economic advancements in the world's poorest countries, such as an increase in the number of cellular phones and internet connections, paints a progressively alarming picture of widening gaps between the North and the South. Between 1960 and 1993, the gap in per capita income between the developing and developed worlds tripled, from $5,700 to $15,400, though all along financial aid and economic stimulus packages were designed to decrease rather than enhance the gap; the per capita income of America in 1900 was nine times more than that of Ethiopia, today it is 45 times as much. In 1960 the income gap between the top 20 percent of the people living in the richest countries and the bottom 20 percent of the poor worldwide was 30–1; in 1990, it had risen to 60–1, and in 1997, it had accelerated to 75–1. The same statistics reappear in different forms. To quote from the introductory summary of the *UN Human Development Report 2001*, which in turns relies upon global studies of wealth and poverty, in 1993 the poorest 10 percent of the world's people had only 1.6 percent of the wealth of the richest 10 percent; the poorest 57 percent of the world's people had about the same income as the richest 1 percent; and the richest 10 percent of the US population, or about 25 million people, had more combined income than the poorest 43 percent of the world's people, or around 2 billion people.[53] This data, moreover, adjusts income levels using purchasing power parity conversions.

The statistics about the wealth of the super-rich are easily complemented, then, by far more encompassing studies of global inequality as well as ethnographic and sociological studies of poverty. It would be a mistake, however, to dismiss the quantitative trivia which forms the narrative of the lives of the very rich – the $20,000 gowns worn by the late Diana, Princess of Wales, the 3,000 pairs of shoes found in Imelda Marcos' house, the 93 Rolls-Royces owned by "Bhagwan" Shree Rajneesh – as the detritus, even the surplus, of more conventionally sophisticated analyses of income and wealth distribution grounded in the histories of capitalism, technology, innovation, marketing, monopoly, and corporate transnationalism. Some forms of apparent trivia should occupy the same place in frameworks of social knowledge as garbage does in urban and industrial archaeology: if we wish to divine the nature of modern societies, and understand patterns of consumption, lifestyles, and culinary habits, we can profitably turn to the garbage heaps that we so profusely generate. The extreme affluence and wastefulness of American society, for instance, is comprehended the instant we register the fact that it alone produces half of the world's garbage.

The dominant paradigm insists that we think of the poor as a problem, and the magnitude of the problem is conveyed with the formula, which is meant to awaken the more enlightened to their responsibilities, that over 1 billion people live on less than $1 a day, and half of the world's population lives on $2 a day. Yet when we consider who generates the garbage, it is an open question whether the rich or the poor should be viewed as constituting a problem for global society. The lifestyles of the very rich and the very poor – do the grossly indigent have a "lifestyle"?, some will doubtless ask – are almost always written as discrete histories, but there is no better way of writing a history of poverty than by writing about the super-rich. Such a mode of thinking does not presuppose that the poor lead more spiritually enhanced lives, nor does it require one to glorify poverty or to pretend that the fulfillment of essential requirements and a modicum of comfort may not contribute to the well-being of people. But the dialectical and dialogic modes may give a deeper appreciation of how poverty is intertwined into the lives of the very rich, the dependency of the very rich upon the very poor, and the contingencies of wealth and poverty. There is an old saying that the poor will always be with us; but its complementary half, namely that the rich will always be with us, is less a portion of the popular wisdom that we have inherited. How can we think of what may be called dissenting futures until we start dissenting from the lives of the rich?

6 Dissenting Futures

Classification is integral to all knowledge systems. The back cover of most scholarly books indicates the discipline, or area of inquiry, to which the work in question belongs, and where more than one discipline is listed, the reader's expectations are at once raised at the prospect of a work that promises to be interdisciplinary. A recent study of a Muslim society in Gayo, in highland Sumatra, lists "Anthropology/Religion" as its subjects,[1] while the reading constituencies of another book, entitled *Children of Ezekiel: Aliens, UFOS, the Crisis of Race, and the Advent of End Time*, can be inferred from the pairing of "Religion/Popular Culture" found on the back cover.[2] Anthropology and religion, within the academic universe, can be interpreted as something of a *natural* pairing: though anthropology has greatly diversified, and its practitioners are just as likely to study tourism, violence, globalization, material culture, visual representations, and food as kinship, symbolic systems, and sexual practices, anthropologists have always assumed that one thing all "natives" or "primitives" have is a system of religious belief. The conception of some divinity, or of transcendence, was not lacking from the lives of those traditionally studied by anthropologists. Indeed, since sophisticated moderns profess secularism, religion has now become the domain of the less developed world as well as the relatively un(in)formed masses within the developed world. "Popular culture" furnishes the necessary clue that the subject matter of the book is the developed world, or the urban, more modern sector of a Third World country: the "natives" that were the bread and butter of anthropology have no popular, only a folk, culture. Without some form of print or visual media, and a system to facilitate widespread dissemination of cultural phenomena, popular culture cannot be sustained.

We can be reasonably certain, then, that there will be very few works which will be described as belonging simultaneously to the triple realms of anthropology, religion, and popular culture. While we also recognize that the lines which divide history, anthropology, and sociology from each other might on occasion be razor thin, much recent work purports to partake of the insights of a more eclectic mix of disciplines and has created its own gray area called "cultural studies." Though most universities have been slow in conferring formal recognition – such as the establishment of departments, doctoral programs, and professorial chairs – upon cultural studies, good bookstores, especially those trading in second-hand scholarly and fine books, almost invariably have a cultural studies section. Often one gets the impression, however, that cultural studies hosts the surplus, the remainder, the excess, the uncategorizable: thus the aforementioned book, *Children of Ezekiel*, is likely to end up under "cultural studies." It is evidently not a work of science fiction; and science fiction itself was not a subject of rigorous academic inquiry until a decade or two ago, and then only among critics of literature. But the subtitle of the work indicates that it would resonate among those with interests in millennium studies, eschatology, theology, and race studies: indeed, "race" in the subtitle would be nearly enough to place it under the rubric of cultural studies unless one could, for obvious reasons, deposit the book into the category of sociology. From the vantagepoint of the public, the term "cultural studies" poses a more elementary problem: it presupposes a particular conceit, namely that the study of culture had no prior history before cultural studies. The practitioners of cultural studies know, of course, that their work has been fed by a diverse array of theoretical trajectories, extending from psychoanalysis and post-Marxism to postcolonial theory and poststructuralism, and that cultural studies helped to pose new kinds of questions about the politics of representation and the constitution of subjects.[3] Nonetheless, cultural studies practitioners must always be prepared to face the question, "Have we not all been studying culture?"[4]

To that apparently naive query, cultural studies is unable to give an innocent answer, and not only because cultural studies is the study of culture as well. Stuart Hall, one of its most inspirational figures and sometimes viewed as one of the "founding fathers," admitted nearly two decades after the first emergence of cultural studies in Britain that "cultural studies is not one thing, it has never been one thing."[5] Hall did not think it likely that cultural studies, itself born of a profound unhappiness with the disciplinary structure of modern academic knowledge, would ever become a discipline. Besides, if cultural studies is not one thing, it evokes the strongest suspicion that it is in fact anything that its practitioners might want it to be, which is another mode of suggesting that it is largely fluff. Its opponents have charged cultural studies with being lazy, undisciplined, prone to encourage moral relativism, and lacking "rigor" –

rigor is one of those qualities that is almost never defined, and there is an unstated presumption that the study of economics, statistics, and the pure sciences, even classical languages, entails rigor but a vague, theory-laden commitment to the study of culture represents a form of mere, generally decadent, flirtation with knowledge. In American parlance, cultural studies is not quite rocket science – the latter apparently being the undisputed standard for what might be described as difficult and erudite work requiring long years of training and brilliance. Such is the tyrannical grasp of common notions that scarcely anyone who invokes rocket science bothers to ask what precisely is so admirable about rocket science, and whether the world would not be better without this science of dubious merit.

Sandwiched between the disciplines, which in principle it disowns, and the popular conception of the study of culture, as an endeavor that perhaps might lead people to the appreciation of other cultures and to more enhanced forms of cultural dialogue, cultural studies has nonetheless achieved an extraordinary degree of success in the academy, nowhere more so than in the United States. Its somewhat liminal status belies the degree of institutionalization that cultural studies has managed without the formal support that traditional departments expect and receive from institutions of higher education. There are legions of conferences devoted to cultural studies, and numerous prestigious journals – *Cultural Studies, New Formations, Social Text, Cultural Critique, boundary 2, Public Culture, Differences, Arena*, among many others – have emerged in the course of the last two decades with reputations for publishing work at the "cutting edge." Its most famous practitioners, a disproportionately large number of whom trace their national origins to the formerly colonized world, are practically the superstars – they are referred to as such – of the American academy, commanding not merely awesome salaries and chaired professorships at the leading universities but the kind of public attention to which film stars and social celebrities are accustomed. The recent departure of Homi Bhabha, a professor of literature whose name is indelibly linked with cultural studies, from the University of Chicago for Harvard became the subject of a lengthy article in the *New York Times*, and the reporter described Harvard's achievement in luring Bhabha as a "major coup, as if Sammy Sosa had defected to the Boston Red Sox."[6]

Though the fanciest of academic salaries are but pocket change for professional American sportsmen playing in the major leagues, it is instructive that the reporter should have thought of the trading which characterizes the world of American sport as the template for the more rarified transactions that beset the Ivy League set. No one can argue that Bhabha moved to the Boston area to escape the bitter winters of Chicago, or that Chicago is intellectually less robust than Harvard. But Chicago has much less of the glitter that Harvard's name conveys, and for a former colonial subject, most particularly a member of the Parsi community that located its own aspirations in the moral and intellectual histories of the modern West,[7] there is a particular sweetness in lodging oneself at the very nexus of intellectual glamour. Scholars do not typically wish to have their own carefully crafted theories – such as the ideas of hybridity, in-betweenness, and colonial ambivalence, which have become Bhabha's trademarks[8] – seen as the partial products of their own anxieties, but the disjunctiveness of such intellectual positions seems perhaps somewhat less excusable in scholars who have spent a lifetime studying the inadequate moral worlds of the colonizers and the discursive aspects of oppressive regimes. Bhabha, who migrated to the US after a long spell at a good British university, has seen enough of "in-betweenness"; there is only the "top" for him.

Trading for superstars among the major American universities has now become so marked a feature of the landscape that it is not uncommon to hear rumors of the departure of someone who just arrived at his or her new location – and sometimes not arrived at all. In the academy, as in the corporate world, hard bargains are driven – and quite unabashedly, with scarcely a thought for the old and apparently worthless pieties about knowledge being its own reward, the pleasures of leading the life of the mind, and so on. Such economic transactions are, needless to say, not the subject of the ruminations of cultural studies practitioners and postcolonial theorists, whose predilection for Marxist critiques of advanced capitalism is otherwise openly on display. Unlike earlier generations of scholars, whose reputation was to a very great extent also determined by the students they trained and the academic positions their proteges came to occupy, superstars and their nearest competitors seldom stay at a single university long enough to give shape to a new generation of scholars. The institutional affiliations of these superstars are the most immediate instantiation of the cultural capital that they embody, but they belong to the world, and they certainly conduct themselves in that belief: they have followings everywhere, and clusters of their devotees and hangers-on are easily found at every conference or university that they might grace with their presence. Though, once again, many of these cultural studies practitioners and postcolonial theorists have put master narratives under great scrutiny, and showed the precise parochial underpinnings of Enlightenment discourses pretending to universalism, their own works are treated much like reverential objects, and often subjected to exegetical analysis in the manner of biblical criticism. Citations to their work are nearly obligatory in analyses of colonial cultures, identity politics, popular culture, and a vast range of work pertaining to the literature, culture, and artifacts of modern societies. These superstars and their near successors have their own little fiefdoms, little kingdoms that echo the empires that they study and deconstruct.

The place of cultural studies and its most eminent practitioners in the academy is no trivial matter, because cultural studies' very domestication, and the ease with which it inserted itself into the capacious and extremely well-funded world of American scholarship, raises uneasy questions about the relationship of knowledge to politics and the public sphere, the diminishing possibilities for dissenting frameworks of knowledge, and the limited conception of the future held by those who might have thought of themselves as the vanguard of progressive thinking on university campuses. Cultural studies began to emerge and then flourish on American campuses precisely at that time when the country elected to its highest office a man whose entire political thinking was driven by the overwhelming ambition to contain and eliminate the "evil empire"; discipline, chastise, and humiliate its real or alleged satellites and surrogates, and celebrate, at the price of diminishing the influence of government, private enterprise as "the American way" of handling a vast array of economic, social, and political problems. In the 1980s, as cultural studies entrenched itself on university campuses, most particularly in its more activist and student-led incarnations of multiculturalism and identity politics, the Republican ascendancy ensured that social welfare programs were cut and numerous people imagined as recalcitrants were taught the virtues of restraint, abstinence, and disciplined work. Corporations became leaner and meaner as the managerial revolution led to the exaltation of efficiency, downsizing, increased corporate earnings, and obscene compensations for senior executives. Class differences, measured for instance by the significant increase both in the numbers of people falling below the poverty line and in the astronomical increase of the super-wealthy, sharpened throughout the 1980s and 1990s as cultural studies was allowed to hold sway over campuses. These trends were seldom the subject of cultural studies, which in its American variant remained shockingly oblivious to class.[9]

Universities have often imagined themselves as spaces of freedom, as autonomous realms relatively free of the nefarious influence of the dirty world of politics where pure thought could be entertained. The prevailing political view appears to have been to encourage them in this tendency. On the one hand, identity politics flourished, and attempts were made to form rainbow coalitions of all oppressed, marginalized, and largely or wholly silenced voices. The narrative of cultural studies, Lata Mani was to write in the early 1990s, "sets up problematic chains of equivalences, between, say, women, people of color in the U.S., people from the third world, lesbians, gay men. It implies that these groups are caught in the webs of postmodernity in analogous ways." But the making of "inventories of difference" is not the same as a substantive engagement with difference, as Mani suggested, and she found the "unrealistic, utopian conceptions of collectivity" making "a mockery of the escalating racial, class, and social tensions" characterizing the United States.[10] On the other hand, the principal theorists, or at least their followers, fondly imagined that their interrogations of received narratives and foundational discourses were liable to make a profound difference in the conduct of practical politics, and that the world would be a better place on account of their interventions.[11] The operative words, such as "resistance," "alterity" ["otherness"], and "subaltern," all conveyed the impression that much thought was being expended on the invisible and the marginalized and their valiant struggles to make their own histories.

Thus, while cultural studies made its mark, the United States was unleashing mayhem in central America, supporting reactionary or anti-anti-colonial movements in Southern Africa, encouraging militant Islam in Afghanistan and central Asia, and bombing Iraq to smithereens. This catalog of crimes could be extended with ease, but the point scarcely requires belaboring. Meanwhile, on the economic front, the entire world was being cajoled, through the mechanisms of the NAFTA, structural adjustment programs in developing countries, and the GATT and its successor regime, WTO, into the acceptance of what was euphemistically called free trade. Three decades ago, as the United States was engaged "in a criminal war, criminally conducted," the philosopher Thomas Nagel says that it produced in him "a heightened sense of the absurdity of [his] theo-retical pursuits." The feelings of "rage and horror" produced by the United States' crimes in Vietnam led to "serious professional work by philosophers on public issues."[12] But, in the 1980s and 1990s, as large parts of the world were subjected to a campaign of pacification by bandits camouflaged as presidents and leaders of the free world, and the United States' inner cities were allowed to putrefy, becoming virtual war zones, academic radicals satisfied themselves with cultural studies.

Within the American university, and likewise in Britain and Australia, cultural studies, broadly conceived, established itself as the dissenting model – or at least as far dissenting as the modern culture of universities permits. Since no one has been able to place even remotely precise parameters around cultural studies, the rela-tionship of cultural studies to postcolonial theory and poststructuralism,[13] and even to science studies,[14] the new American studies,[15] race studies,[16] and a range of other recent academic phenomena (not to mention "queer theory" and gay and lesbian studies) remains a matter of debate. The achievements of the last twenty-odd years in opening up the traditional disciplines to new kinds of questions and voices, as well as more illuminating strategies of interpretation – reading texts for their betrayals and slippages, cracking wide open what Ranajit Guha has called the "prose of counter-insurgency" for its fissures,[17] questioning the myriad ways in which texts are gendered – cannot be doubted. Nonetheless, viewed against the backdrop of increasing American hegemony, the pauperization of much of the Third World, the incarceration of an alarming number of African-American males, and the globalization of knowledge systems, cultural practices, corporate cultures, and consumer goods, the consolidation of cultural studies appears to have done little if anything to promote what I have described as the ecological survival of plurality. If universities can put on offer nothing better than cultural studies, the prospects for an emanci-patory politics of knowledge look slim. The university cannot be the site for dissenting futures.[18]

FINITE GAMES: HOSTAGE TO "THE CLASH OF CIVILIZATIONS"

I began with some unfinished ruminations on the categorization or, shall we say, disciplining of books. I recall an occasion in the mid-1980s when, as a graduate student at the University of Chicago, I went looking in the university library for a copy of the journal *Alter-*

natives. To my utter surprise, and some consternation, I found that it had been shelved in the section reserved for journals in economics and operations research in the library of the university's business school. I could not have expected that *Alternatives*, which had featured some of the most insightful work on alternative futures and visions of modern society, besides offering trenchant critiques of dominant models of war, violence, and political and economic repression, would be placed alongside journals in economics. Not everyone is agreed that economics remains, singularly, the "dismal science"; nonetheless, its pretensions exceed those of the other social sciences, and its practitioners increasingly fancy themselves mathematicians. In near proximity to *Alternatives*, on the other side of the shelf, lay various journals on forecasting, technological planning, and strategic management, as though the only conception of the future that we are permitted to have is one which the cormorant crew of economists, management specialists, and tech-nocrats, who have hitherto failed miserably in giving us a more desirable society, have ordained as worthy of the attention of humankind. Economists have flourished, just as many of the societies they have been called to manage have decayed; but unlike the tribes to which they are likened, economists have scarcely had the decency to live in self-sufficiency.

It is quite possible, of course, to describe the peculiar place that *Alternatives* occupies in the shelves of more than one university library as a technical problem in classification, or to attribute the error to the quirkiness of a few, perhaps ill-informed, librarians. That benign view, for instance, would appear to explain why I once found Ashis Nandy's *The Tao of Cricket* (1989), a subtle exploration, with cricket as the regnant metaphor, of colonialism, the culture of mas-culinity, and the ethos of amateurism in Victorian England, in the section of a bookstore where it shared space with books on motor racing, boxing, and football. All knowledge systems have relied on forms of classification, and the disposition towards one form of clas-sification rather than another might be no less than the difference between competing visions of culture and society. Problems of clas-sification and categorization, I have argued in this book, are almost never mere trivialities: thus the history of Sikhs in post-independent India might have been quite different had not the British classified them as a "martial race,"[19] nor would the Gurkhas have continued to do the dirty work for British imperialists had they not fallen under the same rubric. Similarly, to reiterate an argument advanced earlier, if the deaths on account of development could be counted alongside the countless victims of numerous genocides, the twentieth century might appear still more barbaric than it does even to the mere observer of history. It is through classification that otherness is marked, boundaries are marked, and entire cultures are construed as being civilized or rendered as outside the pale of civilization.

There is in the tale of the not-mislaid journal, then, a rather more ominous warning, both about the oppressiveness of modern knowledge systems and the manner in which, as the Pakistani intellectual Ziauddin Sardar has described it, "the future has been colonised."[20] At a considerable distance in the past, the future was the provenance of astrologers, soothsayers, palmists, and various other traditional specialists in magic, fortune-telling, and curses. Every storyteller was a futurist, since stories (though they are generally located in the past) are invariably interventions in the future. Storytelling is especially associated with children not only because, as is commonly thought, children do not have a developed capacity for understanding abstractions, and consequently are immersed in the concrete detail. Everyone recognizes that stories are vehicles for the transmission of moral lessons, but it is pre-eminently through stories that we convey to children our ideas of, and hopes for, the future: the future has no meaning without children, and it is in them that we invest our futures. The ancient Greeks certainly recognized that no matter where one went, one was bound to encounter a story. It is no accident that the greatest of the Greek writers in the post-Homeric period was the boisterous and mythomaniac storyteller, Herodotus; indeed, to take a heretical view, the demise of Greek civilization can be marked by the advent of the historian Thucydides, who set out to correct the record, tame Herodotus's flights of imagination, and present a more realistic account of Greek society. While the most outlandish and egregious of Herodotus's representations of the Other were absorbed over time into the West's huge corpus of ideas about purportedly barbaric, primitive, or otherwise inferior and exotic civilizations, in every other respect Herodotus was deemed in need of discipline. Herodotus' depictions of northern Africa as inhabited by headless or dog-headed people, with eyes in their breasts, or of black men as producers of black sperm, were considered as quite authentic representations of the Other,[21] but in other respects Thucydides' ruthless devotion to *realpolitik* and his rejection of sentimentality were seen as more reliable signposts to the future and the exercise of power.

Western civilization's desire to scientize its narratives, which must be associated with its increasing loss of capacity for storytelling, evidently has a long history.

If at the lower end the astrologers and palmists reigned supreme, at the higher end the lot of envisioning the future fell to the utopian visionary and the prophet. Many utopian thinkers were, however, inclined to locate their utopia not in the future but in the past, in some imagined "Golden Age" when law and order prevailed, and when justice was not so easily mocked. Though the tradition of utopian thinking survives in the twentieth century, judging from the works of H. G. Wells, Eugene Zamiatin, Aldous Huxley, George Orwell, and many other lesser writers, it has been showing a precipitous decline for some time, and has now largely been relegated to the ranks of science fiction writers and their admirers who are determined to establish that the American government has been conspiring to keep knowledge of Martians and other extraterrestrials a secret. In the United States, a country uniquely built on the promise of the future, nothing is as prized as the past, and the achievements of record-setters, which last but a short time, are at once earmarked as "historic." Prophecy has been even more effectively pushed into complete extinction, asphyxiated on the one hand by the increasing dominance of the historical mode, and condemned on the other hand as a regrettable residue of medieval superstition, the remaining sibling of alchemy and black magic. In the English-speaking West, Blake appears to be the last in the line of the prophets, but the entire West remains alienated from the prophetic mode, and not only because of the loss of orality, the transformation of the countryside, the overwhelming ascendancy of the print (and now visual) media, the declining emphasis on memory, the submission of civilizational entities to the nation-state, and the disappearance of the classic itinerant. Though Marx and Freud might well be hailed as prophets in their own right, they remain resolutely the creatures of knowledge formations which envision no possibility for dissent other than in the language of those formations themselves. Thus Marxism can allow for no critique that is not historical, and indeed to be non-historical, or even ahistorical, is to open oneself to the charge of belonging with the primitive, with those hordes still vegetating in the frozen vestibule of time.

It must come as a surprise to many, then, to find that the future is striking again. In the public domain, most particularly in the

United States, the future is most often recalled in the conventional pieties of politicians' pronouncements, in their exhortation to us to remember what is good for "our children's children." It is to assure our children, and in turn their children, a bright future, free of biological weapons and poisonous gases, that Clinton initiated a new round of the carpet-bombing of Iraq; and his successor has affirmed that our children deserve to inherit a world free of the scourge of terrorism. If under colonialism the preservation of the honor of Englishwomen was seen as conferring upon their menfolk the right to commit mayhem around the world,[22] the invocation of "our children's future" now similarly provides a sanctimonious license to discipline a recalcitrant world. More generally, however, the American tendency, now increasingly emulated around the world, is to turn the future over to policy planners, management specialists, technocrats, and computer nerds. In this "vision," a rather lofty word for shrunken thinking, the world wide web and the internet will keep us all connected. Chat rooms and cyber cafes, we are induced to believe, will suitably substitute for table talk and what once everyone understood as conversation; virtual communities herald the end of the nation-state.[23]

We may all be connected, but apropos Thoreau's comment upon learning of the invention of the telegraph, do we all have something to say to each other? While diagnosing the failures of the English in the colonies, E. M. Forster – who divined as well the madness that men are capable of to preserve the sanctity of women and children – came upon the sacred mantra to bring together the East and the West: "Only connect."[24] But our modern form of connectedness is only a travesty of the feeling of community that now seems irretrievably lost, and a lesser degree of connectedness would do a great deal to render the world more pluralistic, more impermeable to the dominant categories of knowledge and homogenizing contours of culture. Had we been more attentive to the political economy of hybridity, we might sooner have come to the recognition that multiculturalism has often flowered in the most insipid, not to mention insidious, ways – in the elimination of *multi*plicity, and in the promotion of mono*culturalism*. We are connected, most surely, but only by the barest threads and lifelines that the dominant culture of the West deigns to place in other palms.

No doubt, if the future was left to technoplanners and compuexperts, we would achieve the same results envisioned by the creators of the neutron bomb, which while destroying all signs of life leaves buildings intact. Since the human being is the one unpredictable animal, many planners for the future find *Homo sapiens* to be a rather unpleasant obstacle in the formation of a perfect blueprint. Yet, since the essence of the Western ethos is to strive, mastery over the future – following the now-contested mastery over nature, women, and children – is deemed an imperative. Consequently, like everything else, the future too has become a subject of study. Though the study of the future has only a fraction of the trappings associated with the traditional disciplines, future trends are there to be seen. The futurists have their own associations and organizations, their annual conventions, and their own organs of research and communication. Across the globe, especially in the "advanced" Western nations, even a few university departments of future studies have cropped up.[25]

Though in some sectors the futurist has yet to gain academic respectability, since his or her calling is still associated with astrology, numerology, palmistry, and other supposed superstitions, the study of the future is nonetheless now poised to become a big business. As the rest of the world embraces the market morality, and countries consent to the structural readjustment mandates of the IMF, the same breed that rules the roost in Western countries is beginning to flex its muscles in developing countries. In a country like India, where business schools were something of an anomaly less than two decades ago, and where business had less than the tinge of respectability, no degree is now more coveted than the MBA. Suited and booted financial planners, consultants, management experts, and computer specialists, who have learned the tools of their trade from the West (thereby enacting the modern form of *Vishwakarma puja*, or a Hindu religious rite in which the worship of tools, which signify the Lord's creation, is undertaken), partake of the hotel lobby culture mentioned by James Clifford, and it is at their business seminars and lunches that they hatch those schemes designed to render the future of India (and much of the Third World) like the present of the West. Truly, the future of the greater part of the non-West, if the forecasters, planners, and technoexperts are to be believed, is to be without any intimations of the future: it is to live someone else's life, to dream someone else's dream, to inhabit someone else's skin, and to become someone else's merchandise.

In the matter of the future, one might then reasonably infer, it will be business as usual. For a very brief moment, it appeared as though this business would be fatally interrupted by the demise of communism in Eastern Europe and the Soviet Union. Some disciplines, such as anthropology, Oriental studies, and historical studies, which served as the handmaiden to the West in its efforts to colonize the world, had as it seemed long ago outlived their usefulness; other disciplines, such as political science, which had flourished during the Cold War, and had, in a substantial number of its practitioners, no other reason for being than to be the foot-soldiers of the United States' consumerist ambitions, political self-aggrandizement, and ideological war on communism, should have faced extinction. But no species has ever willed its own destruction, however close human beings have been to eliminating themselves (and other species, who are not granted the dignity of survival in themselves, but only for humans); moreover, Western man knows little else if he does not know the art of retooling. All the questionable disciplines, as I have argued in a previous chapter, adroitly reinvented themselves and even became indispensable. Oriental studies, to take one example, was reconceptualized as area studies, a matter even of vital national security,[26] and to this have been added various forms of ethnic and minority studies. This form of self-fashioning, of acquiring an acquaintance with the Other, sampling various cuisines, and acquiring a library of world music, is now even championed as multiculturalism, as an instance of the West's unique thirst for knowledge and capacity for curiosity. It has almost nothing to do with the opening or closing of the so-called American mind.[27]

What, then, of the political scientists, those members of the American academy who so shamelessly thrived on the foreign policy and defense establishments, or of the economists, who were so warmly embraced by the authoritarian regimes of Latin America or Asia? The economists must have more lives than cats: they found new clients as the former Soviet bloc opened itself up to the rapacious drives of corporate Euro-America, and the booming tiger economies of Asia began to show unmistakable and alarming signs of weariness, poor management, and what Western economists describe as an inadequate comprehension of the working of the invisible hand. Nickel-and-dime capitalists once again can provide hoary testimony to the endurance of the American dream: the rags-to-riches narrative survives, though if one looked beyond the United States, more complex versions of this narrative would be witnessed on the horizon – the ascendancy to the Presidency of India of a man from the class of *dalits*, once commonly described as "untouchables," or the recent prime ministership of a man from a peasant community. Indeed, never has the economist had such a large playing field as he does now, when the entire developing world seems on the brink of liberalization and privatization: the academic economist is easily transformed into a corporate economist.

This apparent shrinking of the world, which we are told will make of the world a global village, is music to the ears of the capitalist and the economist alike. Globalization in effect means that the colonization of the developing world, which in its time was not even financially lucrative for European powers in some cases, can now be rendered complete. Moreover, when the exercise of power was once naked, and the victories of the battlefield were won by the Maxim gun and the ruthless bombing of villages, ironically termed pacification, now domination will take place under the sweeter and gently-killing dispensation of McDonald's and Coca-Cola. McDonald's has even convinced the world that it is no multinational, but rather a multicultural corporation: in India, its burgers are prepared without beef; in Israel, the Big Macs are served without cheese, so honoring the requirement under kosher dietary laws of the separation of meat and cheese; in France, wine appears on the menu at McDonald's, unthinkable in the child-friendly US.[28] Who can say that McDonald's is not sensitive, caring, even nurturing of local traditions? Cows must be fattened before they can be slaughtered.

But the story of globalization scarcely ends here. Though the shape of the future under globalization suggests unequivocally the narrowing of cultural options, the reduction of democracy to largely meaningless gestures at the electoral booth, the beggaring of the Third World, and the instillation of the warped mentality of the West into people not so utterly incapable of dealing with the Other except by habitual recourse to various forms of total violence, what is most at stake, as the burden of this book has been to establish, is the future of knowledge itself. The debate, however, is most often cast in terms of culture. The "battle lines of the future," the political scientist Samuel Huntington was to argue a few years ago, will be the "fault lines between civilization," and he sees the future as one in which the center stage will be occupied by a conflict between "Western civilization" on the one hand, and Chinese nationalists and "Muslim fanatics," acting singly or in concert, on the other hand.[29] (It is axiomatic that Western and civilization are supposed to be in natural apposition to each other, just as Muslim and fanatics are presumed as making happy bed-fellows. Perhaps we ought to place Western and fanatics in apposition to each other, and the two together in opposition to Muslim civilization.) That this thesis should have been advanced by Huntington is scarcely surprising. First an avid proponent of the United States' involvement in the Vietnam War, and then an advocate of the nuking of Vietnam,[30] Huntington became one of the foremost ideologues of the Cold War and was subsequently to find himself much in demand as a mercenary, offering such advice to despotic regimes as would enable them to be properly authoritarian, all to equip themselves for a future of democracy. Since the end of the Cold War threatened to run him out of business, leaving him with a mere Harvard sinecure, Huntington had to reinvent himself, and rather adeptly – as the millennium was drawing to a close – he chose a Spenglerian worldview to paint the picture of the future.

Huntington's thesis is all too simple: where previously world conflicts were largely political or economic, the new conflicts will be largely cultural. Having identified seven or eight civilizations – "Western, Confucian, Japanese, Islamic, Hindu, Slavic-Orthodox, Latin American and 'possibly' African," one suspects in approximate descending order of importance and worthiness – Huntington advances the view that these civilizations are bound to be in conflict with each other. "Western ideas of individualism, liberalism, constitutionalism, human rights, equality, liberty, the rule of law, democracy, free markets, [and] the separation of church and state, often have little resonance" in other cultures. These differences, "the product of centuries," will endure; they are more lasting than "differences among political ideologies and political regimes." Many developed countries modernized, introducing such technology and administrative efficiency as would enable them to raise the standards of living for their people and compete in the world market; but these countries did not Westernize, as it was scarcely to be expected that they would compromise, for example, their collectivist spirit (as in the case of China and Japan) for the individualism that is ingrained in the Western psyche.

Huntington takes it as axiomatic that these alleged differences will lead to conflict, which he sees as exacerbated by the increasing tendency towards "economic regionalism." Many of these civilizations, in other words, are developing, or have developed, their own trading blocs, and the increasing worldwide trade is not so much between different trading blocs, as it is within these blocs. Thus, however inadvertently, Huntington returns to the thesis that world conflict will be bound up with economic competition, as though numerous forecasters have not been laboring to make this transparent for a very long time. (One discerns even, in some of these prognoses, the desire that trade wars should lead to something more manly and rougher. War has been good to the West: if Germany was the classic case of a nation built on a war machine in the first half of this century, it is the armaments industry and the military-industrial complex that powered the United States to the status of the world's pre-eminent power in our times.[31]) The attempts of the West to impose its values upon other cultures are countered by other civilizations, Huntington argues, and as non-Western civilizations are no longer mere objects but "movers and shapers of history," violent resistance is to be expected. The clash of civilizations "will dominate global politics" and determine the shape of the future.

Though Huntington already finds such clashes between civilizations taking place around the world, the brunt of his thesis is that the West should expect conflict between itself and the two entities, China and the Muslim world, which have the power to resist the West's continuing influence. Islam is most hostile to everything from which the West draws its sustenance, and drawing upon an earlier and somewhat lesser-known piece by his fellow Ivy League cohort, the Orientalist Bernard Lewis, Huntington is inclined to believe that Muslims can tolerate neither the separation of church and state, nor submission to infidels. It is not that imperialism and domination are unacceptable in themselves to Muslims: rather, as Lewis was to put it, "What is truly evil and unacceptable [to Muslims] is the domination of infidels over true believers."[32] In Huntington's cryptic formulation, "Islam has bloody borders." The "roots of Muslim rage" are an ambition that is thwarted and the paramountcy of Christianity over Islam; on the other hand, the insularity, arrogance, and self-centeredness of China, which is now poised to rule over the Pacific, and where since time immemorial totalitarian regimes have crushed the rights of the people, make it an implacable foe of Western democracies.

It is evident that Huntington is unable to make the most elementary distinctions between the nation-state and civilization, or understand the consequences of injecting essences into politics. So the dispute over Kashmir becomes part of the fabric of "the historic clash between Muslim and Hindu in the subcontinent," and since "Hindu" and "Islam" point to two kinds of civilizations, a conflict between nation-states, themselves the product of forms of reification of identity under the oppressive political paramountcy of a colonial power, becomes a conflict between civilizations. Just how historic is the "historic clash" between Islam and Hinduism on the Indian subcontinent, and does this history take us back to 1947, to the early part of the nineteenth century and the inauguration of what the historian Gyan Pandey has described as the "communal riot narrative,"[33] or to the beginnings of Islam (as Huntington would no doubt like to believe) in India in the eighth century? This fiction of a clash makes a mockery of the largely syncretic history of India's past, of the richness of Hindu–Muslim encounters; indeed, even of colonial accounts that, against the grain, offered dense layers of evidence suggesting that in the daily lives of many Indians Hindu and Islamic practices weaved so seamlessly into each other as to be all but indistinguishable.[34] Huntington recognizes no "Indian" civilization, which has been infinitely more pluralistic than anything European Christendom has ever known, just as he transposes the experience of Europe's bloody religious past on to every other place, assuming of course that there could have been no superior form of social organization, and more elastic conception of self, outside Europe. Huntington's view here is the primitive one that religion must remain the fault line between civilizations, because howsoever insistent the West may be on retaining the separation between church and state, other civilizations have their essential and inescapable grounding in religion. Though the West orients itself spatially, the Orient renounces spatiality: thus we have Confucian but not Chinese civilization, Hindu but not Indian civilization, and Slavic-Orthodox but not Eurasian civilization. Huntington's essences are the stuff from which the proponents of the national-character industry made their living and killing some decades ago.

If Huntington fatally substitutes "Hindu" for "Indian," and supposes that Indian Muslims are of little interest as Muslims (the more authentic specimens of that faith being in the Middle East) and of even less consequence as Indians, no less egregious is it to suppose that the West is the repository of such ideas as human rights and the rule of law. This leads us, of course, to such nauseating spectacles as the report of Madeleine Albright, the then US Secretary of State, lecturing the Vietnamese on her visit in 1997 about their inadequate respect for human rights, which the United States did everything to decimate in Vietnam and has done little to respect around the rest of the world. It leads to such obscenities as the passage in the House of Representatives, in the week before the terrorist attacks of September 11th 2001 tore into Fortress America, of a law that set aside $2 million for the promotion of human rights and democracy in Vietnam.[35] After having engineered the first genocides of the modern period, and being responsible for the most gruesome ones of our own bloody century, the West can applaud itself for having successfully induced some other peoples to act in its mirror image.

Since the hypocrisy of the West in these matters is now amply documented, and its record in perpetuating unspeakable atrocities can no longer be denied or camouflaged, a species of American or Western exceptionalism is introduced to differentiate the actions of the West from the rest of the world. This disturbing and less-noticed strategy to colonise the future of much of the world deserves scrutiny. "The accusations" against the West "are familiar," concedes Bernard Lewis, and to them, he continues, "we have no option but to plead guilty – not as Americans, nor yet as Westerners, but simply as human beings, as members of the human race." Since this is too prosaic for words, Lewis moves to a higher level of comparison: so the treatment of women, deplorable as it has been in the West, "unequal and often oppressive," is nonetheless said "at its worst" to be "rather better than the rule of polygamy and concubinage that has otherwise been the almost universal lot of womankind on this planet." But as even this is not wholly convincing, and certainly subject to dispute, Lewis moves on to what he imagines is the loftier form of the argument. What is "peculiar" about the "peculiar institution"[36] of slavery is that in the United States it was eventually abolished – and so from here impeccably to the *non sequitur* that Westerners "were the first to break the consensus of acceptance and to outlaw slavery, first at home, then in the other territories they controlled, and finally wherever in the world they were able to exercise power or influence – in a word, by means of imperialism." Having first introduced slavery to many parts of the world where it was never practiced, Western powers conspired, against their own self-interest, to outlaw it: Lewis finds that a charming thought. Apparently, since imperialism led to the abolition of slavery, we might think about its restoration: some other good may yet come out of imperialism.[37] So the West is "distinct from all other civilizations in having recognized, named, and tried, not entirely without success, to remedy those historic diseases" such as racism, sexism, and slavery: herein is the exceptionalism of the West.[38] The West, we should all unhesitatingly believe, has the decency at least to seek forgiveness for its sins.

While the general tenor of American or Western exceptionalism similarly defines Huntington's enterprise, he follows the complementary strategy of demonstrating the ills that must result when the rest of the world emulates the West. It is not that the West must not, in principle, be emulated: we should all aspire to the greater good. Moreover, since the natives thrive on mimicry, a good course must be left for the non-West to follow. If there is to be a universalism, it can only be universalism on the Western model; but what sort of universalism is it which makes the world capable of equating America not with democracy, the Bill of Rights, the spirit of freedom, and the inalienable right to the pursuits of happiness and liberty, but with Pepsi, Madonna, and McDonald's, in short with "US pop culture and consumer goods." The "essence of western culture," Huntington is at pains to persuade, "is the Magna Carta, not the Magna Mac," the English of Shakespeare and not of pure instrumentality, and the conflation between the two cheapens the inestimable achievements of the West. Nor is this all: if the West can even turn its evils into good, as Bernard Lewis pleads apropos imperialism, Huntington inclines to the opposite formulation that the non-West habitually renders all that is good into evil. Most notably, Huntington sees this in the trend to accept modernization but not Westernization; and if this appears to be merely innocuous, or at most mildly self-serving, consider that "when non-western societies adopt western-style elections, democracy often brings to power anti-western political movements." The warped minds of tin-pot Asian and African despots render democracy instrumental to totalitarian impulses and designs: "Democracy tends to make a society more parochial, not more cosmopolitan." It must perforce, on Huntington's view, be Western exceptionalism, rather than Western universalism, that will mark the future.

It is an extraordinarily telling comment on the state of knowledge and the academy that arguments so poorly conceived should have received the accolades that Huntington's work has garnered. If the future is to be defined between the polarities of Western exceptionalism and Western universalism, then the only future that remains is to disown this debilitating and diseased choice. This is less than easily attained, since the West has even attempted to foreclose all dissenting futures. No dissent that does not take place in a form understandable to the West, or according to its canons of civility, is constituted as dissent; and every act of dissent that calls into question the purportedly dissenting frameworks of knowledge thrown up by the West in recent years, whether encapsulated under the terms "postcolonial" or "postmodern," is construed as a retreat into romanticism, indigenism, nativism, or tribalism.[39] As our very idea of the future has been held subject to the dominant ideas purveyed by the experts, it becomes inescapably clear that no better future can be expected unless we can decolonize the dominant framework of knowledge. The twentieth-century university, with its disciplinary formations and (more recently) its well-intentioned multicultural brigades, will have to number among the first of the victims. The earliest measure of our new-found wisdom and knowledge might well be to recognize that when the experts are removed from their area of expertise, the future will begin to manifest itself as more ecological, multifarious, and just.

INFINITE GAMES: DISSENT IN THE GANDHIAN MODE

One person who emphatically repudiated the idea that Hindus and Muslims comprised the membership of distinct civilizations was Mohandas ("Mahatma") Gandhi, and he paid for his belief in interculturality with his life. His assassination on January 30th 1948 at the hands of a Hindu fanatic, Nathuram Godse, who claimed that Gandhi had emasculated the Hindu nation and fathered Pakistan, was only the first of many assassinations to which Gandhi would be subjected.[40] But Godse was far more than a Hindu fanatic: he was the self-appointed spokesperson for all the modernizing elites of Indian society who were desirous of seeing India emerge from the end of colonial rule as a strong nation-state, fully committed to grandiose projects of development, capable of exerting its will in the world, and ready to embrace the wisdom of modern science. Gandhi, with his insistence on the "inner voice," his unorthodox political views and practices, his disavowal of *realpolitik*, and his trenchant critique of modern, industrial civilization, provoked the most acute anxieties among his detractors who between themselves represented the entire spectrum of political opinion.[41] Gandhi, a "half-naked fakir" in the eyes of not only Churchill but many modernists who deprecated his supposed glorification of poverty, was an obstacle in the path of India's future greatness – and so Godse pulled off the killing to which many others were silent and approving witnesses.[42]

In the aftermath of Gandhi's murder, the rituals of obeisance to the "Father of the Nation," which were really enactments of ritual assassination, would be performed at appointed times: with each passing year, every wreath laid at his *samadhi*, or national memorial, meant that India was coming closer to extinguishing Gandhi's influence from the life of the nation-state. The man who toiled

ceaselessly became the pretext for a national day of leisure. Yet the
spectre of Gandhi could not be removed; the old man refused to go
away, and in his death was almost as much of a nuisance as he had
been while alive. When the world took any interest in India, it was
largely on account of Gandhi; when the likes of Martin Luther King,
Jr. visited India, they did so because of Gandhi's unique articulation
of the principles of non-violent struggle and the worldwide attention
that the Indian independence movement garnered under his
leadership. Political activists and leaders of anti-colonial movements
would take succor from Gandhi's political struggles against colonialism in South Africa and India; the burgeoning vegetarian
movements in the West would find inspiration from Gandhi's
writings and strong attachment to vegetarianism; and environmental activists, again in India and abroad alike, declared themselves
emboldened by Gandhi's far-reaching critiques of consumption,
greed, and capitalist exploitation.

India's advocacy of non-alignment played a part as well in keeping
alive some of Gandhi's principles when many others wished to see
his memory buried. Declaring himself opposed to both the Soviet
bloc and the US-led NATO, Jawaharlal Nehru offered his services as
mediator in many conflicts; he had imbibed the spirit of honorable
negotiation from Gandhi. The Gandhian legacy of non-violence
demanded of India that it adhere to more principled conduct in its
foreign relations, and there would be some attempt to show the
world that India had been deserving of someone like the Mahatma.
But the difficulty in adhering to Gandhian-like ideas while operating
in a world of zero-sum politics was transparently on display when
India conducted its first experiments with nuclear weapons. The
world was informed by Prime Minister Indira Gandhi in 1973 that
India had exploded a "peaceful nuclear device." Can there be such
a thing? What does it mean to wedge "nuclear" between "peaceful"
and "device"? The hawks in India's defense and foreign policy establishments were doubtless pleased, but the profound ambiguity which
marked the emergence of India's nuclear program suggested that
Gandhi's spell had not been entirely broken.

In May 1998, in the fiftieth year after Gandhi's assassination, the
Indian nation-state finally laid to rest his spectre; it completed the
task that Godse had left unfinished. That month, India conducted
five nuclear tests. Having finally achieved its long-desired quest for
the summit of power in Indian politics, the Bharatiya Janata Party
(BJP), some of whose supporters have openly declared their

membership in organizations that were implicated in the assassination of Mahatma Gandhi, was eager to stake a place for India in world politics. Previous Indian governments had shared this ambition, and for some years India had quietly been lobbying to secure, in however distant a future, a permanent seat for itself at the Security Council on the grounds that it was poised to become an important player in Asia and the Pacific. Many Indian politicians and commentators were inclined to think that India's population, then nearing 1 billion, alone warranted the country's inclusion in the Security Council, while others pointed to the scientific and technical Indian manpower widely dispersed around the world; yet others thought that the recognition of India as more than another "pipsqueak nation," to use the none too charitable language of more than one arrogant American foreign policy expert, was owed to it on account of its great civilization. No Indian government functionary paused to consider whether the United States would ever contemplate the admission of a new country as a permanent member of the Security Council without the alteration of the Council itself to reflect a yet more complex hierarchy that would still allow the United States to remain *primus inter pares*, or whether the United Nations would not become an obsolete entity by such time as India was permitted to enjoy the paltry remains of an abandoned feast. The militarists in India recognized only one fact, namely that the five permanent members of the Security Council were also the world's only declared and recognized nuclear powers, and drew from this circumstance the only obvious conclusion. If India had to make a bid for power, it would have to acquire membership in the nuclear club.

The most resounding failure of our times, as India's nuclear tests of 1998 indubitably established, is that no nation that seeks to be a great player in the world feels it can do so other than by embracing the brutal and xenophobic zero-sum politics of the nation-state system. India has been a nation-state for only a little over fifty years, and it has been a part of one empire or another for several centuries; but it has been a civilization for around 5,000 years. Though the members of the BJP and other Hindu militants proudly describe themselves as adherents of a "glorious Hindu civilization," they know this civilization only as a historical fact, and understand almost nothing of its sensibility. They little know that "civilization" derives from "*civilitas*," or "civility," and that the loudest Hindus have seldom been the best Hindus, and sometimes not Hindus at all. Only a political leadership profoundly ignorant of India as a civilizational entity could have thought that it was destined to be a great player in the modern world system as a nation-state, and that in any other mode India was bound to be unappreciated and ignored; and only those contemptuous of the spiritual heritage of a civilization would have had the effrontery to explode nuclear devices on the auspicious occasion of the Buddha's birthday, and have the message relayed to them, upon the successful detonation of the bombs, that "Lord Buddha is smiling." In this matter they were perhaps emulating their political heroes: when the first test of the atomic bomb was successfully conducted by Robert Oppenheimer and his associates, Churchill received a telegram with the following words: "Babies satisfactorily born."[43]

With its attempted entry into the grotesquely named "nuclear club," India signified its willingness to accede to the rules by which its members conduct themselves. That India should have done so shortly after it marked the fiftieth anniversary of the assassination of Gandhi is the most palpable indication of how India has increasingly stripped itself of its capacity to dissent from the mandates of *realpolitik* and the narrowing options for dissent in contemporary times. Gandhi throughout sought to engage the British, and indeed even his many Indian critics, on terms that, from his standpoint, would be morally compromising neither to himself nor to any of his opponents. If freedom is indivisible, then the adversary has as much to gain from the struggle as does the victim: that was Gandhi's first principle of dissent from the world of what James Carse has described as "finite games."[44] In such games, there are always winners and losers; and if some people might be inclined to the rejoinder that neither India nor Pakistan are winners, and consequently there are only losers, it would do well to remember that the armaments industry, the military-industrial complex, and the nation-state system itself emerged triumphant from the nuclearization of South Asia. Gandhi's peculiar mode of dissent was to enter into what Carse characterizes as an "infinite" game, the purpose of which is not to win (as it is with the finite game) but to continue playing, and thereby give our assent to the proposition that as human beings we are morally bound to the principle that the conversation must never cease. In infinite games, rules are not set, and if they are, their transgression is tolerated if not encouraged. Conjoined to this philosophical dimension of play were the rudimentary elements of a Gandhian grammar of dissent: thus, during the crucial negotiations leading to India's independence, the numerous parties to the deliberations had to bear with the fact that once a week Gandhi was bound to the complete observance of silence, a silence that allowed him to listen to the still voice within, much as it rendered mute the chatter of endless voices. Where, to the British, Gandhi's resort to fasting was merely another instance of the unpredictability if not irrationality of the Oriental politician masquerading as a saint, to Gandhi it was an expressive and healing mode of communicative action. Gandhi uniquely came to formulate an engaging dissent and a dissenting engagement.

As we ponder, then, over the deeper significance of India's forays into militaristic nuclearization, it becomes imperative to inquire into the possibilities of dissent in our times. From a Foucauldian standpoint, doubtless, the prospects for dissent must look slim. As Foucault was to argue, the apparently dissenting practices found in modern democracies themselves constitute the apparatus of power, and power sustains itself by generating discourses which are apparently opposed to it but which in fact sustain the network of power. Dissent is permitted to flourish on the understanding that it ultimately enhance the very same structures of power that it appears to defy: "Power is tolerable only on condition," Foucault writes, "that it mask a substantial part of itself."[45] What, then, are the languages in which dissent can be expressed, and how does one signify one's dissent from those very political processes, economic forces, and epistemological structures that have made even of dissent a sexy commodity?

THE CIVILIZATIONAL ETHOS AND THE FUTURE OF DISSENT

I have suggested that in thinking of how we could work towards a future that will be fulfilling for every human being, and where dissent will be allowed to have an existence other than as a normal oppositional practice which subtly performs the work of oppression, it may be desirable to lavish some attention on the teachings, writings, and social practices of Gandhi. There are many, perhaps insuperable, problems in pursuing this line of inquiry. His name is associated with no particularly complex set of theories, and the only full-fledged doctrine that can be attributed to him is the technique he forged of non-violent resistance, or *satyagraha*. Gandhi himself gave every appearance of endorsing the view that he was to be construed as a doer rather than thinker, when he declared quite unambiguously that his life was his message,[46] and that his writings were to be "cremated" with him at his death.[47] Thus even intellectuals from whom one might have expected greater sophistication and some sensitivity to dissenting frameworks of knowledge, such as postcolonial theorists, have had little use for Gandhi.[48] But this is not surprising: most academics, even those who are associated with calls for resistance, and who imagine themselves as constituting the sole voices of dissent in an academic world that is increasingly taking on overtones of corporate management, are ultimately aesthetes: they have virtually created the discipline of non-dissenting dissent.

If the intellectuals who are presently in fashion have not made any time for Gandhi, his admirers have also had a rather limited conception of the Gandhian worldview. Gandhi may not have been the consummate theorist, though perhaps even that can be disputed, but there is scarcely a subject on which he did not express himself. More so than other figures, Gandhi is easily appropriable by those with particular and partial interests. Even Marxists have found useful at trying moments Gandhi's many pronouncements on communal harmony, but it is understandable, considering their own philo-sophical predisposition, that they should dismiss his views on science, industrialization, and modernity as the thoughts of a cranky old man. The advocates of non-violence have perhaps the most holistic approach to Gandhi, and some among them have come to a more complex understanding of the relationship of Gandhi's views on non-violent thought and conduct to his views on the violence perpetrated in the name of industrialization and progress, the dese-cration of the earth, and the degradation of women. But their interpretations of Gandhi are, as I shall suggest shortly, static: they are often more Gandhian than Gandhi himself, and thus they have taken the politics out of Gandhi.

Though it is customary to see Gandhi as a well-meaning if occa-sionally naive advocate of the rights of the oppressed, as a champion of human rights, Gandhi's various constituencies are united in their common inability to see Gandhi as the ultimate dissenter. He did not, let it be stated emphatically, opt out of society: that was neither his form of religion nor of politics, and Orwell was shrewd in his assessment that after Gandhi, the saintly life would have to be led in the slums of politics rather than the monastery.[49] Perhaps dissent (as disagreement, opposed to assent or agreement) has a strange and unremarked upon affinity to non-violence: it too is cast in what for our times is the much detested negative modality, and few self-proclaimed revolutionaries would prefer non-violence to violence. It is a portent of the unwillingness of intellectuals even to conceive of dissent that Raymond Williams, in his famous *Keywords*,[50] could find no place for "dissent," or even "non-violence," in his essential vocabulary, though "violence" is predictably given recognition. No scholar who has pored through Gandhi's writings can, however, miss the extraordinarily razor-sharp and subtle distinctions that Gandhi made between non-violence and violence, and his delineation of violence that is non-violent, the non-violence of the weak as opposed to non-violence of the strong, and the violence of some forms of non-violence.[51] Marxist critics, postcolonial theorists, and poststructuralists, however, are seldom biographers, and since it is an unstated assumption that Gandhi's life is richer than his thought, the onus of interpretation has disproportionately fallen upon Gandhi's (mainly mediocre) biographers.[52] That the supposed dissenters of the American and British academy, who are impugned by their conservative critics in the academy and media for their political radicalism and intellectual relativism, should be construed as beacons of an emancipatory politics of knowledge is only one of the minor absurdities of our times.

It is my submission that, in innumerable respects, Gandhi shows us the path to the future, though ironically he is often denounced for his allegedly hidebound adherence to some noxious traditions. I shall point here only to three considerations. First, the "talisman" he offered shortly before his death reminds us that thinking about futures cannot be merely left to the forecasters, economists, and management specialists, and that all concern for the future must simultaneously be read as an intervention in the present:

> Whenever you are in doubt or when the self becomes too much with you, apply the following test: Recall the face of the poorest and the weakest man whom you may have seen and ask yourself if the step you contemplate is going to be of any use to him. Will he gain anything by it? Will it restore him to a control over his own life and destiny? In other words, will it lead to Swaraj [freedom] for the hungry and spiritually starving millions? Then you will find your doubts and your self melting away.[53]

Second, Gandhi was firmly bound to the idea that freedom is indivisible: no person is truly free when others are unfree. So, in the struggle for Indian independence, he was guided by the principle that the emancipation of Indians was incomplete if the British could not be freed from themselves. The British colonized themselves, perhaps far more effectively and resolutely, before they colonized others; and the profound unease they experienced in the midst of Indians stemmed precisely from the fact that they recognized in some Indians a part of their own expurgated selves, a part of histories from which they had been sundered.[54] A Wajid Ali Shah suggested that a ruler could be playful, a dancer and a poet, even "effeminate";[55] a Gandhi suggested that resistance could be other than in the mode of violence and masculinity, and that the colonized had perhaps something to teach the colonizers in those very domains – the courtroom and the newspaper office – which the British were inclined to see as their own proprietary fiefdoms.[56] Thus Gandhi recognized that sometimes the emancipation of the oppressor requires greater reservoirs of strength and fortitude than does the emancipation of their victims. We must strive to ensure that our future will encompass a moral inclusiveness, and, as well, our very dissent is incomplete if it does not allow others to partake in the dissent, and if it does not create the conditions for further dissent. The dissenters within British society, consequently, had a role to play in the emancipation of Britain as well as India: they were the natural allies of those condemned as the underdeveloped. There is an egalitarianism in dissent, too.

Third, as Gandhi's own life shows, our conception of the truth must remain hermeneutic, dialectical, and dialogic. Gandhi's vegetarianism has been inspirational for many, and it is his reverence for all living beings that has made him important to Indian environmentalists, the Greens in Germany, and the advocates of deep ecology. Unlike the "deep ecologists," to whom he is sometimes likened, Gandhi would not have been ecocentric, and he would have been aghast at the misanthropic tendencies of many who style themselves friends of the environment. Though the word "environment" almost never appears in his writings, he nurtured every living thing that came into his care, and he was the most meticulous practitioner of recycling long before the idea had crept into the lexicon and sensibility of affluent citizens of the industrialized nations. While deeply caring for animals, Gandhi would have disavowed the keeping of personal pets, and he would have asked the ferocious defender of animal rights to ponder over their own propensity towards violent intimidation of women wearing furs. Gandhi could be quite irreverent, though the Gandhians will be among the last to arrive at that understanding.

Paradoxically, as the leader of the nationalist movement, Gandhi alone had almost nothing invested in the nation-state. On August 15th 1947, as power was handed over to Indians in Lutyens' Delhi and the rest of the country celebrated its deliverance from British rule, the principal architect of Indian independence was endeavoring to bring peace between Hindus and Muslims in far-away Calcutta. Gandhi was surely the first (and quite likely the last) political leader in modern India to understand that power exists to be disowned, and that there can be strength without power. His political negotiations stemmed not from considerations of expediency, nor even from the principle of reciprocity, which would be considered an honorable achievement on the part of any modern politician, but from his notion of the gift. He gave his endorsement to the Khilafat, a movement aimed at restoring the authority of the Caliphate over the Muslim holy places while Britain sought to dismember the Ottoman empire, but not in exchange for any promise from Indian Muslim leaders that they would forbid cow-slaughter; nor did he champion Hindu–Muslim unity principally on the noble grounds that peace is to be preferred to violence, much less on the expedient grounds that together Hindus and Muslims could more effectively resist colonial rule. He took the view, rather, that Hindus and Muslims were incomplete without each other, and that Indian civilization would be irreparably fractured by the separation of the two faiths.

To locate the sources of Gandhi's strength, and his unique appeal across the most diverse strands of Indian society, it is imperative to recall the deep mythic structuring of Indian civilization. The modernizers and rationalists have trivialized myth, opposing it to history and science, tarnishing it with responsibility for the worst evils of our times (thus the "myth of the Aryan race," or the "myth of the white man's superiority," both of which ironically point to the wholly destructive manner in which science and history were conjoined in the service of debased ideologies), when it is myth alone which has retained the open-endedness that the formal disciplines and discourses no longer possess. "Myth provokes explanation but accepts none of it," writes Carse, adding: "Where explanation absorbs the unspeakable into the speakable, myth reintroduces the silence that makes original discourse possible."[57] The idea of civilization has similarly been denuded of its immense possibilities. Gandhi himself was anchored in Indian civilization, from the syncretistic customs of Indian villagers to the multitudinous depths of the Mahabharata. He also came to mirror, as even the best of men and women must do, the shortcomings of that civilization: while purporting to speak for the nation, his critics charged, he was unable to look after his own family, and his eldest son turned against his stentorian authority. India has never seemed to be able to look out for the material needs of its body politic, though this was undoubtedly part of Gandhi's endeavor when he pleaded with the nation to turn to spinning. Nonetheless, though Gandhi came to represent Indian civilization in much of its spiritual complexity and cultural efflorescence, just as figures like Ramana Maharishi, Sri Ramakrishna, and Rabindranath Tagore have drawn out some other aspects of Indian civilization to which Gandhi was unable to give adequate expression, it is necessary that we move from Gandhi to the larger civilizational ethos of which he was the most eloquent spokesman.

Not everyone will give their assent to the category of civilization, even when they are sympathetic to critiques of the nation-state: as every student of the history of European discourses knows, much exploitation has also taken place in the name of civilization. It is invariable that some people should think of themselves as more civilized than others, and the mission assumed by European colonial regimes to civilize the primitives, heathens, savages – "natives" all – scarcely requires comment. The phrase "civilizing mission" was not coined in jest. One has only to go through the pages of the popular nineteenth-century American periodical, *Harper's Weekly*, which carried on its masthead the adumbrative subtitle, "A Journal of Civilization," to understand how a great many people have always been construed as being without civilization. The recent revival of the term by Huntington, as I have already argued, will do nothing to place it on more civilized terrain – and if the speeches of American officials in the wake of the terrorist attacks of September 11th are any indication, civilization will continue to be deployed in the service of differentiating between the forces of freedom and the evil-doers and justifying the chastisement of the latter. There is also the treasured injunction of Benjamin, who reminds us that "there is no document of civilization that is not at the same time a document of barbarism."[58] Nonetheless, there is no reason why those limitations which are attached to certain historical discourses of civilization should restrain us from probing its ecumenical and emancipatory possibilities, just as there is no compelling argument for supposing that the terms through which Western civilization is understood can be suitably deployed for understanding civilization in its more general and expansive sense.

The difficulties attendant upon the word "civilization" should not obscure the inestimable insights that the civilizational sensibility, and its discourses, make available to us. It is a pointed fact that the supporters of India's decision to conduct nuclear tests argued that the country removed the "ambiguity" in which its nuclear program had been shrouded. The modern nation-state has never found it easy to live with ambiguity, and it cannot countenance open-endedness. Civilizations have been more tolerant in this respect, and once again India furnishes many examples. We like to imagine that gender-bending is characteristic of the modern endeavor to free ourselves of repressive sexual mores, but the Odissi tradition of Indian dance has for a very long time given expression to the view that a man might feel himself like a woman trapped in a man's body. In some Indian traditions of painting and poetry, Krishna often appears as his consort Radha, just as Radha appears as Krishna. Recalling my earlier discussion of *hijras*, that third sex, we can think of them as expressive of the kind of ambiguity which has always been integral to Indian self-understanding and self-realization.[59] The myths of liminality derive not from modern India, but from a civilization that could tolerate ambiguity and uncertainty; today, on the contrary, it is demanded of Indians that they unequivocally declare whether they wish to be construed as Hindu or Muslim, Hindu or Sikh, secular or religious, modern or traditional.[60] The modern nation-state is always insistent on the preservation of its borders, whether construed in geographic, cultural, or epistemological terms. For dissent to have any future, we will surely have to forgo our allegiance to the nation-state and to impoverished notions of home, while we embrace in its fullness the more nurturant ethos of civilization.

No future can be promising unless it entails a thoroughgoing critique, and dismantling, of modern knowledge systems that have given us the interpretive devices with which we have sought to make sense of our lives and the world around us. For much too long, the spokespersons for the West have not merely pretended they had the solutions to the world's problems, but they have been allowed to exercise a monopoly over what kind of questions are asked and the manner in which they are to be asked. Had Gandhi, for instance, allowed the British to frame his choices for him, he would not merely have been consigned to deploying those modes of "resistance," whether that be constituted as the recourse to arms or the adoption of parliamentary and polite procedures of redress, which the British considered to be legitimate expressions of dissent; rather, his entire moral and cognitive framework would have been captive to a colonial epistemology which had firm notions about the "self," the "other," and the respective place of colonizers and colonized in a moral universe. We would have needed, in the first instance, a different sartorial Gandhi.[61] His critique of modernity was mistaken for a crude assault on the West, just as his scathing attack on industrial civilization was caricatured as an obscurantist retreat into agrarian primitivism; and if Gandhi's politics of the body – from his endeavor to embrace womanhood to his espousal of the predominantly feminine practices of spinning and fasting – was ridiculed as the unmanly and effete politics of a cowardly race of people, so his unabashed defense of the centrality of religion to politics was dismissed as characteristic of the Indian's inability to think in other than religious terms. That Marxists, liberals, and modernizers, not to mention his virulent critics in India who describe him as the "father of Pakistan," have been unable to disavow these criticisms of Gandhi is a sure sign that no emancipatory politics of dissent can emanate from these quarters. Gandhi's example suggests how Western universalisms might be brought into some engagement with other universalisms – yes, other universalisms, not particularisms – and how we could be moving towards formulations of dissent that are not merely disguised forms of oppression. If my exposition of Gandhi is not without merit, we arrive then at this caveat: before we deliver our future to those mandarins in the "civilized" West who would be its custodians, it would be best to ask if their conception of the future has room enough for more elastic and expansive conversations on truth.

Postscript:
9–11, or The Terrorism
That Has No Name

The United States remains distinct among the nations of the world with respect to one little-noticed detail that has generally not found its way into the copious commentary on the events of 9–11: in the American convention, the month precedes the day. One might have thought that there is an intrinsic logic in moving from the small unit (day) to the larger (month), and from thence to the largest (the year), but American exceptionalism extends from the feeling of "divine dispensation" as a guide to American history and the characterization of league championships in baseball as the World Series to obduracy in many other matters, including a refusal to convert to the metric system and to fall into line with the rest of the world on the vexed question of representing dates. As investigations into the terrorist attacks of September 11th have suggested, the attacks appear to have been executed according to extraordinarily well-laid plans first hatched perhaps a few years ago. Evading the security systems installed at American airports, the hijackers boarded four different aircraft and brought on board box-cutters and knives, and then flew three of the planes – with the full fuel tanks required for long flights, to ensure a huge explosion at the moment of impact, and relatively few passengers, to minimize the risk of an altercation on board – into the World Trade Center and the Pentagon. Who could have scripted this instantiation of the cunning of reason – and the morbid but grotesquely articulate union of the rational and the symbolic? Two of the planes belonged to American Airlines, the other two to United; two aimed at the twin towers of the World Trade Center, supremely iconic of American economic prowess, and two (we can reasonably assume) were targeted at the principal installations representing the might of the American government. (Only one plane crashed into the Pentagon; the other, judging from the plane's recovered black box, crashed into a field after the passengers apparently struggled with the hijackers.) Swirling around in a macabre dance of death, these planes appear to have entered into their own peculiar engagement with the military-industrial complex.

No one can say with a degree of assurance why the terrorists – that is the category into which they have been absorbed, though they started their journeys modestly as passengers, and were transmuted into hijackers somewhere along the way, before being transmogrified into terrorists – chose 9–11, but they could not have been unaware that 911 is the telephone number dialed in the United States to report an emergency or seek immediate help.[1] With their suicidal attack, the terrorists turned 9–11 into a national crisis: I use the word "crisis" advisedly, however, for as Walter Benjamin has written, we are in a perpetual state of crisis.[2] It is both the extraordinariness of the ordinary, and the ordinariness of the extraordinary, that the terrorist actions brought into full play. Remarkably, in the midst of turmoil from which many parts of the world – the Balkans, Indonesia, Algeria, Iraq, Afghanistan, Sudan, Chechnya, Israel, Palestine, Kashmir – have been reeling, Americans had come to accept it as axiomatic that they would lead lives of nearly complete security, or at least as much security as a country can expect when it is generally subject to no other assaults upon its sensibility barring the periodic outbursts of gunfire in high schools and usual homicides with which American cities are afflicted. They have never expended much thought about how the sheer ordinariness of their lives could be construed as extraordinary by those who are much less fortunate; nor have they had to contemplate the prospects of living, night after night, with the sound of bombs, the flash of explosions, and immense firestorms. Thus, in the events of 9–11 are writ large many reversals, not least of which is the fact that though 911 is a distress call, the terrorists apparently meant it as a wake-up call. Or is it the case that, having designated the terrorists perpetrators of unmentionably evil acts, we have shut our ears to the desperation in their voices? What manner of men are they, and what have they been reduced to, who think nothing of taking their own lives?

Perhaps the terrorists may have been alive to more complex nuances of recent history captured by 9–11. On November 9th (as the rest of the world knows 9–11), a reign of terror was unleashed against the Jews in Germany in 1938. The pretext was furnished by the assassination that day, which marked the fifteenth anniversary of the failed *putsch* which almost brought Hitler into power, of a minor German diplomat in Paris by a Jew. The same evening, when informed by Propaganda Minister Josef Goebbels that riots had broken out against Jews in certain districts of Germany, Hitler reportedly said that the riots were 'not to be discouraged.' Party officials, as Raul Hillberg has written, thought this statement capable of only one interpretation: the Nazis, working in the background, were to facilitate and orchestrate the riots. Jewish businesses were attacked; synagogues were burnt down: every Jew was put on notice that he or she no longer had any claim over his or her life or property.[3] It is not possible to conjecture about Osama bin Laden's awareness of this *other* history of 9–11, though anti-semitism is one common thread that stitches together the two narratives. That bin Laden, at any rate, should be thinking through the category of history comes as no surprise. On October 2nd, the birth anniversary of Mohandas Gandhi, the US launched the war on Afghanistan; that same day, bin Laden released a taped video message, where he refers to the 80 years that Muslims have been living in fear.[4] The reference is obviously to the disintegration of the Ottoman Empire following the conclusion of World War I, and the official abolition of the caliphate in 1923. Whether bin Laden, who has also denounced the desecration of the holy land of Arabia by the presence of American troops, might not be thinking of the restoration of the caliphate as his own form of millenarianism is another question.

ISLAMIC FUNDAMENTALISM: SO WHAT'S IN A NAME?

That fateful day, 9–11, the holiest day in the Nazi calendar,[5] marked the beginning of the end for the Third Reich. The terror of that day has a name – it is called *Kristallnacht*, "the crystal night," or "the night of the broken glass." What name shall we give to the terror of September 11th? In what language shall we designate that event? No sooner had it transpired than the US, with the world following in tow, called that act of terrorism "Islamic fundamentalism." Soon thereafter, a strenuous effort would be made, and it can be witnessed down to the present day, to disassociate Islam from the events of 9–11. We all have heard countless times from the lips of George Bush, senior American officials, and leaders of various communities that Islam is a "peace-loving religion," and that acting in the name of Islam, the terrorists had blasphemed the very religion they professed to adore and serve. When stories about attacks upon Muslims (among others) on American streets began to proliferate, several days after Bush had already delineated a sharp difference between the forces of civilization and the enemies of freedom, so giving perhaps something of a free rein to white supremacists, he paid a visit to the Islamic Center in Washington.[6]

Everyone still presumed to know what is constituted by Islamic fundamentalism, and few people doubted the wisdom of the category itself. If anything, Islamic fundamentalism was at times construed as a redundancy, since Islam – on this view – is itself fundamentalist. Of course the adherents of this view seldom express themselves openly in this vein, but mainstream commentary should be read for its numerous slippages and betrayals. The editorialists for the *New York Times* weighed in immediately after 9–11 with the assurance that the attacks arose from "religious fanaticism" and from the "the distaste of Western civilization and cultural values" among the perpetrators, but when they added that the attacks represented the "anger [of] those left behind by globalization,"[7] we begin to understand that those implicated are not only the terrorists but nearly all the Muslims of the Middle East, Indonesia, South Asia, and Central Asia who clearly have gained nothing, and perhaps lost much, from globalization and the structural adjustment policies imposed purportedly for their benefit by the IMF. All these millions of people are potential terrorists. What the *New York Times* is loath to admit, the militant Hindu embraces openly. Thus HinduUnity.Org, a group which espouses the same worldview that one has come to associate with organizations advocating Hindu hegemony such as the Vishwa Hindu Parishad (VHP) and the Rashtriya Swayamsevak Sangh (RSS), in a press release on September 12th declared that

> Islamic fundamentalism will forever stay and plague our world as its "roots" are deeply embedded in Islam itself. The conquests and plunder that have been committed by hordes of Islamic barbarians to continents like North Africa, Europe and India cannot ever be blamed [on] any type of Islamic Fundamentalism but Islam itself.[8]

Robert Burns wrote that the greatest gift is the ability to see ourselves as others see us. The ways of life followed by others seem laden with terror, and the supposition that terrorism has become a way of life among some Muslim men in most Islamic countries runs deep in the Western press and academic world. A decade ago, Bernard Lewis spoke rather incomprehensibly of the "roots of Muslims rage,"[9] which he located in the inability of Muslims to live in the modern world, their antiquated social and political institutions, their loss of power and failure to cope with that loss, and their exclusion from the orbit of world political activity. Lewis was not the first to represent Islam as an obscurantist faith that had clumsily inserted itself into modernity, nor should one think that his style of thinking does not resonate widely among educated and influential Americans. Francis Fukuyama has, in the aftermath of September 11th, assured us that "Islam ... is the only cultural system that seems regularly to produce people like Osama Bin Laden or the Taliban who reject modernity lock, stock and barrel," and that "of all contemporary cultural systems, the Islamic world has the fewest democracies." While certain that "there are no insuperable cultural barriers" to prevent underdeveloped people "from getting there" (that is, to the mountain-top occupied by the free market economies), Fukuyama evidently thinks that Muslims may have to be exempted from the circle of optimism.[10]

This chorus of voices has been joined by Asians. Recalling Lewis' "The Roots of Muslim Rage," the Indian-born editor of *Newsweek International*, Fareed Zakaria, presses forth the view in his article "The Roots of Rage" that Islamic fundamentalism is akin to fascism, Nazism, and even populism in the US, having widespread acceptance in Muslim-dominated societies. The anger and despair of unemployed young men, conjoined to the success of fundamentalist organizations in offering various social, cultural and political services that the state is unable to provide, accounts for the success which the "medievalists" have had in recruiting youth to their cause.[11] *Madrassas* in Saudi Arabia, Pakistan, and Afghanistan are said to churn out tens of thousands of pupils steeped in parochial versions of Islamic history and theology and ill-equipped to face up to the modern world. Terrorism can be an attractive way of life when all other options have disappeared.

For Salman Rushdie, even this much analysis is unnecessary. Purporting to speak as a New Yorker, and – one suspects – slyly exploiting his own experience with the terror of Khomeini's *fatwas*, the recently arrived immigrant celebrity deplores "the savaging of America by the left" and finds it heartless that a "country in a state of deep mourning and horrible grief" should have been told that its own policies may have contributed to the culture of terror. To prove the fundamentalists wrong, Rushdie avers, "We must agree on what matters: kissing in public places, bacon sandwiches, disagreement, cutting-edge fashion, literature, generosity ... movies, music, freedom of thought, beauty, love." For good measure, and to counter the reasonable suspicion that he has precipitously declined into a state of senility, Rushdie adds "a more equitable distribution of the world's resources" to his list.[12] Rushdie's fondness for bacon sandwiches – a rather telling comment on how little interested he really is in interculturality – apart, his conviction that Islam to most Muslims means little more than "the sermons delivered by their mullahs of choice; a loathing of modern society in general, riddled as it is with music, godlessness and sex; and a more particularized loathing (and fear) of the prospect that their own immediate sur-roundings could be taken over – 'Westoxicated' – by the liberal Western-style way of life" is underscored by his more recent *New York Times* editorial. Here Rushdie affirms that the events of September 11th have everything to do with Islam, and more partic-ularly with Islam's failure to become modern. "If terrorism is to be defeated," he writes in the mode of the man who feels vindicated, "the world of Islam must take on board the secularist-humanist principles on which the modern is based, and without which Muslim countries' freedom will remain a distant dream."[13]

The sentiments expressed by Zakaria and Rushdie, whom it would be a mistake to dismiss as specimens of deracinated ex-colonials, are shared far more widely across the educated, middle-class, and urban sectors of Indian society and the far-flung Indian diaspora;[14] they are also sentiments, as I have suggested, with which the West is very sympathetic. The very culture of others becomes construed as the breeding ground of terror: we all have heard of Islam's culture of the sequestration of women, the culture of fanaticism bred by a harsh and unrelenting monotheistic faith born in the inhospitable envir-onment of an unyielding land, the culture of the *madrassas*, and so on. Thus, even those who wish to implicate only Islamic Funda-mentalism rather than Islam constantly betray themselves, and it is becoming transparent that the mere exoneration of Islam will not suffice. The problem of the elision of Islamic Fundamentalism into Islam cannot be wished away, or arrested by the heartfelt expression of ideas about the universal goodness of all religions and the "true, peaceful face of Islam,"[15] or contested by the plea that a fundamen-tal misunderstanding informs the West's conception of *jihad*. Among Orientalists, the Indian Muslim writer and politician Rafiq Zakaria reminds us, there is a saying that "Islam reformed is no Islam."[16] There remains, as well, the lengthy history of the troubled relations between Christianity and Islam, and interpreters who are inclined to see the two faiths as set on a collision course are also prone to viewing Islam itself as the source of misery for the modern West. President Bush, who spoke in the early days following September 11th of the "crusade" that had to be launched against terrorism, probably had to be coached by his advisers in the immense historical weight carried by the word, just as the ineptly named operation against terrorism, "Infinite Justice," had to be renamed "Enduring Freedom" after it was pointed out that Muslims believe that Allah alone can dispense infinite justice. In the innumerable fissures of the discourses surrounding terrorism, it appears that the distinction between Islamic fundamentalism and Islam will be difficult to uphold without the most sustained moral effort and rigorous analysis. One can hope for neither in the present climate of opinion.

It could be argued, of course, that among US government officials the plea to separate Islam from the terrorists purporting to act in its name was never motivated by anything but expediency. The administration was putting together a coalition to fight "the war against terrorism," and everyone recognized that it would be prudent to include Muslim nations – do we speak of "Christian nations," even when the preponderant number of the people in Western European countries, Australia, New Zealand, and North America are Christians? – in the broad-based endeavor to bring bin Laden and the al-Qaeda network to justice. Moreover, though one can understand that the American hostility to revolutionary Iran, the Taliban, and radical armed Islamic groups such as Hezbollah and Hamas is animated by the desire to combat Islamic fundamentalism, the American indifference to the plight of Muslims in Bosnia, not to mention the devastation of Iraq during the Gulf War, and the retention of a brutal regime of sanctions said to have accounted for at least 1 million lives in Iraq, conveys the widespread impression that the United States is at war with the entire Muslim world. The suspicion that in the last analysis the West is inclined to attribute responsibility for the terrorist actions to Muslim nations and certain tendencies within Islam itself, is strengthened by the fact that the "clash of civilizations" hypothesis associated with Bernard Lewis and (more famously) Samuel Huntington has received an extraordinary resuscitation since September 11th.[17] Even Huntington and his ilk may choose not to see the al-Qaeda operatives and the Taliban as representing any kind of civilization, but on the other hand it is by no means apparent that they would construe Islamic fundamentalism as a phenomenon removed from the center of Islam. The perpetrators of terror, as commentators have often written, certainly thought of themselves as good Muslims, as *shahids* (martyrs) of a *jihad* that will earn them a place in paradise where they can enjoy limitless wine and the company of doe-eyed virgins.[18]

FUNDAMENTALISMS: FAMILY RESEMBLANCES

Huntington identified China and the Islamic world as the two civilizations with which the West was most likely to enter into a conflict. This conflict, his followers in the media have suggested, first takes the form of a "civil war" within Islam fought between the modernists and the medievalists, between those who wish to see Islam become as progressive as the modern West and those who are prone to sulk, reminiscing about the ascendancy of Islam in its early days and the glorious attainments of the Ottoman Empire, or do much worse.[19] The modernists, in a manner of speaking, represent the West within Islam; they are the objects of the extremists' wrath, but on occasion the target is the West itself, which is seen as encouraging the modernists or moderates. The modernist is the terrorist's own repressed other half, which may be why he or she evokes such hatred. But this analysis is perhaps a little too distant from the stark manicheanism preferred by most American commentators and their commander-in-chief, who are rather more accustomed to thinking of "evil-doers," or of the opposition of "those who believe in open societies against those who believe in revenge and chaos instead of civilisation."[20] But the moral imperative cannot be doubted: it must be to assist the forces of "freedom" in the war against the forces of "evil" and "darkness." In the primitive language of Thomas Friedman, "We need to strengthen the good guys in this civil war."[21]

Many others besides myself have noted how acts of terrorism were translated into war, and the resort to the language of war should be understood as having several referents, all doubtless related: the civil war within Islam; the war between Islam and the West; and the war between ways of life. As I have argued, terrorism is now assumed to be a way of life among many young Muslim men, but it is in implied juxtaposition with the notion of the American way of life that the claim acquires more nuanced and troubling resonances. We should recall that in his evening address to the nation on September 11th, Bush put the matter unequivocally: "Today, our fellow citizens, *our way of life*, our very freedom came under attack in a series of deliberate and deadly terrorist acts" (emphasis added).[22] The US, Bush told FBI agents a few days later, is "the most free nation in the world," and it has a special calling which can be inferred from the fact that it is a "nation built on fundamental values that reject hate, reject violence, reject murderers and reject evil."[23] Four weeks later, as the US began its air war against Afghanistan, British Prime Minister Tony Blair was still speaking of the murder of innocents in the US as "an attack on our freedom, our way of life ... ."[24]

Arguably there is no one "American way of life," but the vast bulk of American commentators, as even a cursory examination of the print and visual media suggests, are firmly persuaded that the United States is the most eminent custodian of those eternal values of freedom, democracy, and compassion without which a people cannot be viewed as civilized. This has been the daily refrain of Bush's briefings, his radio addresses, his speeches before the CIA and forums of businessmen: the civilized world and freedom themselves are under attack, the US is a good and compassionate country, its people have moral values and place a premium on the sanctity of life, and their opponents are faceless cowards who are evil-doers hiding in caves and waging a new kind of war. To the overwhelming question, "What is it that the terrorists so hate about America?," Bush replied in Congress: "They hate our freedoms – our freedom of religion, our freedom of speech, our freedom to vote and assemble and disagree with each other." We might ask why in an elected body with over 430 members, only one Congressperson (Barbara Lee) had the daring to cast a dissenting vote when Congress decided to give the President untrammeled authority to prosecute the war. We might ask why a lone Senator (Joseph Biden) later ventured to suggest – and merely suggest, not affirm – that the actions of the US in bombing one of the poorest and most war-torn countries in the world might "play into every stereotypical criticism of [the US] that we're this high-tech bully," and for this mildest of indiscretions received the reprimand of his colleagues, who described his comments as "outrageous and negligent."[25] In a similar vein, chastising postmodernists, relativists, pacifists, and other critics of "modern-day American imperialism," William Bennett assured his readers that "America's support for human rights and democracy is our noblest export to the world," and that "America was not punished because we are bad, but because we are good."[26] Little do Bush, Bennett, and their ilk realize that the very self-righteousness of the US, particularly when it is brought into service as the ideological plank of American domination, is read by many people around the world as a license for the United States to engage in terror.

If maudlin sentimentality should appear to render these expressions about the American way of life somewhat embarrassing, other commentators, who can claim to be more than journalists or populists, have attempted readings that purport to be more complex. Thus the burden of an editorial by Joyce Appleby, who recently served as the President of the American Historical Association, the premier scholarly organization in the United States for the public and professional advancement of historical research, is that the inheritance of the Enlightenment divides the 'modern West' from those determined upon a course of obscurantism and violence. This specialist in the intellectual history of the American Revolution says with supreme confidence that "Muslim culture is not Western culture 300 years earlier. Its bias against individual autonomy and self-interested economic exchanges runs deep."[27] There is not much scope for interpretation here, the message is writ large: the terrorists, and their Muslim brethren, share a profound dislike for the free market and that emblematic figure of the American West and rugged individualism, the Lone Ranger. Could Muslims be further removed from the American way of life?

Orientalist discourse has always insisted that the non-West has no idea of the individual, and that collectivities – organized around religion, caste, tribal loyalties, and the like – alone matter among the less civilized and those without a conception of the free market. If, moreover, anyone should be foolish enough to hazard the speculation that interculturality is a far more promising avenue to the understanding of diverse histories, Appleby has this rejoinder: "Sexual relations, so basic to all social organizations, are ordered along entirely different principles [among Muslims]." Presumably this bland opinion, masquerading as sheer fact, should be read to mean that Muslim societies understand little of that bliss enjoyed by the Western heterosexual couple, and that conceptions of family, fatherhood, and motherhood are mutually unintelligible across Muslim and Western societies. The day may not be far away when we will be informed by Western experts that Muslims and "we" moderns in the West have different anatomies. Judging from the attacks upon Arabs, Sikhs, Hindus, Afghans, Muslims, Pakistanis, and Iranians in the immediate aftermath of September 11th, some Americans, whose premise for action is the formula that "they who look different, are different," are already enacting the street versions of this particular superstition derived from the Enlightenment. Should we not ask if this is also the American way of life?

Ruminations about the relationship of the terrorist attacks of September 11th to the American way of life are not an idle matter, judging from the first of two impassioned pieces by Arundhati Roy on the gross excesses of the American state and the sheer immorality of the United States' bombing of Afghanistan. Recalling the long historical record of the United States' genocidal intent and behavior, Roy's denunciation of US conduct abroad is just as interesting for its reticence, common to the left-liberal critique of American foreign policy, in entertaining more daring questions about the widespread animus against the US which, not unfairly, can now be described as a distinct characteristic of "world consciousness." Roy finds it altogether inexplicable, even inexcusable, that the US government should have represented the attacks as an assault upon the American Way of Life. It's "an easy notion to peddle" amidst rage and grief, Roy writes, but she urges us to resist the thought, and "wonders why the symbols of America's economic and military dominance – the World Trade Center and the Pentagon – were chosen as the targets of the attack. Why not the Statue of Liberty?"[28]

If the business of the US is business, and the military is deeply interwoven into nearly all the political, social, and civil institutions of American society, then Roy is evidently missing the pulse of the US. She has the idea, particularly quaint in someone as astute as her, that the voice of the American people remains unheard in the web of military institutions, as though the entrails of the military did not extend into tens of thousands of American communities and homes. The return of an aircraft carrier or battleship to its American home is the subject of the evening news; and the immense lobbying in Congress for military contracts, retention of military bases, and defense-related research is fueled as well by popular constituencies. Roy is obviously aware of the yellow ribbons and the display of flags, which come out far more quickly and in embarrassing abundance in the United States than they do in any other country,[29] but somehow, to her this appears disconnected from the meanings generated by the Pentagon. "American people ought to know that it is not them," Roy declaims, "but the government's policies that are so hated," and she points to the acclaim with which the country's many "extraordinary" musicians, writers, actors, and sportsmen are received worldwide. If the disjunction between the government and the people is so vast, then American democracy must be dismissed as an entirely farcical exercise – a view that the farce of the last presidential race would appear to support, but one that neither the US government nor the American people will accept as credible. To imagine that the American people have a government wholly at odds with their sensibilities is to commit the folly of supposing that they are entirely gullible and ignorant, and yet wiser than their leaders; it also makes a mockery of the idea of representation, which is the formal mainstay of all democratic polities. Since leaders in the US are elected, one cannot but think that elections must mean something, however inane the exercise may seem of choosing between indistinguishable Democrats and Republicans.

Variations of Roy's argument are frequently encountered among those critical of the US government but eager to exculpate, as perhaps the moral imperative must be to do so, "the people" and civil society. The American people, I might note incidentally, have many spokespersons: certainly in no other country does the government, and similarly its critics, purport to act and speak as frequently in the name of the people. In India, the Prime Minister or President addresses "the nation"; the American President addresses "the American people," the ultimate tribunal of civilized values, humanity, and reasoned opinion. The world is constantly reminded that "the American people" will not tolerate assaults on freedom, democracy, human decency, and civilization, and it is striking that Bush began his address to a special joint session of Congress on September 20th with the observation that "the American people" had already delivered a report on the State of the Union. The people were, in effect, the answer to bin Laden, rebutting his terror-laden acts with unforgettable scenes of courage and compassion: the Union remained strong. Thus even as seasoned a political commentator as Noam Chomsky, a relentless chronicler over three decades of American state terrorism, gallantly persists in the belief that *if* "the American people" *really knew* of their government's widespread complicity in the perpetration of gross abuses of human rights, their outrage would be sufficient to arrest the government in its tracks. (If Chomsky can be in the know, what prevents the people amidst the information explosion of our times from shedding their ignorance?) It is perhaps superfluous to add, then, that Roy, Chomsky, and many others persuaded about the inherently democratic propensities of American civil society – while persuaded that American state terrorism represents the greatest threat to global society – ignore as well the consistent poll findings that show massive public support for military intervention, whether at the time of the Gulf War or in the immediate and distant aftermath of September 11th. Polls are, doubtless, not innocuous exercises in the calibration of public opinion, but their instrumentality in matters of policy, governance, and opinion-making is widely acknowledged, and the left has just as eagerly embraced poll findings when it has been in their interest to do so.

A TALE OF TWO COUNTRIES: THE UNITED STATES (REVISITED) AND AFGHANISTAN (DISCOVERED)

The most conventional definition of terrorism adverts to violence that is indiscriminate, targeting not only soldiers and functionaries of the state but civilians, not only government installations but the pillars of civil society. The distinction between the government and the American people is precisely what the terrorist actions of September 11th sought to undermine, and the conservative elements in American society may be much closer to the truth than left commentators in recognizing that an attempt was made to put the American way of life under the bomb. It has been the American way of life to assume that one can live without fear; indeed, that one is entitled to live with as much security as a multicultural democracy can promise, while being perfectly free to inflict, through one's representatives in government, fear and terror upon others. Who in the US can presume to understand the trauma, what Ernest Jones described in the 1940s as the "mutism and emotional paralysis," followed by "practical cessation of all mental activity and even death," of those who have had to endure night after night of intensive bombing with missiles, cluster bombs, and extensive payloads of 50,000 lb?[30]

Osama bin Laden has sought to carry the war to the American public and disrupt the American way of life, and no other reading is suggested by his ardently expressed desire that America should be "full of fear from its north to its south, from its west to its east." It is another matter altogether that his actions will only reinforce the American way of life, whether witnessed in the immense surge of militarism, the extraordinarily disproportionate use of airpower against a people who have little else but the clothes on their back, the shameless pretense at internationalism, the pathetic air drops of packages of peanut butter and strawberry jam, or the scarcely veiled threats of death and destruction for those states that are less than willing partners in the coalition against terrorism. Osama bin Laden does not appear to have understood that it is also the American way of life to lace terror with a tinge of kindness. Bush has talked endlessly about this being a "new kind of war," but there is nothing new in the bombing of Afghanistan: that country has been the laboratory of European powers for a very long period of time, and it is significant that the modern exercise of air power originated with the aerial bombing of Afghanistan by the British in 1919.[31] Bush appears to have been thinking about fighting invisible cavemen and cowards who refuse to show their faces, but the bombing of people from the safety of 15,000 feet is scarcely evidence of the manliness of American soldiers. It is the Americans who, since the last days of World War II, have been endeavoring to make their forces invisible while making their threats as visible as possible.

It is demonstrably true that the terrorist acts of September 11th were undertaken with utter deliberation and executed according to a plan perversely admirable in its devotion to detail. The terrorists conjoined this means–end rationality, at the altar of which all great powers have worshipped, to another form of life equally well-understood by Americans, namely that captured by the domain of the symbolic. One of the most visible symbols of the American way of life in late modernity is the Sport Utility Vehicle (SUV), which now accounts for 50 percent of sales of consumer vehicles. Commercials invariably show the SUV traversing over rugged terrain, taking the intrepid "explorer" to remote backlands, helping the "expedition" leader bridge the awesome chasm of the Grand Canyon. The SUV, as everyone knows, is far more likely to be found on the freeways of Southern California, and generally the driver is its only occupant. Elbowing other vehicles off the road, terrorizing other drivers into caution and submission, the SUV is the battle tank of highways and surface streets. Its track record on safety is widely acknowledged to be severely wanting. It has almost nothing to do with sports, and its only utility is to feed the coffers of an automobile industry that has moved from one form of oppression to another, from Fordization to more expansive forms of exploitation of the earth's resources. The SUV is illustrative, even in its mere designation, of the terrorism of hegemony: the hegemon retains the power of naming, and so embellishes what we might call the Road Bully Monster (RBM) with the trappings of both functionalism (utility) and leisure (sport). Even in American parlance, the SUV is a gas guzzler, a significant admission in a country where the unhindered supply of cheap gasoline is virtually a constitutional right.

Installed in this monstrosity of a vehicle, the American takes it as an axiomatic truth that the world's oil supply exists for the satisfaction of his or her wants. This *is* the American way of life, and it is its own form of terror, and not only for the most obvious reason that with 4 percent of the world's population, the United States consumes nearly a third of the world's oil and other resources. No cliche has proliferated as much in recent months as the assertion that "the world is forever changed," or that "life will never be the same again," but the American way of life is not so easily disrupted. An article in one American newspaper admits that "sales of SUVs and vans actually went up in October, the month after the attacks in New York and near Washington"[32] – most Americans, evidently, are unable to discern the slightest connection between terrorism, oil consumption, and American exceptionalism. For all one knows, SUVs are to American roads what bomb shelters were to exercises guarding against nuclear war: the illusion that foolproof security is possible will never have an easy death.

A profligate consumer, sworn to criminal levels of waste, the United States has succeeded admirably well in exporting the ideology of consumerism to the entire world. Its academics have also made an industry of exporting critiques of consumerism, but this should not surprise us, considering that as by far the largest manufacturer and exporter of arms and military hardware, the United States also describes itself as the greatest force for peace in the world. Hegemonic powers, to recall once again Tacitus' maxim, have always thought themselves entitled to call war peace. The trail that leads from the gross energy-abusing SUVs to the United States' huge oil bill, the Middle East, the Gulf War, and now the conflagration in Afghanistan and the untapped petroleum reserves of Central Asia, is covered in blood. Oil flows through the veins of George Bush and Osama bin Laden,[33] both scions of wealthy families, both molded by the fatherly presence of George Bush, Sr.: this is the happy marriage of the American way of life and terrorism as a way of life. One can only hope that there will be no progeny from this horribly deformed union.

Having said this, the atrocities of September 11th can be known by no name other than terrorism. While it would be cruel to speak of chickens coming home to roost, or callous to think that the US had it coming, as though human lives were expendable for no other purpose than to instruct the powerful that the universe is governed by strange and unfathomable laws of compensation, it is also imperative to recognize that much of the world has been living with terror for years and decades. The greater part of terrorism is the fact that the United States, indeed nearly the entire "civilized" West, has never had the courage to admit that it purchased its long night of peace with a long night of terror abroad. Terrorism has been incubating and flourishing in the American way of life and Western civilization – that thing of which Gandhi said that "it *would* be a good idea." Curiously, the Taliban shares with the United States this history. In the conventionally accepted narrative, the withdrawal of the Soviet Union in 1989 led to bitter internecine warfare among Afghans of different tribes and political persuasions, and the Taliban are said to have rescued the country from the chaos, murderous anarchy and wild bloodshed into which it was plunged. The peace of the Taliban, too, was purchased with terror, but the world seems largely not to have been awake to this phenomenon until it was much too late.

Thus the narrative of September 11th, and especially its aftermath, involves far more than the United States – however difficult it is for some people to think of Afghanistan. History is a pact between the powerful and the powerless, the voiced and the voiceless, the visible and the invisible. Whilst the perpetrators of the bombings made no immediate demands and claimed no responsibility for the events, nothing in their actions suggests any inclination to enter into a conversation or dialogue. Their bombing of the World Trade Center appears to have represented an exercise in the metaphysics of power. The Twin Towers have often been described as having fallen down like a stack of cards, but the sand mandalas of the Buddhists offer perhaps a more instructive analogy: here is the play of presence and absence, construction and destruction, fullness and nothingness. Every action generates multiple trails, and belongs to communicative universes, and the terrorists could not but have known that their actions would tie the United States into a strange relationship with its putative enemy, the Taliban. Nothing could have been calculated to give Afghanistan, which appears to have left a small impress upon the United States for a few days earlier in 2001 when the Taliban blasted the Bamiyan Buddhas into pieces before disappearing into the swamp of American self-obsession,[34] more visibility than the bombings of September 11th.

It would be no exaggeration to speak, in fact, of the United States' recent discovery of Afghanistan, and the profuse writing on the atrocities and aftermath of September 11th furnishes an extraordinary instance of what I have described throughout this book as the imperialism of categories and the alarmingly narrow scope for dissenting perspectives. It is a striking fact that, in the aftermath of 9–11, it was at once assumed by the American media that there are two constituencies *naturally* positioned to enlighten the public on the atrocities and terrorism in general; namely, experts in the history, politics and culture of Middle Eastern societies, and American foreign policy specialists. The left in the United States, India, the UK, and elsewhere assimilated the terrorist attacks into the general category marked as bearing a relationship to American foreign policy failures. The other tendency, which apparently necessitates the expertise of specialists in Middle Eastern politics and Islamic history and theology, is to assign the terrorist attacks to the pre-existing category of Islamic fundamentalism. But the possibility that the history of Afghanistan belongs in great measure, and not merely in recent fragments, to the history of South Asia appears never to have been contemplated. What is Afghanistan's place on the map of knowledge, what categories does it occupy, and what have been the consequences of viewing it through these categories?

The salience of these queries might better be appreciated when we consider that no less a person than Gandhi, who insisted upon the most exacting standards of non-violence, considered the Pathans, the ancestors of the contemporary Taliban and now denounced as "barbarians," as the most perfect practitioners of non-violence that he had ever encountered. In the late 1920s, the Pathan leader, Khan Abdul Ghaffar Khan, later nicknamed the "Frontier Gandhi," came to embrace the Gandhian doctrine of *satyagraha*.[35] He forged an army of volunteers and disciplined them into a fighting force of *satyagrahis*: these were no effete rice-eating vegetarians or banias, to use the mocking language of some of Gandhi's critics, but towering men. Their reputation for military prowess was legendary. Such was the strength and resolve of the *Khudai Khidmatgars*, "the Servants of God," that they even paralyzed the British administration in Peshawar.[36] Years later, the Pathans, who hold aloft the banner of their faith in Islam with pride, repudiated the two-nation theory on the basis of which Pakistan was carved out of India as a Muslim-majority state and openly declared themselves unhappy with the partition of India. Afghanistan would also be the only country to oppose Pakistan's admission into the United Nations. Where is this history, and what is the politics of this amnesia? Apparently Afghanistan required a Soviet invasion so that it could at least enter into the consciousness of the West and become the slum and marginalia of Western existence. This is the condition of the wretched of the earth: they must be impregnated by Europe, or by ideological movements of Western provenance, before they can be said to have entered into the pages of history. What possibilities of politics were abjured when Abdul Ghaffar Khan and the Pathans were sidelined and browbeaten into submission? What alternative histories might have been generated had the Pathans then received the ear of the world?

That the left in the US, as in India, should be oblivious to anything which cannot be comprehended under the conception of an "authentic" left history is no surprise. That failure of imagination, which I have hinted at throughout the book, is also witnessed elsewhere. Within the American academy, with its two-pronged focus on disciplinary formations and area studies, Afghanistan has never had anything of a presence. Specialists in Middle Eastern history and Islamic studies, who are accustomed to thinking of the Middle East – which is itself an invention of area studies programs – as the "authentic" home of Islam, have characteristically displayed not the slightest interest in Afghanistan; indeed – with the obvious exception of that very small fraternity of scholars working on Indo-Islamic history – not even in South Asian Islam. There remains more than a lingering feeling among scholars of Islam that the Muslims of South Asia, who number about 400 million, embody an inauthentic, compromised, hybrid, adulterated, even "bastardized" version of Islam. Ernest Gellner's widely acclaimed study, *Muslim Society* (1981),[37] the scope of which is not qualified by any subtitle or the demands of geography, barely mentions India, the home of the second-largest Muslim population in the world; similarly R. Stephen Humphreys' *Islamic History: A Framework for Inquiry* (1991),[38] ignores South Asia.

Close proximity to the idolatrous beliefs of polytheistic Hinduism is supposed to have contaminated the Muslims of South Asia, and since Islam is presumably best studied in its pure form, scholars have turned to Islam's primordial home in the Middle East. Now that the Taliban have come to the attention of the West, one should not marvel at the recent spate of articles which seek to establish, not without justification, that the Taliban are inspired by that puritanical strand of Islam which goes by the name of Wahhabism, apparently the state religion of Saudi Arabia.[39] In the eighteenth century, Sheikh Mohammed ibn Abdul Wahhab sought to return the practices of Islam to the pristine state of the seventh century. As Edward Said has argued, the "myth of the arrested development of the Semites" remains critical to the Orientalist worldview;[40] and to study the Taliban is perforce to gain an insight into the origins and early history of Islam. However despised the Taliban might be, they are useful to the scientific and scholarly community in the West as part of the fossil record of humanity.

The social organization of knowledge is such that, for very different reasons, Afghanistan has similarly never been part of South Asian area studies programs in the United States. Sandwiched between the Islamic and Indic worlds, Afghanistan has been seen as belonging to neither, and has suffered the fate of those who cannot be accommodated within the known categories.[41] (Pashto, the language of the Pathans, the dominant ethnic group in Afghanistan, is not taught at a single American university.[42]) It matters little to American "experts" that South Asians themselves are cognizant of the longstanding relations between the Indian subcontinent and Afghanistan, and that Afghanistan, Pakistan, and India are seen as sharing an intertwined history. Many Indians might not remember that north India was governed by Afghans for the greater part of the first half of the second millennium, but the tombs of the Lodi kings in Delhi are a palpable reminder of the times when Afghanistan was the source not of terrorist networks but of ruling dynasties. Perhaps even fewer will have experienced a familiar sense of recall at hearing the news that the most widely mentioned political resolution of "the Afghanistan problem" until early November entailed the restoration from exile of the former monarch, Muhammad Zahir Shah, who is now in his mid-eighties and has been living in Europe for nearly three decades.[43] Nearly 150 years ago, when Hindu and Muslim mutineers took to arms and momentarily threatened to bring British rule in India to a swift conclusion, they marched to the residence of the last monarch of the great Mughal dynasty, Bahadur Shah Zafar, and persuaded him to lead the rebellion against the colonial pretenders. For about the same time as Muhammad Zahir Shah has been living in exile as the deposed King of Afghanistan, Bahadur Shah, also in his eighties, had been confined to the grounds of the Red Fort as the titular King of Delhi. Then, as now, it remains the supposition, even among many formerly colonized subjects, that democracy is not for these countries, and that only the transcendent figure of the monarch, however old or distant from his people, can bring together a fractious people torn apart by ties of religion, ethnicity, and language. What will have changed for the people of Afghanistan?

Notes

INTRODUCTION

1. *"Solitudinem faciunt pacem appellant."*
2. Michael Renner, "Ending Violent Conflict", in Lester Thurow (ed.), *State of the World 1999* (New York: W.W. Norton, 1999), pp. 151–68. The figure may be as high as 200 million; World War II alone accounted for nearly 54 million lives, 60 percent of those being civilians.
3. The resignation of Ravi Kanbur, the lead author of the World Development Report on Poverty, commissioned by the World Bank, is but one of many illustrations of the American inability to allow dissenting opinions to flourish within institutions that it views as falling entirely within its jurisdiction or spheres of influence. Kanbur, who rather unusually for an economist sought to incorporate the voices of the poor in his report, and pointed to numerous non-income dimensions of poverty, pleaded that aggregate statistics could not be relied upon to provide a more nuanced understanding of the reasons that make some groups more vulnerable than others. The model of globalization, he suggested, is insensitive to such considerations, and to the necessity of removing political obstacles to the implementation of policies designed to assist the poor. He is also on record as having stated that "unreasonable pressure" was placed on him by then US Treasury Secretary Laurence Summers to alter his report. Summers then proceeded to rewrite what he deemed to be objectionable portions of Kanbur's report. See <http://www.brettonwoodsproject.org/action/wdr/kanbur.html>
4. James P. Carse, *Finite and Infinite Games: A Vision of Life as Play and Possibility* (New York: Ballantine Books, 1986).
5. I am echoing the phrase of Eric Wolf, *Europe and the People Without History* (Berkeley: University of California Press, 1982).
6. Ziauddin Sardar, *Postmodernism and the Other: The New Imperialism of Western Culture* (London: Pluto Press, 1998).
7. For some extraordinary insights on the questions of plurality and cosmopolitanism, see Ashis Nandy, "Time Travel to a Possible Self: Searching for the Alternative Cosmopolitanism of Cochin", *Japanese Journal of Political Science* 1, no. 2 (2000), pp. 295–327.

CHAPTER 1

1. The most insightful epistemological treatment of temporal colonization, with particular reference to anthropology's deployment of time in its construction of other societies, is Johannes Fabian, *Time and the Other: How Anthropology Makes its Object* (New York: Columbia University Press, 1983).

2. Cited by Robert Levine, *A Geography of Time: The Temporal Misadventures of a Social Psychologist* (New York: Basic Books/HarperCollins, 1997), p. 63. The quotation is slightly inaccurate: see Lewis Mumford, *Technics and Civilization* (New York: Harcourt, Brace & World, 1934; paperback edn, 1963), p. 14.

3. Juliet Schor, *The Overworked American: The Unexpected Decline of Leisure* (New York: Basic Books, 1992); see also Stephen Bertman, *Hyperculture: The Human Cost of Speed* (Westport, Conn.: Praeger, 1998), p. 9. These findings are anticipated in Jerry Mander, *In the Absence of the Sacred: The Failure of Technology and the Survival of the Indian Nations* (San Francisco, Calif.: Sierra Club Books, 1991), pp. 254–5.

4. Sebastian de Grazia, *Of Time, Work, and Leisure* (New York: Anchor Books, 1962), p. 313.

5. David S. Landes, *Revolution in Time: Clocks and the Making of the Modern World* (Cambridge, Mass.: Harvard University Press, 1983), p. 12.

6. Pitirim A. Sorokin, *Sociocultural Causality, Space, Time* (Durham, N.C.: Duke University Press, 1943).

7. Jeremy Rifkin, *Time Wars: The Primary Conflict in Human History* (New York: Henry Holt & Co., 1987), p. 73.

8. For further discussion, see Eviatar Zerubavel, *Hidden Rhythms: Schedules and Calendars in Social Life* (Chicago, Ill.: University of Chicago Press, 1981), pp. 70–7.

9. S. D. Goitein has written that "Muhammad chose Friday as [the] day of public worship, because on that day the people of Medina gathered anyhow to do their shopping. There was no intention of polemics against the older religions." The Friday markets were busy affairs, since the Jews did their shopping on the eve of the Sabbath; thus Friday was an opportune day to bring together Muslims under a common roof for worship. Goitein adds that the "Friday service was of more than religious significance," as participation in it "demonstrated the participants' joining of the Muslim community." See "The Origin and Nature of the Muslim Friday Worship", *The Muslim World* 49, no. 3 (July 1959), pp. 195, 192.

10. Eviatar Zerubavel, *The Seven Day Circle: The History and Meaning of the Week* (New York: The Free Press, 1985), p. 25.

11. Pitrim A. Sorokin and Robert K. Merton, "Social Time: A Metholodogical and Functional Analysis", *The American Journal of Sociology* 42, no. 5 (March 1937), pp. 624–5.

12. Daniel Defoe, *The Life and Strange Surprising Adventures of Robinson Crusoe, Mariner* (London: Oxford University Press), p. 64.

13. The discussion in Anthony Aveni, *Empires of Time: Calendars, Clocks, and Cultures* (New York: Basic Books, 1989), is useful.

14. M. N. Saha and N. C. Lahiri, *History of the Calendar* (New Delhi: Council of Scientific and Industrial Research, 1992). D. D. Kosambi, *Ancient India: A History of Its Culture and Civilization* (New York: Meridian Books, 1969), has briefly hinted at the place of the calendar in Indian social life in antiquity, suggesting that its use points to at least some degree of literacy among the Brahmins, who consulted calendars to determine when crops

at sowing were to be blessed and gods were to be placated (pp. 168, 196–7).

15. The most authoritative source on the Gregorian calendar is G. Coyne et al. (eds.), *Gregorian Reform of the Calendar, Proceedings of the Vatican Conference to Commemmorate Its 400th Anniversary, 1582–1982* (Vatican City: Pontificia Academia Scientarum, Specola Vaticana, 1983). For a more readable narrative, see David Duncan Ewing, *Calendar: Humanity's Epic Struggle to Determine a True and Accurate Year* (New York: Avon Books, 1998).

16. Gibbon's judgment is not without interest. Writing of the position of Christians under Diocletian (reigned 284–305) and his associate Maximian, he avers that "it was thought necessary to subject to the most intolerable hardships the conditions of those perverse individuals who should still reject the religion of nature, of Rome, and of their ancestors. Persons of a liberal birth were declared incapable of holding any honors or employments; slaves were for ever deprived of the hopes of freedom; and the whole body of the people were put out of the protection of the law." See Rosemary Williams (ed.), *Gibbon's Decline and Fall of the Roman Empire*, abridged and illustrated edn (New York: W. H. Smith/Gallery Books, 1979), p. 118.

17. Stephen Jay Gould, *Questioning the Millennium* (New York: Harmony Books, 1997), pp. 104–8; for an arresting set of reflections on the history of zero, see Dick Teresi, "Zero", *Atlantic Monthly* (July 1997), pp. 88–94.

18. A detailed discussion will be found in Gordon Moyer, "The Gregorian Calendar", *Scientific American* 246, no. 5 (1982), pp. 104–11; see also Aveni, *Empires of Time*, pp. 116–17.

19. See, for example, the discussion in Bailey W. Wiffie and George D. Winius, *Foundations of the Portugese Empire 1415–1580* (Minneapolis: University of Minnesota Press, 1977). As one instance, consider that the Papal Bull issued by Pope Nicholas V to Henry the Navigator in 1454, which gave him the right to all his discoveries up to India, also enjoined Henry to "bring under submission ... the pagans of the countries not yet afflicted with the plague of Islam." This followed a Bull which "conceded to king Affonso, the right, total and absolute, to invade, conquer and subject all the countries which are under the rule of the enemies of Christ, Saracen or Pagan ... ." See K. M. Panikkar, *Asia and Western Dominance*, new edn (London: George Allen & Unwin, 1959), pp. 26–7.

20. Norbert Elias, in *Time: An Essay* (Oxford: Basil Blackwell, 1992), points to another anomaly as a consequence of the edict: the year 1566 extended from April 14 to December 31 and "had only eight months and seventeen days. Thus the months of September, October, November and December which, in accordance with a Roman tradition of beginning the year in March and with the corresponding meaning of their names, had been the seventh, eighth, ninth and tenth months respectively, now became somewhat incongruously the ninth, tenth, eleventh and twelfth months" (p. 55).

21. Estimates of the number of people killed in the massacre (1572) vary immensely, from 10,000 to 100,000. Gregory XIII had a medal struck on the occasion, and the artist Vasari, also known for his biographical

sketches of other painters, was commissioned to paint a mural of the massacre at the Vatican.

22. Zerubavel, *Hidden Rhythms*, p. 99.
23. P. W. Wilson, *Romance of the Calendar* (New York: Norton, 1937), pp. 29–30, cited in ibid., p. 100.
24. Cited in Zerubavel, *Hidden Rhythms*, p. 74.
25. Landes, *Revolution in Time*, p. 286; Derek Howse, *Greenwich Time and the Discovery of the Longitude* (Oxford: Oxford University Press, 1980).
26. Henry David Thoreau, *Walden and Other Writings*, ed. Brooks Atkinson (New York: Modern Library, 1950), pp. 106–7.
27. Stephen Kern, *The Culture of Time and Space 1880–1918* (Cambridge, Mass.: Harvard University Press, 1983), p. 12; Michael O'Malley, *Keeping Watch: A History of American Time* (New York: Penguin Books, 1991), esp. ch. 2.
28. Cited by Levine, *A Geography of Time*, p. 73. See also Sanford Fleming, "Time-Reckoning for the Twentieth Century", *Annual Report of the Board of Regents of the Smithsonian Institution ... for the Year Ending June 30, 1886*, Part I (Washington, D.C.: Government Printing Office, 1889), pp. 345–66, for a discussion of the various ways in which time was sought to be standardized.
29. Jeremy Bentham, *Panopticon*, in John Bowring (ed.), *The Works of Jeremy Bentham* (London, 1843), Vol. IV, and the discussion in Michel Foucault, *Discipline and Punish: The Birth of the Prison*, trans. Alan Sheridan (New York: Viking, 1979), pp. 195–228 esp. pp. 200–1.
30. Cited by O'Malley, *Keeping Watch*, pp. 161–2.
31. Cited by Rifkin, *Time Wars*, pp. 106–7.
32. Ibid., p. 109.
33. Ibid., pp. 110–11.
34. Sumit Sarkar, *Writing Social History* (Delhi: Oxford University Press, 1997; paperback edn, 1998), p. 283.
35. Cited by Sarkar, *Writing Social History*, pp. 307–8.
36. Chinua Achebe, *Arrow of God* (London: Heinemann, 1964). The local population is inclined to trace the District Officer's illness to his humiliation of the priest.
37. The classic interpretation of this remains E. P. Thompson, "Time, Work-Discipline, and Industrial Capitalism", *Past and Present*, no. 38 (December 1967).
38. Cited by Fabian, *Time and the Other*, p. ix.
39. A good instance of the manner in which Indian notions of time are placed in apposition with notions of time said to prevail in preindustrial Europe, aboriginal Australia, and China is furnished by Mircea Eliade, "Time and Eternity in Indian Thought", in Joseph Campbell (ed.), *Man and Time* (New York: Pantheon Books, for the Bollingen Foundation, 1957), p. 174. James Mill, in his *History of British India*, 5th edn (London: James Madden, 1858) had much occasion to remark on the fabulously fecund and extravagant notions of time that he found prevailing in India; but the polemic is not confined to India: "Rude nations seem to derive a peculiar gratification from pretensions to a remote antiquity ... We are informed, in a fragment of Chaldaic history, that there were

written accounts ... comprehending a term of fifteen myriads of years. The pretended duration of the Chinese monarchy, is still more extraordinary. A single king of Egypt was believed to have reigned three myriads of years' (1: 107).

40. E. C. Sachau (ed. and trans.), *Alberuni's India*, 2 vols. (London: Trubner, 1888), chs. 32–43, 49.

41. Some of the Hindu numbers, from the vantage point of later modernity, now seem much less fantastic than they have to earlier observers. The year as measured in oscillations of atomic cesium is 290,091,200,500,000,000. Let me affirm that I do by no means wish to suggest the comical argument, often encountered among Hindu revivalists, that all modern scientific achievements are anticipated in the Vedas or other Hindu texts of antiquity. I do intend to put into question the status of the "fantastic" and the frameworks by which we understand the imaginative and intellectual products of any other civilization.

42. Sachau, *Alberuni's India*, 2: 1–9.

43. Hajime Nakamura, "Time in Indian and Japanese Thought", in J. T. Fraser (ed.), *The Voices of Time*, 2nd edn (Amherst: University of Massachusetts Press, 1981), p. 81.

44. G. S. Kirk and J. E. Rave, *The Presocratic Philosophers*, corrected edn (Cambridge: Cambridge University Press, 1964), p. 197.

45. Karl Marx, "The Future Results of the British Rule in India" [1853], in Karl Marx and Friedrich Engels, *The First Indian War of Independence 1857–1859* (Moscow: Foreign Languages Publishing House, n. d.), pp. 32–8.

46. Thomas R. Trautmann, "Indian Time, European Time", in Diane Owen Hughes and Thomas R. Trautmann (eds.), *Time: Histories and Ethnologies* (Ann Arbor: University of Michigan Press), p. 176; Trautmann, "The Revolution in Ethnological Time", *Man* (1992), p. 380.

47. On passing the time in mindfulness, see Thich Nhat Hanh, *The Miracle of Mindfulness: A Manual on Meditation*, translated into English by Mobi Warren (Boston, Mass.: Beacon Press, 1986).

48. James Beard, "Science supports the three-hour lunch break", *Utne Reader* (September–October 1997), p. 59.

49. Paul Bohannan, "Concepts of Time among the Tiv of Nigeria", *Southwestern Journal of Anthropology* 9, no. 3 (Autumn 1953), p. 253.

50. Zerubavel, *The Seven Day Circle*, p. 98.

51. Herbert Butterfield, *Napoleon* (New York: Collier, 1962).

52. See <http://www.slowfood.com>

53. Levine, *A Geography of Time*, p. 6.

CHAPTER 2

1. Benjamin R. Barber, *Jihad vs. McWorld: How Globalism and Tribalism are Reshaping the World* (New York: Ballantine Books, 1995), p. 239.

2. *New York Times* columnist Thomas Friedman represents one end of the spectrum: see *The Lexus and the Olive Tree: Understanding Globalization* (New York: Farrar, Straus & Giroux, 1999), though his namesakes, Milton and Rose Friedman, in *Free to Choose* (New York: Harcourt Brace

Jovanovich, 1980), anticipated him by two decades. *Free to Choose* doesn't only sound silly, it is: one apparently chooses between political systems, universities, sexual partners, books, toothpastes, and cereals in much the same way. The other end of the spectrum is adequately represented in the popular vein by Thomas Frank, *One Market under God: Extreme Capitalism, Market Populism, and the End of Economic Democracy* (New York: Doubleday, 2000).

3. Michael Hardt and Antonio Negri, *Empire* (Cambridge, Mass.: Harvard University Press, 2000); some of the arguments made a succinct appearance in Masao Miyoshi, "A Borderless World? From Colonialism to Transnationalism and the Decline of the Nation-State", *Critical Inquiry* 19, no. 4 (Summer 1993), pp. 726–51.

4. Ernst Friedrich, *War against War!*, new edn (Seattle: The Real Comet Press, 1987).

5. Christopher Simpson, *The Splendid Blond Beast: Money, Law, and Genocide in the Twentieth Century* (New York: Grove Press, 1993), p. 76.

6. Samuel Huntington, "The Clash of Civilizations?", *Foreign Affairs* 72, no. 3 (Summer 1993), pp. 22–49; Bernard Lewis, "The Roots of Muslim rage", *Atlantic Monthly* (September 1990), pp. 47–54; and, for critiques of various exponents of Western exceptionalism, including David Landes, Eric L. Jones, and Jared Diamond, see J. M. Blaut, *Eight Eurocentric Historians* (New York: Guilford Press, 2000). I have argued elsewhere that "Western universalism" is just as important to Huntington as "Western exceptionalism": see my "Futures and Knowledge", in Ziauddin Sardar (ed.), *Rescuing All Our Futures* (New York: Adamantine Press; London: Praeger, 1998), pp. 210–20, and also Chapter 6 (of this volume). A scathing assessment of Huntington is to be found in Edward Said, "The Clash of Definitions", in his *Reflections on Exile and Other Essays* (Cambridge, Mass.: Harvard University Press, 2000), pp. 569–90.

7. Thomas Pakenham, *The Boer War* (New York: Random House, 1979), ch. 19. The back endpaper has a photograph of "The Camp for Undesirables."

8. John Ellis, *Eye-Deep in Hell: Trench Warfare in World War I* (New York: Pantheon Books, 1976; reprint edn, Baltimore, Md.: Johns Hopkins University Press, 1989).

9. Thomas Pakenham, *The Scramble for Africa 1876–1912* (New York: Random House, 1991), pp. 577–9; Pakenham, *The Boer War*, pp. 511–49.

10. A. J. P. Taylor, *From the Boer War to the Cold War: Essays on Twentieth-Century Europe* (Harmondsworth: Penguin Books, 1996), p. 38.

11. David Stannard, *American Holocaust: Columbus and the Conquest of the New World* (New York: Oxford University Press, 1992). More unusual is Richard Wright, *Stolen Continents: The Americas Through Indian Eyes since 1492* (New York: Houghton Mifflin, 1992). Writing five decades before Stannard, one eminent scholar, who confined himself to the middle Pacific Coast of the United States, came inescapably to the same conclusion, though from a different perspective, on the relative merits of the civilizations that were brought into contact: see Sherbourne F. Cook, *The Conflict between the California Indian and White Civilization* (Berkeley: University of California Press, 1976). "The effect of racial

impact and competition," Cook wrote, "was here unusually complete. It resulted in the substantial disappearance of the primitive population and the utter extinction of its civilization" (p. 1).

12. Richard G. Hovannisian, "Etiology and Sequelae of the Armenian Genocide", in George J. Andrepoulos (ed.), *Genocide: Conceptual and Historical Dimensions* (Philadelphia: University of Pennsylvania Press, 1994), p. 125.

13. Philip Gourevitch, *We Wish to Inform You that Tomorrow We Will be Killed with Our Families: Stories from Rwanda* (New York: Farrar Straus Giroux, 1998).

14. Raymond Aron, *The Century of Total War* (Boston, Mass.: Beacon Press, 1955).

15. Ibid., pp. 109–11.

16. Robert Conquest, *The Harvest of Sorrow: Soviet Collectivization and the Terror-Famine* (New York: Oxford University Press, 1986).

17. Xizhe Peng, "Demographic Consequences of the Great Leap Forward in China's Provinces", *Population and Development Review* 13, no. 4 (December 1987), pp. 639–70; Basil Ashton et al., "Famine in China, 1958–61", *Population and Development Review* 10, no. 4 (December 1984), pp. 613–45; and Carl Riskin, "Feeding China: The Experience since 1949", in Jean Dreze, Amartya Sen, and Athar Hussain (eds.), *The Political Economy of Hunger: Selected Essays* (Oxford: Clarendon Press, 1995), pp. 401–44, esp. pp. 414–19.

18. Amartya Sen, *Poverty and Famines: An Essay on Entitlements and Deprivation* (Oxford: Clarendon Press, 1981), p. 1.

19. The discussion in ch. 3 of Jenny Adkins, *Whose Hunger? Concepts of Famine, Practices of Aid* (Minneapolis: University of Minnesota Press, 2000), is useful.

20. A good summary, already somewhat dated, is offered by Eric Hoskins, "The Humanitarian Impacts of Economic Sanctions and War in Iraq", in Thomas G. Weiss et al. (eds.), *Political Gain and Civilian Pain: Humanitarian Impacts of Economic Sanctions* (Lanham, Md.: Rowman & Littlefield, 1997), pp. 91–147.

21. Cited by Richard Becker, "The Role of Sanctions in the Destruction of Yugoslavia", in Ramsey Clark et al., *NATO in the Balkans: Voices of Opposition* (New York: International Action Center, 1998), p. 107.

22. Wolfgang Sachs, "On the Archaeology of the Development Idea", *Lokayan Bulletin* 8, no. 1 (January–February 1990), p. 18.

23. Richard L. Rubenstein, *The Cunning of History: The Holocaust and the American Future* (New York: Harper Torchbooks, 1987), pp. 6, 21, and 31; Rubinstein, *After Auschwitz: History, Theology, and Contemporary Judaism*, 2nd edn (Baltimore, Md.: Johns Hopkins University Press), esp. pp. 123–39.

24. Zygmunt Bauman, *Modernity and the Holocaust* (Ithaca, N.Y.: Cornell University Press, paperback edn, 1992). Exponents of the view that the Holocaust should be viewed as a particularly German malady include Lucy S. Dawidowicz, *The War Against the Jews, 1933–1945* (New York: Holt, Rinehart & Winston, 1975), and Daniel Jonah Goldhagen, *Hitler's*

Willing Executioners: Ordinary Germans and the Holocaust (New York: Alfred Knopf, 1996).

25. Among the more prominent works of recent years one can enumerate the following: Tom Nairn, *Faces of Nationalism: Janus Revisited* (London: Verso, 1997); Ernest Gellner, *Nations and Nationalism* (Oxford: Basil Blackwell, 1983); Benedict Anderson, *Imagined Communities: Reflections on the Origin and Spread of Nationalism* (London: Verso, 1983), and Partha Chatterjee, *Nationalist Thought and the Colonial World: A Derivative Discourse?* (London: Zed Books, 1986; reprint edn, Minneapolis: University of Minnesota Press, 1993). No work on decolonization as such can be described as having a similar kind of visibility or influence. Gellner's later works, *The Conditions of Liberty: Civil Society and Its Rivals* (Harmondsworth: Penguin Books, 1996) and *Nationalism* (London: Weidenfeld & Nicolson, 1997), likewise make no mention of decolonization. Apparently decolonization should not be seen as the condition of liberty; some commentators have chosen to view it as the condition of servitude and have, it is no exaggeration to say, called for the recolonization of Africa on the grounds that Africans have shown themselves incapable of self-governance. Since it is one of the supreme platitudes of our times that the world is a "global village," and that consequently disorder in one portion of the world has a contagious effect elsewhere, the logical inference is that Africa must be contained, lest the chaos, pestilence, and poverty that afflict it spread outward. "West Africa is becoming the symbol of worldwide demographic, environmental, and societal stress," a widely admired commentator has written, "in which criminal anarchy emerges as the real 'strategic' danger. Disease, overpopulation, unprovoked crime, scarcity of resources, refugee migrations, the increasing emotion of nation states and international borders, and the empowerment of private armies, security firms, and international drug cartels are now most tellingly demonstrated through a West African prism" (p. 45). The article, by Robert Kaplan, is entitled "The Coming Anarchy" (*Atlantic Monthly*, February 1994), and since anarchy already prevails in west Africa, one can be certain that Kaplan fears that it is poised to make inroads into the civilized West. The reference to "increasing erosion of nation states and international borders" is not innocuous.

26. Ronald Robinson, John Gallagher, and Alice Denny, *Africa and the Victorians: The Climax of Imperialism* (London: St. Martin's Press, 1961); Eric Stokes, "Imperialism and the Scramble for Africa: The New View", in William Roger Louis (ed.), *Imperialism: The Robinson and Gallagher Controversy* (New York: New Viewpoints, 1976).

27. The maps and data in Christopher Bayly (ed.), *Atlas of the British Empire* (New York: Facts on File, 1989), are useful, though the enthusiasm of the editor and the contributors for empire makes this a less than salutary reading experience. Histories of the British Empire in broad brushstrokes have become something of an avocation for genteel English writers: among the latest is Lawrence James, *The Rise and Fall of the British Empire* (New York: St. Martin's Griffin, 1997).

28. Peter Clarke, *Hope and Glory: Britain 1900–1990* (Harmondsworth: Penguin Books, 1996), p. 14.

29. "The new organization," Gabriel Kolko wrote of the UN in his magisterial *The Politics of War: The World and United States Foreign Policy, 1943–1945* (New York: Pantheon Books, 1990 [1968]), "failed before it began, for Washington conceived it with loopholes and exceptions ... not as a forum for agreement, but as an instrument in the Great Power conflict" (p. 485).

30. Eugen Weber, *Peasants into Frenchmen: The Modernization of Rural France, 1870–1914* (Stanford, Calif.: Stanford University Press, 1976), remarks that "French was a foreign language for a substantial number of Frenchmen, including almost half the children who would reach adulthood in the last quarter of the [nineteenth] century" (p. 67).

31. Ibid., p. 95, citing Albert Soboul, "The French Revolution in Contemporary World History", lecture delivered at the University of California, Los Angeles, April 1973.

32. This insight constitutes one of the main accomplishments of a group of contemporary Indian thinkers. The classic works are those of Jit Singh Uberoi, *Science and Culture* (Delhi: Oxford University Press, 1978) and *The Other Mind of Europe: Goethe as a Scientist* (Delhi: Oxford University Press, 1984), and the numerous writings of Ashis Nandy, especially *The Intimate Enemy: Loss and Recovery of Self under Colonialism* (Delhi: Oxford University Press, 1983), and some of the essays in *Traditions, Tyranny, and Utopias: Essays in the Politics of Awareness* (New Delhi: Oxford University Press, 1987).

33. Peter Mudford, *Birds of a Different Plumage: A Study of British–Indian Relations from Akbar to Curzon* (London: Collins, 1974), esp. ch. VI; Charles Allen (ed.), *Plain Tales from the Raj: Images of British India in the Twentieth Century* (London: Futura, 1977).

34. The role of the (American) media in the Gulf War is already the subject of several book-length studies: see especially Philip M. Taylor, *War and the Media: Propaganda and Persuasion in the Gulf War*, 2nd edn (Manchester: Manchester University Press, 1998). Of respondents in Britain and the US, 80 percent even declared their support for the bombing of the Amiriya shelter in Baghdad, where the fatalities, extending to several hundred people, were all civilians, mainly women and children (p. 212).

35. The literature is growing, and the two volumes edited by Frederique Apffel-Marglin and Steven Marglin, *Dominating Knowledge: Development, Culture and Resistance* (Oxford: Clarendon, 1990), and *Decolonizing Knowledge: From Development to Dialogue* (Oxford: Clarendon, 1996), are superb examples of dissenting scholarship. Many works do not find their way into the circuits of well-traveled books: for example, Linda Tuhiwai Smith, *Decolonizing Methodologies: Research and Indigenous Peoples* (London: Zed Books; Dunedin, N.Z.: University of Otago Press, 1999), which offers a Maori perspective on Western knowledge.

36. F. E. Manuel, *A Portrait of Isaac Newton* (Cambridge, Mass.: Harvard University Press, 1968), pp. 160–90.

37. Quoted in David Seamon and Arthur Zajonc (eds.), *Goethe's Way of Science: A Phenomenology of Nature* (New York: SUNY Press, 1998), p. 72.
38. Cited by Uberoi, *Science and Culture*, p. 69.
39. The essays collected in Ashis Nandy (ed.), *Science, Hegemony and Violence: A Requiem for Modernity* (Tokyo: The United Nations University; Delhi: Oxford University Press, 1988; paperback edn, 1990), offer a dissenting perspective on modern science. On science as vivisection, see the essay in this collection by Vandana Shiva, "Reductionist Science as Epistemological Violence", pp. 232–56; a more elaborate treatment will be found in *Staying Alive: Women, Ecology and Survival in India* (London: Zed Books, 1988; Delhi: Kali for Women, 1988). Shiva's work has been the focus of much critical scrutiny, and the most common objections are that she has a "romantic" idea of the premodern and prescientific world, and that her work is informed by sterile oppositions, such as that (for example) women are falsely seen as being attuned to nature. Shiva's critics, however, are much less imaginative and inventive than they imagine themselves to be; this is particularly true of Meera Nanda, "Is Modern Science a Western, Patriarchal Myth? A Critique of the Populist Orthodoxy", *South Asia Bulletin* 11, nos. 1–2 (1991), pp. 32–61.
40. The classic work is Paul Starr, *The Social Transformation of American Medicine* (New York: Basic Books, 1982). A briefer discussion, which offers a more comparative perspective of British, American, French, and Kong [Zairean] medicinal practices, and is placed within a larger discussion of knowledge systems, is to be found in Peter Worsley, *Knowledges: Culture, Counterculture, Subculture* (London: Profile Books, 1997; New York: The New Press, 1997), pp. 169–240.
41. Manu Kothari and Lopa Mehta, *Cancer: Myths and Realities of Cause and Cure* (London: Marion Boyars, 1979), reprinted (with a new preface) as *The Other Face of Cancer* (Mapusa, Goa: The Other India Press, 1994).
42. V. S. Naipaul, "Our Universal Civilization", The 1990 Wriston Lecture (October 30th 1990), *New York Times* (November 5th 1990), also available at <http://www.manhattan-institute.org/html/wl1990.htm>
43. Paul Gordon Lauren, *The Evolution of International Human Rights* (Philadelphia: University of Pennsylvania Press, 1998), p. 17.
44. Jared Diamond, *Guns, Germs, and Steel: The Fate of Human Societies* (New York: W. W. Norton, 1997), p. 410.
45. David Landes, *The Wealth and Poverty of Nations: Why Some Are So Rich and Some So Poor* (New York: W. W. Norton, 1998), p. 31.
46. Nathan Katz, *Who Are the Jews of India?* (Berkeley: University of California Press, 2000).
47. Lynn Hunt, "The Paradoxical Origins of Human Rights", in Jeffrey N. Wasserstrom, Lynn Hunt, and Marilyn B. Young (eds.), *Human Rights and Revolutions* (Lanham, Md.: Rowman & Littlefield, 2000), p. 5.
48. The Constitution stated that a state would be entitled to count three-fifths of its slave population to determine its representation in the House of Representatives and its votes in the electoral college. See Eric Foner, *The Story of American Freedom* (New York: W. W. Norton, 1998), p. 35.
49. The usual formulation is to speak of one law for the powerful and one for the powerless; for some subtle reflections on the "rule of law", see E.

P. Thompson, *Whigs and Hunters: The Origin of the Black Act* (New York: Pantheon Books, 1975), particularly pp. 258–69.

50. One noted Indian commentator wrote of the US Supreme Court judgment, "We are thus back in the 15th, 16th and 17th century world of piracy and pillage." See Ashok Mitra, "No Holds Barred for the US", *Deccan Herald* (July 3rd 1992).

51. A far more nuanced reading of "Asian values," which stresses the difficulties in unitary models emanating from the modern West, is to be found in Anwar Ibrahim, *The Asian Renaissance* (Singapore: Times Books International, 1996).

52. The obvious exception would be intellectuals such as W. E. B. Du Bois, who claimed full rights for African-Americans as Americans. "We will not be satisfied," Du Bois told members of the National Association for the Advancement of Colored People (NAACP), "to take one jot or title less than our full manhood rights. We claim for ourselves every single right that belongs to a freeborn American, political, civil, and social; and until we get these rights we will never cease to protest and assail the ears of America." See P. S. Foner (ed.), *W. E. B. Du Bois Speaks: Speeches and Addresses, 1890–1919* (New York: Pathfinder Press, 1970), p. 170.

53. D. G. Tendulkar, *Mahatma: The Life of Mohandas Karamchand Gandhi*, 8 vols. (New Delhi: Publications Division, Ministry of Information and Broadcasting, Government of India, 1951–54), vol. 8, pp. 283–5.

54. *Asia-Africa Speaks from Bandung* (Jakarta: Indonesian Ministry of Foreign Affairs, 1955; reprinted, Jakarta: The National Committee for the Commemmoration of the Thirtieth Anniversary of the Asian-African Conference, 1985).

55. Noam Chomsky, *The New World Order*, Open Magazine Pamphlet no. 6 (Westfield, N.J.: Open Magazine Pamphlet Series, 1991), pp. 14–15.

56. Vinay Lal, "An Epidemic of Apologies", *Humanscape* 6, no. 4 (April 1999), pp. 38–41.

CHAPTER 3

1. Cited by Benjamin Schwarz, "A Serious Case of Mistaken Identity", *Los Angeles Times* (June 22nd 2000), p. B15, who reminds readers that the one "indispensable nation" in World War II was most likely Russia, which accounted for 88 percent of all German casualties.

2. Alexander Cockburn, "Another Way: 'Hello, Saddam? This is Bill ...'", *Los Angeles Times* (February 19th 1998), section B.

3. John R. Lott Jr., *More Guns, Less Crime* (Chicago, Ill.: University of Chicago Press, 2000).

4. "Amnesty International Savages US Over Human Rights Record", *Agence France Presse* (May 30th 2001). The year 2001 is not the first that the US has faced sustained criticism over its use of the death penalty and other violations of human rights. *The Human Rights Watch World Report 1998* faulted the US for actively obstructing human rights efforts in numerous areas, and it concluded with the following observation: "U.S. arrogance suggests that in Washington's view, human rights standards should be embraced only if they codify what the U.S. government already does,

not what the United States ought to achieve." See Robin Wright, "Human Rights Group Assails 'Setbacks' by U.S. in Report", *Los Angeles Times* (December 5th 1997), p. A25. Mike Farrell, co-chair of Human Rights Watch in California, offers some reflections on what it means for the US "to share the killing stage with some of the world's worst human rights violators." See "Executions Put State and Nation on the Killing Stage", *Los Angeles Times* (December 22nd 1999), p. B13.

5. Iran, Iraq, Nigeria, and Saudi Arabia execute juvenile offenders. Texas, under George W. Bush, led all states in execution of the mentally retarded: see Joseph Margulies, Robert L. McGlasson, and Susan C. Casey, "Executing the Retarded Is a Shameful Legal Relic", *Los Angeles Times* (June 26th 2001), p. B17. For an exhaustive treatment of capital punishment, see Hugo Adam Bedau (ed.), *The Death Penalty in America: Current Controversies* (New York: Oxford University Press, 1997).

6. Norman Kempster, "U.S. 'Impediment' to Human Rights, Report Declares", *Los Angeles Times* (May 30th 2001), p. A18.

7. Robert E. Hunter, "Europe's Own Painful Past Shapes Its Reaction to U.S. Death Penalty", *Los Angeles Times* (June 12th 2001), p. B17.

8. Cited by Graham Dunkley, *The Free Trade Adventure: The WTO, the Uruguay Round and Globalism – A Critique* (London: Zed Books, 1997), p. 7.

9. Carey Ker, "U.S. Loses Seat on U.N. Narcotics Board", *National Post* (May 9th 2001), p. A11 (Canada).

10. Perry Miller, *Errand Into the Wilderness* (Cambridge, Mass.: Harvard University Press, 1957).

11. Edward Lytton Bulwer, *England and the English* [1833], ed. Standish Meacham (Chicago, Ill: University of Chicago Press, 1970), p. 21.

12. Robert Bellah has written about the widespread prevalence in America of the view that God is "actively interested and involved in history, with a special concern for America." Cited by Barbara Ehrenreich, *Blood Rites: Origins and History of the Passions of War* (New York: Henry Holt & Co., 1997), pp. 219–20.

13. Andrew Bacevich, "Different Drummers, Same Drum", *National Interest*, no. 64 (Summer 2001), p. 70.

14. Ibid. China, declared Clinton, was on "the wrong side of history."

15. Cited by Paul Drake, "From Good Men to Good Neighbors: 1912–1932", in Abraham F. Lowenthal (ed.), *Exporting Democracy: The United States and Latin America* (Baltimore, Md.: Johns Hopkins University Press, 1991), p. 11.

16. See, for example, Robert Scheer, "Do as We Say, Not as We Do", *Los Angeles Times* (June 26th 2001), p. B17; Nora King, "How Dr. Henry Kissinger orchestrated global repression", *Covert Action Quarterly* (April–June 2001), and Christopher Hitchens, *The Trial of Henry Kissinger* (London: Verso, 2001).

17. "The Sentencing Project", <www.sentencingproject.org>

18. Ibid., "Felony Disenfranchisement Laws in the United States". See also Jesse Katz, "For Many Ex-Cons, Ban on Voting Can Be for Life", *Los Angeles Times* (April 2nd 2000), pp. A1, 20; Tamar Lewin, "Crime Costs

Many Black Men the Vote, Study Says", *New York Times* (October 23rd 1998), p. A12.

19. Eric Schlosser, "The Prison-Industrial Complex", *Atlantic Monthly* (December 1998), pp. 51–77.

20. A good introductory work is William Blum, *Killing Hope: U.S. Military and CIA Interventions since World War II* (Monroe, Me.: Common Courage Press, 1995).

21. Michael Renner, "Ending Violent Conflict", in Lester R. Brown et al., *State of the World 1999* (New York: W. W. Norton, 1999), p. 154, relying upon Stephen Schwartz (ed.), *Atomic Audit: The Costs and Consequences of U.S. Nuclear Weapons Since 1940* (Washington, D.C.: Brookings Institution Press, 1998).

22. Cited by Stewart L. Udall, *The Myths of August: A Personal Exploration of Our Tragic Cold War Affair with the Atom* (New York: Pantheon Books, 1994; paperback edn, New Brunswick, N.J.: Rutgers University Press, 1998), p. 95. An official announcement issued by the US included the following lines addressed to the Japanese, described by Truman in his diary as "savages, ruthless, merciless, and fanatic": "If they do not now accept our terms, they may expect a rain of ruin from the air, the like of which has never been seen on this earth." Quoted in Herbert Feis, *The Atomic Bomb and the End of World War II* (Princeton, N.J.: Princeton University Press, 1970), p. 123, Truman's words are cited by Udall, *Myths of August*, p. 95.

23. Cited by Udall, *Myths of August*, p. 57.

24. Michael Sherry, *The Rise of American Airpower: The Creation of Armageddon* (New Haven, Conn.: Yale University Press, 1987); John Dower, *War Without Mercy: Race and Power in the Pacific War* (New York: Pantheon, 1986). Sherry shows (p. 406 n. 76 and p. 413 n. 43) that the estimates vary considerably: at the lowest end, 80,000 people were reportedly killed in the March 10th raid over Tokyo, while at the other extreme is the frequently encountered argument that more people were killed in Tokyo alone than were killed in Hiroshima and Nagasaki put together, which would suggest a figure of at least 200,000 dead.

25. Dower, *War Without Mercy*, pp. 40–1. The author adds, "When Tokyo was incinerated, there was scarcely a murmur of protest on the home front."

26. Peter Calvocoressi and Guy Wint, *Total War: Causes and Courses of the Second World War* (Harmondsworth: Penguin Books, 1974), p. 873.

27. Cited by Udall, *Myths of August*, p. 94.

28. Michael Klare, *Rogue States and Nuclear Outlaws: America's Search for a New Foreign Policy* (New York: Hill and Wang, 1995), p. 26.

29. Quoted in ibid., p. 27.

30. Quoted in ibid., p. 39.

31. Anthony Lake, "Confronting Backlash States", *Foreign Affairs* 73, no. 2 (March–April 1994).

32. Robert Litwak, "'Rogue State' Label Was a Bad Fit", *Los Angeles Times* (June 28th 2000), p. B13.

33. Anthony Abraham, "'Rogue States' Threaten West: Thatcher", *Hindu* (March 15th 1996), p. 11.

34. William Blum, *Rogue State: A Guide to the World's Only Superpower* (Monroe, Me.: Common Courage Press, 2001).
35. David Horowitz, "Even Standing Alone, the United States Can Still Be Right", *Los Angeles Times* (November 26th 1999), p. B11.
36. Anjali V. Patil, *The UN Veto in World Affairs, 1946–1990* (Sarasota, Fla.: UNIFO, 1992), pp. 485–6.
37. Thucydides, *History of the Peloponnesian War*, 5: 89; the text used is Robert B. Strassler (ed.), *The Landmark Thucydides: A Comprehensive Guide to the Peloponnesian War*, trans. Richard Crawley (New York: The Free Press, 1996), p. 352.
38. Inis Claude Jr., *Swords into Plowshares: The Problems and Progress of International Organization*, 2nd edn (New York: Random House, 1956), p. 87, cited by Giovanni Arrighi and Beverly J. Silver, *Chaos and Governance in the Modern World System* (Minneapolis: University of Minnesota Press, 1999), pp. 209–10.
39. The Commission on Global Governance, *Our Global Neighbourhood* (Oxford: Oxford University Press, 1995), pp. 243–4.
40. Ramsey Clark, *The Fire This Time: US War Crimes in the Gulf* (New York: Thunder's Mouth Press, 1992).
41. Maggie Farley, "2 Cite Iraq Sanctions in Resignations", *Los Angeles Times* (February 18th 2000), p. A6.
42. Jim Mann, "America: Global Arms Superstore", *Los Angeles Times* (October 13th 1999), p. A5. For a more detailed account, see William Hartung, *And Weapons for All: How America's Multibillion Dollars Arms Trade Warps Our Foreign Policy and Subverts Democracy at Home* (New York: HarperCollins, 1995).
43. See the UN's own web pages, <http://www.un.org/Depts/dpko/dpko/pub/pko.htm> Detailed information can be obtained from William J. Burch (ed.), *The Evolution of UN Peacekeeping: Case Studies and Comparative Analysis* (New York: St. Martin's Press, 1993).
44. Commission on Global Governance, *Our Global Neighbourhood*, p. 113.
45. Data here is drawn from Marjorie Ann Browne, "United Nations Peacekeeping: Issues for Congress", December 20th 1996, at <http://www.fas.org/man/crs/90-103.htm> Funding of UN peacekeeping operations is discussed in William J. Durch and Barry M. Blechman, *Keeping the Peace: The United Nations in the Emerging World Order* (Washington, D.C.: Henry L. Stimson Center, 1992), pp. 48–64.
46. Karen A. Mingst and Margaret P. Karns, *The United Nations in the Post-Cold War Era* (Boulder, Colo.: Westview Press, 1995), pp. 92–5. Figures on fatalities can be found at <http://www.un.org/Depts/dpko/dpko/pub/pko.htm>
47. "Military personnel contributions", <http://www.un.org/Depts/dpko/dpko/pub/pko.htm>
48. Cited by Michael A. Sells, *The Bridge Betrayed: Religion and Genocide in Bosnia* (Berkeley: University of California Press, 1996), p. 128.
49. M. S. Rajan, *The Expanding Jurisdiction of the United Nations* (Bombay: N. M. Tripathi Private Ltd.; Dobbs Ferry, New York: Oceana Publications, 1982), p. 115.

50. Jean Dreze and Haris Gazdar, "Hunger and Poverty in Iraq, 1991", *World Development* 20, no. 7 (1992), p. 924.

51. Ibid., p. 929.

52. United Nations, Economic and Social Council, Commission on Human Rights. Sub-Commission on Prevention of Discrimination and Protection of Minorities. 'Forty-third session [August 20th 1991]: Summary Record of the 10th Meeting.' E/CN.4/Sub.2/1991/SR.10, p. 10.

53. Ibid., p. 19.

54. Roger Normand, "Iraqi Sanctions, Human Rights and Humanitarian Law", *Middle East Report* (July–September 1996), p. 41.

55. The data is drawn from a large number of sources, and there are numerous reports published by Human Rights Watch, the International Red Cross, UNICEF, and the International Action Center in New York. The special issue *of Middle East Report*, "Intervention and Responsibility: The Iraq Sanctions Dilemma", no. 193 (March–April 1995), can be usefully supplemented by Eric Hoskins, "The Humanitarian Impacts of Economic Sanctions and War in Iraq", in Thomas G. Weiss et al. (eds.), *Political Gain and Civilian Pain: Humanitarian Impacts of Economic Sanctions* (Lanham, Md.: Rowman & Littlefield, 1997), pp. 91–148, and, most significantly, by Anthony Arnove (ed.), *Iraq Under Siege: The Deadly Impact of Sanctions and War* (Cambridge, Mass.: South End Press; London: Pluto Press, 2000). See also Philip Shenon, "Washington and Baghdad Agree on One Point: Sanctions Hurt", *New York Times* (November 22nd 1998), p. A10; 'UN Curbs on Iraq have Doubled Death Rates Among Children', *Times of India* (August 25th 1999), p. 15 (Mumbai edition); Tariq Ali, "Throttling Iraq", *New Left Review* (September–October 2000), and <http://www.timesofindia.com/300301/30mide4.htm>

56. Clark, *The Fire This Time*, p. 290, furnishes higher estimates.

57. Anthony H. Codesman, *Iraq and the War of Sanctions: Conventional Threats and Weapons of Mass Destruction* (Westport, Conn.: Praeger, 1999), p. 33.

58. [William Jefferson Clinton, "In Clinton's Words: Containing the 'Predators of the 21st Century", *New York Times* (February 18th 1998), p. A9. It is not in the least transparent that most Iraqis at this point hold Saddam Hussein responsible for the continuing devastation of Iraq. One Iraqi intellectual, rejecting a suggestion put forth by a *New York Times* reporter that the Iraqi leadership was alone responsible, stated: "Why? Is it Saddam who has imposed the embargo? Besides, what is America to tell any country what leadership it should have? This is a country with thousands of years of culture that is now watching its babies dying of malnutrition." Youssef M. Ibrahim, "Despite Threats of Missiles, the Iraqi Capital's People Take a Crisis in Stride", *New York Times* (February 23rd 1998), p. A7.

59. Kimberley Ann Elliott, "A Look at the Record", *Bulletin of the Atomic Scientists* 49, no. 9 (November 1993), p. 33.

60. See Jack Patterson, "The Sanctions Dilemma", *Middle East Report* (March–June 1994), pp. 24–7.

61. UN, General Assembly, "Supplement to an Agenda for Peace: Position Paper of the Secretary-General on the Occasion of the Fiftieth Anniversary of the United Nations." S/1995/1 (January 3rd 1995), p. 16.

62. On more than one occasion, American political leaders have declared that nothing but Saddam Hussein's removal would satisfy them. Thus in May 1991, Secretary of State James A. Baker stated that "we are not interested in seeking a relaxation of sanctions as long as Saddam Hussein is in power." See Shenon, "Washington and Baghdad Agree on One Point", *New York Times* (November 22nd 1998), p. A10.

63. Hans Kochler, *The United Nations Sanctions Policy and International Law* (Penang, Malaysia: Just World Trust, 1995), p. 11.

64. UN, Economic and Social Council (1991), p. 20.

65. John Quigley, "Prospects for the International Rule of Law", *Emory International Law Review* 5, no. 2 (Fall 1991), p. 320.

66. United Nations, Security Council, "Provisional Verbatim Record of the Three Thousand and Sixty-Third Meeting." S/PV.3063 (March 31st 1992), p. 267.

67. Robert W. Oliver, *International Economic Co-operation and the World Bank* (New York: Holmes and Meier, 1975), Appendix A, pp. 297–8.

68. See the discussion on Laurence Summers, one-time Chief Economist at the World Bank, in Chapter 4 of this volume.

69. The literature on the United Fruit Company, whose crimes in Central America and Latin America are legion, is immense. A recent study of very wide scope, going far beyond United Fruit, is Richard P. Tucker, *Insatiable Appetite: The United States and the Ecological Degradation of the Tropical World* (Berkeley: University of California Press, 2000).

70. Gordon Fairclough and Darren McDermott, "Fruit of Labor: The Banana Business is Rotten, So Why Do People Fight Over It?", *Wall Street Journal* (August 9th 1999), p. A1. Profits for growers of bananas are so slim that very few of them desire a "truly free market."

71. Ronald Labonte, "Brief to the Genoa Non-Governmental (GNG) Initiative on International Governance and WTO Reform", April 16th 2001, p. 5 [internet].

72. Robert O'Brien, Anne Marie Goetz, Jan Aart Scholte, and Marc Williams, *Contesting Global Governance: Multilateral Economic Institutions and Global Social Movements* (Cambridge: Cambridge University Press, 2000), pp. 69–70.

73. Jeffrey Schott, *The Uruguay Round* (Washington, D.C.: Institute for International Economics, 1994), p. 125.

74. Bhagirath Lal Das, *Some Key Issues Relating to the WTO* (Penang: Third World Network, 1996), p. 5.

75. See the brief discussion in T. N. Srinivasan, *Developing Countries and the Multilateral Trading System* (Boulder, Colo.: Westview Press, 2000), pp. 56–7.

76. Debi Barker and Jerry Mander, *Invisible Government: The World Trade Organization – Global Government for the New Millennium* (San Francisco, Calif.: International Forum on Globalization, 1999), p. 9.

77. Interview of June 29th 1996, cited by Srinivasan, *Developing Countries*, p. 108.

78. Srinivasan, *Developing Countries*, p. 110.
79. Barker and Mander, *Invisible Government*, p. 8.

CHAPTER 4

1. The road is named after an influential Southern California family of the nineteenth century: see Kevin Starr, *Inventing the Dream: California Through the Progressive Era* (New York: Oxford University Press, 1985), pp. 16, 20. On Juan Sepulveda, see Lewis Hanke, *Aristotle and the American Indians* (Chicago, Ill.: Henry Regnery Company, 1959).
2. A quote attributed to the Spanish writer Julian Marias by David Rieff, *Los Angeles: Capital of the Third World* (New York: Simon & Schuster, 1991), p. 50.
3. Reyner Banham, *Los Angeles: The Architecture of Four Ecologies* (Harmondsworth: Penguin Books, 1971), pp. 213–22.
4. Richard Austin Smith, "Los Angeles, Prototype of Supercity", *Fortune* (March 1965), pp. 98–106, 200–2; quotations are from p. 200.
5. Ashis Nandy, "The Future University", *Seminar*, no. 425 (January 1995), p. 95.
6. Paul Fussell, *Class: A Guide Through the American Status System* (New York: Summit Books, 1983), especially pp. 76–96. The American model of cultural studies has revolved around notions of race, ethnicity, and gender; and the advent of identity politics, no less than the attraction of poststructuralist arguments that stress the constructedness of communities and social relations, has further diminished the appeal of class, which had comparatively little resonance in American social analyses. See also the discussion in Chapter 4 of this volume.
7. David J. Brown and Robert Merrill, eds., *Violent Persuasions: The Politics and Imagery of Terrorism* (Seattle, Wash.: Bay Press, 1995), pp. 54–5.
8. On the syncretism of Sikh and Hindu traditions, and indeed the historical difficulties in distinguishing between the two, see Harjot Oberoi, *The Construction of Religious Boundaries: Culture, Identity, and Diversity in the Sikh Tradition* (Chicago, Ill.: University of Chicago Press, 1994). There has been a systematic attempt by orthodox Sikh scholars, who insist on the unique trajectories of the Sikh religion, and profess utter disdain for "Hindu" traditions, to discredit Oberoi's work: see Jasbir Singh Mann, Surinder Singh Sodhi, and Gurbaksh Singh Gill (eds.), *Invasion of Religious Boundaries: A Critique of Harjot Oberoi's Work* (Vancouver: Canadian Sikh Study and Teaching Society, 1995).
9. Michael Stewart, *The Time of the Gypsies* (Boulder, Colo.: Westview Press, 1997), is a remarkable ethnography; 500,000 gypsies are said to have been killed in the genocide (p. 5).
10. Serena Nanda, *Neither Man Nor Woman: The Hijras of India* (Belmont, Calif.: Wadsworth, 1990).
11. Laurence W. Preston, "A Right to Exist: Eunuchs and the State in Nineteenth-Century India", *Modern Asian Studies* 21, no. 2 (1987), pp. 371–87.

12. For a more extended political reading of Hijras, see Vinay Lal, "Not This, Not That: The Hijras of India and the Cultural Politics of Sexuality", *Social Text*, no. 61 (Winter 1999), pp. 119–40.

13. Vladimir I. Lenin, *The Development of Capitalism in Russia: The Process of the Formation of a Home Market for Large-Scale Industry* (Moscow: Progress Publishers, 1956).

14. See Arturo Escobar, *Encountering Development: The Making and Unmaking of the Third World* (Princeton, N.J.: Princeton University Press, 1995).

15. Stephen Greenblatt, *Marvelous Possessions: The Wonder of the New World* (Chicago, Ill.: University of Chicago Press, 1991).

16. Williams Arens, *The Man-Eating Myth* (Oxford: Oxford University Press, 1979), argues vociferously against any evidence of cannibalism; for a recent, protracted debate that also touches on cannibalism, see Gananath Obeyesekere, *The Apotheosis of Captain Cook* (Princeton, N.J.: Princeton University Press, 1992) and the rejoinder by Marshall Sahlins, *How "Natives" Think: About Captain Cook, for Example* (Chicago, Ill.: University of Chicago Press, 1995).

17. United Nations, Department of Social and Economic Affairs, *Measures for the Economic Development of Underdeveloped Countries* (New York: United Nations, 1951), p. 15.

18. Cited by Escobar, *Encountering Development*, pp. 35–6.

19. Vinod Raina, Aditi Chowdhury, and Sumit Chowdhury, eds., *The Dispossessed: Victims of Development in Asia* (2nd edn, Hong Kong: ARENA [Asian Regional Exchange for New Alternatives] Press, 1999), pp. 37–43.

20. Ibid., for detailed discussion of case studies of "development" from several countries in Asia. Madhav Gadgil and Ramachandra Guha, in *Ecology and Equity: The Use and Abuse of Nature in Contemporary India* (Delhi: Penguin Books, 1995), offer a brief discussion of resistance to large dams (pp. 68–76). The Indian government's proposal to build a missile testing range at Baliapal in the Balasore district of Orissa, which would have displaced nearly 70,000 peasants, met with such opposition that for years the project was stalled, before finally being abandoned. As the general secretary of the People's Committee against the proposed test range put it, "No land on earth can compensate for the land we have inherited from our forefathers" (quoted on p. 76).

On large dams, which are profoundly iconic of grandiose projects of state-sponsored development, see Patrick McCully, *Silenced Rivers: The Ecology and Politics of Large Dams* (London: Zed Books, 1996). The recent exhaustive report of the World Commission on Dams, *Dams and Development: A New Framework for Decision-Making* (London: Earthscan, 2000), reflects the consensus view that "an unacceptable and often unnecessary price" has been paid to secure the benefits promised by large dams, especially in social and environmental terms, by people displaced, by communities downstream, by taxpayers and by the natural environment. The commissioners, while agreeing that "dams have made an important and significant contribution to human development," noted that "lack of equity in the distribution of benefits has called into question the value of many dams in meeting water and energy development needs when compared with the alternatives." See "An

Overview" (of the Report), p. 7, also at <http://www.dams.org> The
report is significant because its twelve signatories include government
officials and the CEO of one of the largest private manufacturers of
heavy equipment used in dam construction; only Medha Patkar, the
founder of the Narmada Bachao Andolan, the famous struggle to save
the Narmada from being dammed, added a lengthy note indicating some
of her disagreements with the compromise consensus view. Third World
states are sometimes seen as having an unusual attachment to dams, and
their indifference to, and contempt for, environmental movements has
done nothing to allay that impression; but it should not be forgotten
that the United States invested heavily in dams at a time when such
protests were rare. Moreover, at a time when most industrialized
countries are dismantling some large dams, Japan's Ministry of Construction is planning on adding 500 more to the 2,800 dams in the
country. See Alex Kerr, *Dogs and Demons: Tales from the Dark Side of Japan*
(New York: Hill & Wang, 2001), ch. 1.
21. The idea that colonized people vastly underutilized their natural
resources, and so wasted the gifts endowed by God, proliferates in
European and American literature; it was to serve as one of many
pretexts for colonization. See Patricia Seed, *American Pentimento: The
Invention of Indians and the Pursuit of Riches* (Minneapolis: University of
Minnesota Press, 2001), pp. 30–2. One governor of Indochina protested
that failure to colonize would "leave unutilized resources to lie forever
idle in the hands of incompetents," while a clergyman, speaking in an
equally representative idiom, declared that "Humanity must not, cannot
allow the incompetence, negligence, and laziness of the uncivilized
peoples to leave idle indefinitely the wealth which God has confided to
them, charging them to make it serve the good of all." Both quotations
appear in Aime Cesaire, *Discourse on Colonialism* (1955), trans. Joan
Pinkham (New York: Monthly Review Press, 1972), p. 17.
22. Marian A. L. Miller, *The Third World in Global Environmental Politics*
(Milton Keynes: Open University Press, 1995), offers an account of the
growing trade – one-way, of course – in hazardous wastes. These are
among the "growth" industries that the West is unwilling to disavow.
There is a rapidly growing body of literature which suggests that within
the United States communities that are predominantly black or
Hispanic, and Native American reservations, are likely to have a disproportionate number of hazardous waste disposal sites or otherwise be
exposed to environmental harm. The scholarship of R. D. Bullard is
exemplary: *Unequal Protection: Environmental Justice and Communities of
Color* (San Francisco, Calif.: Sierra Club Books, 1994); see also Bunyan
Bryant and Paul Mohai, eds., *Race and the Incidence of Environmental
Hazards: A Time for Discourse* (Boulder, Colo.: Westview Press, 1992). An
argument often implied and sometimes openly heard in defense of
locating hazardous industries in the Third World, namely that life there
has little value, or that poor people can scarcely afford to exercise choice
in the matter of employment, is also encountered with reference to the
First World's own Third World. A paper mill's stench in a poverty-
afflicted black community in Alabama evoked this memorable remark

from Governor George Wallace: "Yeah, that's the smell of prosperity. Sho' does smell sweet, don't it?" Cited by Robert Bullard, "Environmental Blackmail in Minority Communities", in Bryant and Mohai, *Race and the Incidence of Environmental Hazards*, p. 86. The phrase "environmental justice" first received prominence in the widely cited report prepared by the Commission for Racial Justice, *Toxic Wastes and Race in the United States* (New York: United Church of Christ, 1987).

23. The memo is now reproduced at <http://www.whirledbank.org/ourwords/summers.html>

It was published in *The Economist* in February 1992, after which Brazil's then Secretary of the Environment Jose Lutzenburger wrote a letter to Summers describing his reasoning as "perfectly logical but totally insane." "Your thoughts," Lutzenburger wrote, provide "a concrete example of the unbelievable alienation, reductionist thinking, social ruthlessness and the arrogant ignorance of many conventional 'economists' concerning the nature of the world we live in." Lutzenburger thought the World Bank would lose all credibility if it retained Summers, and expressed the hope that the Bank would "disappear." Lutzenburger was fired shortly thereafter: so much for the dedication to free speech. In June 2000, Ravi Kanbur, lead author of the World Development Report on poverty, tendered his resignation after the report was altered against the authors' wishes at the behest of Summers, who insisted that the report did not pay enough attention to the role of free markets in the alleviation of poverty. (See Mark Weisbrot, "We Need More World and a Lot Less Bank", *Los Angeles Times* (July 6th 2000), p. B15.) Summers' intolerance for dissenting views is legendary.

24. Marshall Sahlins, "Goodbye to *Tristes Tropes:* Ethnography in the Context of Modern World History", *Journal of Modern History* 65 (1993), pp. 3–4.

25. On the uproar over Japanese history textbooks, see K. Connie Kang, "Japan's New Textbook Decried", *Los Angeles Times* (April 18th 2001), p. B5. In the latest episode over the textbook war, 532 of Japan's 542 districts have rejected *The New History Textbook*, published by Fusosha Publishing Company. See Mark Magnier, "School Districts in Japan Reject Controversial History Textbook", *Los Angeles Times* (August 16th 2001), p. A3.

26. The conservatives were much louder in their denunciation of the standards: see Todd Gitlin, *The Twilight of Common Dreams: Why America is Wracked by Culture Wars* (New York: Henry Holt & Co., 1995), pp. 189–97.

27. The literature on this is prolific, and the journals *Economic and Political Weekly* (Mumbai) and particularly *Frontline* (Madras) have had extensive coverage in the last few years: see, for example, Asghar Ali Engineer, "Textbooks and Communalism", *The Hindu* (November 16th 1999); T. K. Rajalakshmi, "Agendas and Appointments", *Frontline* 16, no. 24 (November 13–26 1999); and Parvathi Menon, "The Falsification of History", *Frontline* 17, no. 6 (March 18–31 2000). Disputes over political patronage of historians have surfaced before: see Vinay Lal, "History and Politics" [original title: "Claims of the Past, Shape of the Future: The

Politics of History in Independent India"] in Marshall Bouton and Philip Oldenburg (eds.), *India Briefing: A Transformative Fifty Years* (New York: M. E. Sharpe for Asia Society, 1999), pp. 197–240.

28. For some further observations, see Anil Lal and Vinay Lal, "The Cultural Politics of Hybridity", *Social Scientist* 25, nos. 9–10 (September–October 1997), pp. 67–80.

29. This point has been made as well by Dipesh Chakrabarty, "Postcoloniality and the Artifice of History", *Representations*, no. 37 (Winter 1992), pp. 1–26, also published in a condensed version in *Provincializing Europe: Postcolonial Thought and Historical Difference* (Princeton, N.J.: Princeton University Press, 2000), pp. 27–46. The "West" appears to resonate more than "Europe" in this case, partly because recent discourses, such as those of development, are steeped in historicism – and they are of American provenance. Indeed, the modern study of history is deeply intertwined with the social sciences, which in their present shape are heavily Americanized.

30. I have discussed this at considerable length in "History and the Possibilities of Emancipation; Some Lessons from India", *Journal of the Indian Council of Philosophical Research*, Special Issue: "Historiography of Civilisations" (June 1996), pp. 95–137.

31. Vinay Lal, "The Discourse of History and the Crisis at Ayodhya: Reflections on the Production of Knowledge, Freedom, and the Future of India", *Emergences*, nos. 5–6 (1993–94), pp. 4–44.

32. M. K. Gandhi, "My Jail Experiences – XI", September 4th and 11th September 1924, as reproduced in Raghavan Iyer (ed.), *The Moral and Political Writings of Mahatma Gandhi*, vol. I: *Civilization, Politics, and Religion* (Oxford: Clarendon Press), pp. 183, 187.

33. Sheldon Rampton and John Stauber, *Trust Us, We're Experts: How Industry Manipulates Science and Gambles with Your Future* (New York: Tarcher/Putnam, 2001). This volume familiarizes the reader with the likes of H. W. Lewis, a physics professor at the University of California, Santa Barbara, and a "risk assessor" frequently hired by corporations, who states that only irrational and poorly educated people worry about nuclear waste, pesticides, and toxins. According to him, "the common good is ill served by the democratic process" (p. 111). The book documents the public relations work of the tobacco industry, pharmaceuticals (Wyeth Laboratories, for instance), and other mega-corporations.

34. Eyal Press and Jennifer Washburn, "The Kept University", *Atlantic Monthly* (March 2000), online at <http://www.theatlantic.com/cgi-bin/o/issues/2000/03/press.html> A lengthier, already slightly dated, account is found in Lawrence C. Soley, *Leasing the Ivory Tower: The Corporate Takeover of Academia* (Boston, Mass.: South End Press, 1995); more remarkable still, considering its original date of publication (1918), is Thorstein Veblen, *The Higher Learning in America: A Memorandum on the Conduct of Universities by Businessmen* (New York: Sagamore, 1957), who recognized that higher education would also be turned over to business executives.

35. Cf. Christopher Simpson (ed.), *Universities and Empire: Money and Politics in the Social Sciences during the Cold War* (New York: New Press, 1998).

36. Cf. M. A. Khan, "Islamic Economics: The State of the Art", in *Toward Islamization of Disciplines* (Herndon, Va.: International Institute of Islamic Thought), and T. Kuran, "The Genesis of Islamic Economics: A Chapter in the Politics of Muslim Identity", *Social Research* 64, no. 2 (Summer 1997), pp. 301–38.
37. Sharon Traweek, *Beamtimes and Lifetimes: The World of High Energy Physicists* (Cambridge, Mass.: Harvard University Press, 1988).
38. Peter Wagner and Bjorn Wittrock, "States, Institutions, Discourses: A Comparative Perspective on the Structuration of the Social Sciences", in Peter Wagner, Bjorn Wittrock, and Richard Whitely (eds.), *Discourses on Society: The Shaping of the Social Science Disciplines*, Sociology of the Sciences Yearbook, vol. XV (Dordrecht: Kluwer Academic Publishers, 1991), pp. 331–58.
39. Vandana Shiva, *Stolen Harvest: The Hijacking of the Global Food Supply* (Boston, Mass.: South End Press, 2001).
40. Paul Samuelson, *The Collected Scientific Papers of Paul A. Samuelson*, vol. 5 (Cambridge, Mass.: MIT Press, 1986), p. 793, cited by Narinder Singh, "Samuelson and Hitler", *Economic and Political Weekly* 29, no. 5 (January 29th 1994), Supplement on Political Economy, p. 25.
41. Burton Bledstein, *The Culture of Professionalism: The Middle Class and the Development of Higher Education in America* (New York: W. W. Norton, 1976); also Dorothy Ross, *The Origins of American Social Science* (Cambridge: Cambridge University Press, 1991).
42. Cf. David R. Loy, "Buddhism and Poverty", *Kyoto Journal*, no. 41 (1999), pp. 43–56.
43. Majid Rahnema, "Poverty", in Wolfgang Sachs (ed.), *Development Dictionary: A Guide to Knowledge as Power* (London: Zed Books, 1992).
44. Mahbub ul Haq, *Reflections on Human Development*, new edn (Delhi: Oxford University Press, 1998), p. 46.
45. Marshall Sahlins, *Culture and Practical Reason* (Chicago, Ill.: University of Chicago Press, 1976), p. 1.
46. Ibid., p. 216.
47. Patrick Tierney, "The Fierce Anthropologist", *New Yorker* (October 9th 2000), pp. 50–61.
48. D. Nettle and S. Romaine (eds.), *Vanishing Voices: The Extinction of the World's Languages* (New York: Oxford University Press, 1998).
49. Russell R. Barsh, "Are Anthropologists Hazardous to Indians' Health?", *Journal of Ethnic Studies* 15, no. 4 (1988), pp. 1–38.
50. Felix Padel, *The Sacrifice of Human Being: British Rule and the Konds of Orissa* (Delhi: Oxford University Press, 1995), pp. vii-x, 5, 64–108.
51. Cf. Garry Wills, "The Dramaturgy of Death", *New York Review of Books* (June 21st 2001), pp. 6ff.

CHAPTER 5

1. Vinod Raina, Aditi Chowdhury, and Sumit Chowdhury (eds.), *The Dispossessed: Victims of Development in Asia* (Hong Kong: ARENA Press, 1997), pp. 33, 40, 166, 227, 372, 397.

2. Madhav Gadgil and Ramachandra Guha, *Ecology and Equity* (New Delhi: Penguin Books). See also "State of Forests", in *Survey of the Environment 2001* (Delhi and Chennai: The Hindu, 2001), pp. 199–204.

3. Ziauddin Sardar, *The Consumption of Kuala Lumpur* (London: Reaktion Books, 2000), p. 125.

4. Geoffrey Ward, "Benares, India's Most Holy City, Faces an Unholy Problem", *Smithsonian* 16, no. 6 (September 1985), pp. 83–5.

5. Joachim Blatter and Helen Ingram (eds.), *Reflections on Water: New Approaches to Transboundary Conflicts and Cooperation* (Cambridge, Mass.: MIT Press), explore various political ideas, policies, and conflicts generated by water.

6. The figure may be much higher than 1 billion. One of India's most well-known environmental activists, the late Anil Aggarwal, estimated that "clean water is only obtained by less than one-third of the population of India," which now exceeds 1 billion. See his "Can Hindu Beliefs and Values Help India Meet Its Ecological Crisis?", in Christopher Key Chapple and Mary Evelyn Tucker (eds.), *Hinduism and Ecology: The Intersection of Earth, Sky, and Water* (Cambridge, Mass.: Center for the Study of World Religions, Harvard University), p. 166.

7. Jacques Leslie, "Running Dry", *Harper's Magazine* (July 2000), pp. 37–52.

8. See "Special Water Issue" of *IFG* [International Forum on Globalization] *Bulletin* (Summer 2001).

9. Maude Barlow, "Water Privatization and the Threat to the World's Most Precious Resource", in ibid., p. 1.

10. "The Free Trade Area of the Americas and the Threat to Water", in ibid., p. 7.

11. Antonia Juhasz, "Bolivian Water War Presents Alternative to Globalization of Water", in ibid., p. 4.

12. Raina et al., *The Dispossessed*, p. 372.

13. Marc Reisner, *Cadillac Desert: The American West and Its Disappearing Water*, revised edn (New York: Penguin Books, 1993), p. 78. This is the most exciting work on the subject. The most scholarly is William Kahrl, *Water and Power* (Berkeley: University of California Press, 1982).

14. See the film *Chinatown* (1974), starring Jack Nicholson and directed by Roman Polanski.

15. For one brief impressionistic account of the water crisis in Chennai, see Martha Ann Selby, "Thirst", *Persimmon* 2, no. 3 (Winter 2002), pp. 72–9. There is a gendering of water politics, a subject that I am unable to take up here. In Indian villages, and around the countryside, women draw the water from the wells and walk several miles with heavy water jugs on their head. In the towns and cities, it is the women who stand in line when city water tankers draw up in neighborhoods, or who place their pots and jars under the lone communal water tap. No grand tales have been spun around the lives of these women. In contrast, the heroic narrative we are familiar with of how water was drawn to Los Angeles involves big, cigar-chomping men. The difference between "gatherers" and "hunters" seems to be relived in various ways under modernity.

16. The phrase is borrowed from Ramachandra Guha, *Mahatma Gandhi and the Environmental Movement* (Pune: Parisar, 1993), p. 2.

17. Ibid., p. 20.
18. Cited by T. N. Khoshoo, *Mahatma Gandhi – An Apostle of Applied Human Ecology* (New Delhi: Tata Energy Research Institute, 1995), p 18.
19. For a short account of the Chipko movement, which highlights in particular its Gandhian impetus, see J. Bandyopadhyay and Vandana Shiva, "Chipko", *Seminar*, no. 330 (February 1987), pp. 33–9. A more systematic account is furnished by Anupam Mishra and Satyendra Tripathi, *Chipko Movement: Uttarakhand Women's Bid to Save Forest Wealth* (New Delhi: People's Action for Development with Justice, 1978). For a short account by Bahuguna, which acknowledges the inspiration he received from Gandhi's life, see *The Chipko Message* (Silyara Tehri, Garhwal: Chipko Information Centre, [1987]), esp. pp. 22–6. Also useful is Sunderlal Bahuguna, "The Crisis of Civilization and the Message of Culture in the Context of Environment", *Gandhi Marg* 9, no. 8 (November 1987), pp. 451–68, though Bahuguna reads much better in Hindi. A complex political, historical, and philosophical reading is furnished by George A. James, "Ethical and Religious Dimensions of Chipko Resistance", in Chapple and Tucker (eds.), *Hinduism and Ecology*, pp. 499–527. On the women of Chipko, see Vandana Shiva, *Staying Alive: Women, Ecology, and Survival in India* (New Delhi: Kali for Women, 1988), pp. 67–77. Mirabehn's work in the Himalayan region is ably and touchingly evoked in Krishna Murti Gupta, *Mira Behn: Gandhiji's Daughter Disciple*, Birth Centenary Volume (New Delhi: Himalaya Seva Sangh, 1992).
20. Arne Naess, *Gandhi and the Nuclear Age* (Totowa, N.J.: Bedminster Press, 1965).
21. Cited by David Rothenberg, *Is It Painful to Think? Conversations with Arne Naess* (Minneapolis: University of Minnesota Press, 1993), p. xix.
22. Burke's accusations against Hastings for his crimes in India ran to hundreds of pages. In his inimitable language, Burke wrote of his adversary: "He has gorged his ravenous maw with an allowance of 200 pounds a day ... He never dines without creating a famine." See *History of the Trial of Warren Hastings* (London, 1796), vol. 7, p. 152.
23. Gupta, *Mira Behn*, pp. 286–7.
24. Kalelkar, *Stray Glimpses of Bapu* (Ahmedabad: Navajivan Publishing House, 1950; 2nd revised edn, 1960), pp. 165–6.
25. Manubehn Gandhi, *Bapu – My Mother* (Ahmedabad: Navajivan Publishing House, 1948).
26. Naess, "Self-Realization: An Ecological Approach to Being in the World", *The Trumpeter* 4, no. 3 (1987), pp. 35–42, reprinted in Alan Drengson and Yuichi Inoue (eds.), *The Deep Ecology Movement: An Introductory Anthology* (Berkeley, Calif.: North Atlantic Books, 1995), p. 28.
27. M. K. Gandhi, *Truth is God* (Ahmedabad: Navajivan Publishing House, 1959), p. 102.
28. Kalelkar, *Stray Glimpses of Bapu*, pp. 54–5. See also Mukulbhai Kalarthi, *Anecdotes from Bapu's Life*, translated from Gujarati by H. M. Vyas (Ahmedabad: Navajivan Publishing House, 1960), pp. 22–3.
29. Gandhi, *Truth is God*, p. 50.

30. Kalarthi, *Anecdotes from Bapu's Life*, p. 31. Mirabehn has recounted having had a similar experience and being reprimanded by Gandhi for plucking too many leaves, that too at night when trees are resting. See Gupta, *Mira Behn*, p. 130.

31. Gupta, *Mira Behn*, p. 130.

32. This subject is given a moving and poignant treatment in the 1935 novel by Mulk Raj Anand, *Untouchable* (reprint edn, Harmondsworth: Penguin Books, 1995). For a Dalit perspective on scavenging, see the chilling documentary directed by Stalin K., *Lesser Humans* (1998).

33. Khoshoo, *Mahatma Gandhi*, p. 19.

34. Jeremy Rifkin, *Beyond Beef: The Rise and Fall of the Cattle Culture* (New York: Plume Books, 1993), and Geoff Tansey and Joyce D'Silva (eds.), *The Meat Business: Devouring a Hungry Planet* (London: Earthscan, 1999).

35. Jehangir P. Patel and Marjorie Sykes, *Gandhi: His Gift of the Fight* (Rasulia, Madhya Pradesh: Friends Rural Centre, 1987), pp. 103–4.

36. See, for instance, James P. Lester, David W. Allen, and Kelly M. Hill, *Environmental Injustice in the United States: Myths and Realities* (Boulder, Colo.: Westview Press, 2001). At the University of California's Research Conference on Political Economy, "Why do International Institutions Matter (If They Do?)", at Lake Arrowhead in February 2000, an advanced graduate student in political science assured me that he could model "desire" and "love" with precision.

37. James S. Coleman, "Equality", in John Eatwell, Murray Milgate, and Peter Newman (eds.), *Social Economics* (New York: W. W. Norton, 1989), p. 52.

38. Andrew Bacevich, "Different Drummers, Same Drum", *National Interest*, no. 64 (Summer 2001).

39. Cited by Lewis H. Lapham, *Money and Class in America: Notes and Observations on Our Civil Religion* (New York: Weidenfeld & Nicolson, 1988), p. 9.

40. Laura M. Holson, "Pity the Poor Rich", *Herald International Tribune* (March 4–5th 2000). The number of households with net worth of $10 million grew in the last decade from 67,700 to nearly 350,000.

41. Shweta Rajpal, "Reality Check", *Hindustan Times* (April 28th 2001), accessible at <http://www.hindustantimes.com/nonfram/280401/htm02.asp>

42. A television show, moderated by India's most famous filmstar, Amitabh Bhachan, and modeled after *Who Wants to Be a Millionaire?*, is called *Kaun Banega Crorepati?* [*Who Shall Become a Crorepati?*] The show is in Hindi, which explains why the term used is "*crorepati*" rather than "millionaire." Those who appear on it are not technological wizards or computer geeks, but rather are drawn from all walks of life. The retention of the term "*crorepati*" poses no problems, because indigenous terms can be made over in the language of the new economy.

43. Between 1991 and 1993, GDP by person decreased across sub-Saharan Africa by 2.5 percent. The last figure is cited by Julius O. Ihonvbere, *Africa and the New World Order* (New York: Peter Lang, 2000), p. 29. The *Human Development Report 1999* reported that 55 countries, mainly in sub-Saharan Africa and the former Soviet Union and Warsaw Pact countries, had declining per capita incomes ("Overview", p. 3). See also

Human Development Report 2001 (New York: United Nations, 2001), p. 13. Sub-Saharan Africa's share of world trade in manufactures declined, as early as the mid-1980s, to 0.2 percent of the world's total from 0.4 percent in 1965. See Paul Kennedy, "Preparing for the 21st Century: Winners and Losers", *New York Review of Books* (February 11th 1993), p. 33, citing S. Dardoust and A. Dhareshwan, *Long-Term Outlook for the World Economy: Issues and Projections for the 1990s*, A World Bank Report (February 1990), p. 9, Table 3.

"Winners" and "losers" also appear in Edward Luttwak, *Turbo Capitalism: Winners and Losers in the Global Economy* (London: Orion Business, 1999). These are the preferred terms of modern political commentators, and scarcely innocuous. The First World, the developed nations, and the winners are all on one side; the other end of the polarity is characterized by the Third World, the underdeveloped nations, and the losers. The entire scenario of global politics and economics is cast in the metaphor of games, and in the American conception of games a draw – or the even distribution of rewards – is seldom if ever permitted. Americans cannot countenance an inconclusive game; thus when the game is tied, it goes into overtime, or extended innings, until a decisive result is achieved and clear winners and losers emerge. Since this militates against sentimental notions of sportsmanship, the players and coach congratulate the losers on a great game at the post-game interview, and it is even hinted that there are no losers; the only winners are declared to be the great games of basketball, football, and baseball, as though the advertisers who pay monstrous sums of money to market their beers, colas, cars, and burgers were mark(et)ing their presence for some charitable end. I suspect it is not only the length of a cricket game – now often only a day long – that makes it unattractive to Americans, but the fact that at end of the five playing days of a conventional test match, punctuated by a day of rest, the whole game often dwindles down to a draw. Football [or "soccer" in the American idiom] games also often end in a tie, and only World Cup matches in the final rounds are so cast that a decisive result must emerge from the game. Other cultures have been able to live with ambiguity better than Americans. There is also the consideration, though far removed from modern anemic thinking about games and sports, that the only worthwhile games are those which are played for the purpose of continuing the play. James P. Carse, *Finite and Infinite Games: A Vision of Life as Play and Possibility* (New York: Ballantine Books, 1986), remains unmatched for his reflections on games.

44. The *Human Development Report 2001* suggests unequivocally the extent of the crisis afflicting sub-Saharan Africa. Even girls' net secondary school enrollments declined between 1985 and 1997 in Angola, Cameroon, the Central African Republic, Congo, the Ivory Coast, Equatorial Guinea, Guinea, Lesotho, and Mozambique (ibid., p. 15).

45. *Wall Street Journal* (June 24th 1999), p. 1, cited by Thomas Frank, *One Market under God: Extreme Capitalism, Market Populism, and the End of Economic Democracy* (New York: Doubleday, 2000), p. 13.

46. Curtis Keim, *Mistaking Africa: Curiosities and Inventions of the American Mind* (Boulder, Colo.: Westview Press, 1999), discusses the prevalence of the evolutionary models in American representations of Africa (pp. 39–51).

47. Cited by Rieff, *Los Angeles*, p. 85. Former MIT economist Lester Thurow has written, not with any evident disapproval, that Americans are "comfortable with inequalities," and he admits to difficulty in finding "anyone of importance to suggest that Americans ought to change the system." See his *Building WEALTH* (New York: HarperCollins, 1999), pp. xii, 36, cited by Frank, *One Market Under God*, p. 14.

48. <http://www.webho.com/WealthClock>

49. <http://www.templetons.com/brad/billg.html>

50. <http://www.quuxuum.org/~evan/bgnw.html>

51. Jeff Gates, "Keep an Eye on the Monopolists", *Los Angeles Times* (January 12th 2000), p. B11.

52. Ibid. See also Roger C. Altman, "The Fourth World", *Los Angeles Times* (December 12th 1999), p. M1; Holly Sklar, "Booming Economic Inequality, Falling Voter Turnout", and Holly Sklar, *Divided Decade: Economic Disparity at the Century's Turn* (Boston: United for a Fair Economy, 2000), available at <www.stw.org>

53. *UN Human Development Report 2001*, p. 19; Altman, "The Fourth World".

CHAPTER 6

1. John R. Bowen, *Muslims through Discourse: Religion and Ritual in Gayo Society* (Princeton, N.J.: Princeton University Press, 1993).

2. Michael Lieb, *Children of Ezekiel* (Durham, N.C.: Duke University Press, 1998).

3. The literature on cultural studies is itself immense: for a brief bibliography of some principal texts, see Vinay Lal, *South Asian Cultural Studies: A Bibliography* (Delhi: Manohar, 1996), Appendix Two and the discussion at pp. 11–14.

4. See Ziauddin Sardar and Borin van Loon, *Cultural Studies for Beginners* (Cambridge: Icon Books, 1997).

5. Stuart Hall, 'The Emergence of Cultural Studies and the Crisis of the Humanities', *October*, no. 53 (1990), p. 11.

6. Emily Eakin, 'Harvard's Prize Catch, a Delphic Postcolonialist', *New York Times* (January 17th 2001). Bhabha was previously named the shining star of the academic firmament by *Time* magazine, but one suspects that *Time* has few, if any, reporters capable of understanding Bhabha's prose, which even many seasoned academics view as impenetrable.

7. Cf. Tanya Luhrmann, *The Good Parsi: The Fate of a Colonial Elite in a Postcolonial Society* (Cambridge, Mass.: Harvard University Press, 1996).

8. Homi Bhabha, *The Location of Culture* (New York: Routledge, 1994).

9. The omission of class from cultural studies is discussed by Stanley Aronowitz, *The Politics of Identity: Class, Culture, Social Movements* (New York and London: Routledge, 1992).

10. Lata Mani, "Cultural Theory, Colonial Texts: Reading Eyewitness Accounts of Widow Burning", in Lawrence Grossberg, Cary Nelson, and

Paula Treichler (eds.), *Cultural Studies* (New York and London: Routledge, 1992), p. 393.

11. Cf. Benita Parry, "Problems in Current Theories of Colonial Discourse", *Oxford Literary Review* 9, nos. 1–2 (1987).

12. Thomas Nagel, *Mortal Questions* (Cambridge: Cambridge University Press, 1979), p. xii, cited by Gayatri Chakravorty Spivak, *Outside in the Teaching Machine* (London and New York: Routledge, 1993), p. 122.

13. Cf. Grossberg et al., *Cultural Studies*; Simon During (ed.), *The Cultural Studies Reader* (New York and London: Routledge, 1993); Robert Young, *White Mythologies: Writing History and the West* (London and New York: Routledge, 1990).

14. Cf. Donna Haraway, *Primate Visions: Gender, Race and Nature in the World of Modern Science* (New York and London: Routledge, 1989); Sandra Harding (ed.), *The 'Racial' Economy of Science: Towards a Democratic Future* (Bloomington: Indiana University Press, 1993); Mario Biagioli (ed.), *The Science Studies Reader* (New York and London: Routledge, 1999). It is perfectly illustrative of some of the arguments I have advanced that Biagioli's recent volume, which is gargantuan in scope and the most ambitious reader of science studies, has virtually nothing to say of the relations between science and colonialism. One wouldn't know from this road-map to science studies that science was enlisted in the cause of colonialism, that the colonized were browbeaten into submission under the authority of science, that the colonies served as laboratories for scientific experiments, and that the histories of science and colonialism share many trajectories in common. Nor would one know from this massive volume that science studies in India has made rapid advances, and that serious debates, even in the West, about the cultural contexts of science, the gendering of science, and the place of science in constructions of modernity can ill afford to ignore the work of scholars such as Jit Singh Uberoi, Claude Alvares, Ashis Nandy, Shiv Viswanathan, Deepak Kumar, and other writers from the South such as Ziauddin Sardar and Susantha Goonatilake. I am not making a case for equitable, or even anything more than cosmetic, mention of Indian or Third World scholarship in science studies (or indeed in any other field), merely on the model of multiculturalism; rather, such scholarship is important because it offers radically different perspectives.

15. Cf. Amy Kaplan and Donald Pease (eds.), *Cultures of United States Imperialism* (Durham, N.C.: Duke University Press, 1993).

16. Richard Delgado (ed.), *Critical Race Theory: The Cutting Edge* (Philadelphia, Pa: Temple University Press, 1995).

17. Ranajit Guha, "The Prose of Counter-Insurgency", in Ranajit Guha (ed.), *Subaltern Studies II: Writings on South Asian History and Society* (New Delhi: Oxford University Press, 1983), pp. 1–42.

18. Cf. Bill Readings, *The University in Ruins* (Cambridge, Mass.: Harvard University Press, 1996).

19. Major G. F. MacMunn, *The Martial Races of India* (London: Sampson Row, Marston & Co., n.d.).

20. Ziauddin Sardar (ed.), *Rescuing All Our Futures: The Future of Future Studies*, Adamantine Studies on the 21st Century, no. 32 (Twickenham: Adamantine Press, 1998; Westport Conn.: Praegar Publishers, 1998).

21. V. Y. Mudimbe, *The Idea of Africa* (Bloomington: Indiana University Press, 1994).

22. Brigadier-General Dyer, the perpetrator of the infamous Jallianwala Bagh massacre, in which a meeting of over 10,000 unarmed Indians was fired upon until the ammunition was exhausted, leading to nearly 400 deaths, admitted that he had been enraged because earlier an Englishwoman had been beaten by a few Indians. In his testimony before the official inquiry committee, Dyer stated that "women are sacred." For a lengthier discussion, see Vinay Lal, "The Incident of the Crawling Lane: Women in the Punjab Disturbances of 1919", *Genders*, no. 16 (Spring 1993), pp. 35–60.

23. Jean-Marie Guehenno, *The End of the Nation-State*, trans. Victoria Elliott (Minneapolis: University of Minnesota Press, 1995).

24. The source of "only connect" is *Howards End* (New York: Bantam Books, 1985), p. 147 [ch. 22], but it might as well have been from *A Passage to India*.

25. The Hawaii Center for Future Studies, University of Hawaii, even confers doctorates in "future studies." International organizations include the World Future Studies Federation (with shifting headquarters) and the Futures Study Centre, Victoria, Australia.

26. It is not commonly known *outside the academy* that many American students learning non-European languages in graduate school do so with the assistance of a fellowship awarded by the Department of Defense.

27. The obvious reference is Allan Bloom, *The Closing of the American Mind* (New York: Simon & Schuster, 1987).

28. Cf. James L. Watson (ed.), *Golden Arches East: McDonald's in East Asia* (Stanford, Calif.: Stanford University Press, 1998).

29. Samuel Huntington, "The Clash of Civilizations?" *Foreign Affairs* 72, no. 3 (Summer 1993), pp. 22–49, and 'The West and the Rest', *Prospect* (February 1997), pp. 34–9.

30. On Huntington's enthusiasm for pacification of Vietnamese villagers, see Marilyn B. Young, *The Vietnam Wars 1945–1990* (New York: Harper-Collins, 1991), p. 177.

31. For a narrow, but nonetheless illuminating, perspective on this question see Stuart D. Brandes, *Warhogs: A History of War Profits in America* (Lexington: University Press of Kentucky, 1997). Banks were also critical in raising both Germany and the US to the ranks of world powers: see Harold James, *The Deutsche Bank and the Nazi Economic War Against the Jews* (Cambridge: Cambridge University Press, 2001).

32. Bernard Lewis, "The Roots of Muslim Rage", *Atlantic Monthly* (September 1990), pp. 47–54.

33. Gyanendra Pandey, "The Colonial Construction of 'Communalism': British Writings on Banaras in the Nineteenth Century", in Ranajit Guha (ed.), *Subaltern Studies VI* (Delhi: Oxford University Press, 1988), pp. 132–68.

34. The literature is immense. For a variety of readings, see Indian National Congress, Cawnpore Riots Enquiry Committee, *A History of the Hindu–Muslim Problem in India* … [1933], reprinted as Gerald Barrier (ed.), *The Roots of Communal Conflict* (New Delhi: Arnold Heinemann, 1976); Tara Chand, *Influence of Islam on Indian Culture* (Allahabad: The Indian Press, 1963); Amaresh Misra, *Lucknow, Fire of Grace* (Delhi: HarperCollins, 1998), and M. Mujeeb, *The Indian Muslims* (London: George Allen & Unwin), especially pp. 9–25. Mujeeb quotes copiously from nineteenth-century colonial gazetteers of Indian districts, which offer astounding evidence of the extent to which Hindus and Muslims had come to embrace practices characteristic of the other faith. Even the more ecumenical conception of Hinduism and Islam rests on the erroneous assumption that these were discrete, monolithic faiths, but historians have not yet found the language to describe the religious tapestry of India before the hardening in modern times of religious communities.

35. Vietnam Human Rights Act: see Sitaram Yechury, "We Must be Neither With the Terrorists Nor With the U.S.", *Hindu* (28 September 2001), p. 11.

36. Kenneth Stampp, *The Peculiar Institution: Slavery in the Ante-Bellum South*, reprint edn (New York: Vintage Books, 1989).

37. This thought has not been far from the mind of Paul Johnson, "Colonialism's Back – And Not a Moment Too Soon", *New York Times Magazine* (April 18th 1993).

38. Lewis, "The Roots of Muslim Rage". It is also characteristic of this mode of argument, which attributes agency only to the white man, that it ignores the place of slave rebellions in the abolition of slavery. The abolition of slavery in the New World was initiated by the slave Toussaint L'Ouverture, and yet, as one prominent scholar has written, the Haitian Revolution has been largely excised from historical narratives, and even progressive writers such as Eric Hobsbawm have managed to ignore it in their histories of the modern world. See Michel-Rolph Trouillot, *Silencing the Past: Power and the Production of History* (Boston, Mass.: Beacon Press, 1995), pp. 98–9. The most gripping account of the Haitian Revolution remains C. L. R. James, *The Black Jacobins*, 2nd revised edn (New York: Vintage Books, 1963).

39. Illustrative of this tendency are the ferocious assaults waged by the Indian left upon those Indian intellectuals who are viewed as indulging romantic ideas about the precolonial past or retreating into various forms of indigenism and nativism on account of their suspicion of modern science and Enlightenment rationality. See, for instance, Achin Vanaik, *The Furies of Indian Communalism* (London: Verso, 1997), and Meera Nanda, "The Science Wars in India", *Dissent* 44, no. 1 (Winter 1997), who considers any departure from Western science as a retreat, a concession to fundamentalism.

40. Nathuram Godse, *May It Please Your Honor* (Delhi: Surya Prakashan, 1987).

41. Gandhi was disliked by both the Hindu right and the left, but rationalists, liberals, and modernizers also deprecated his critiques of modernity and industrial civilization. See B. R. Nanda, *Gandhi and His Critics* (Delhi: Oxford India Paperbacks, 1994), though this is inadequate.

42. Ashis Nandy, "The Final Encounter: The Politics of the Assassination of Mahatma Gandhi", in his *At the Edge of Psychology: Essays in Politics and Culture* (Delhi: Oxford University Press, 1980), is the single best piece on the assassination. See also Vinay Lal, "'He Ram': The Politics of Gandhi's Last Words", *Humanscape* 8, no. 1 (January 2001), pp. 34–8.

43. Cited by J. P. S. Uberoi, *Science and Culture* (Delhi: Oxford University Press, 1978), p. 80.

44. James P. Carse, *Finite and Infinite Games: A Vision of Life as Play and Possibility* (New York: Ballantine Books, 1986).

45. Michel Foucault, *A History of Sexuality*, Vol. 1 (New York: Vintage Books, 1980), p. 94.

46. "My life is my message," wrote Gandhi on September 5th 1947. See Raghavan Iyer (ed.), *The Moral and Political Writings of Mahatma Gandhi*, vol. 3: *Non-Violent Resistance and Social Transformation* (Oxford: Clarendon Press, 1987), p. 609.

47. Gandhi added, "What I have done will endure, not what I have said or written." Cited by Sunil Khilnani, "A Bodily Drama", *Times Literary Supplement* (8 August 1997). I would also like readers to recall my arguments about the ahistoricism of the Indian sensibility and the unimportance of history as a mode of thought among Hindus at least, and can add at this juncture that among Hindus the dead body is cremated rather than buried – perfectly apposite for a civilization that cared little for its past and often knew nothing of even its traces.

48. This is true of Edward Said, Gayatri Chakravorty Spivak, Homi Bhabha, and Stuart Hall, to name but a few.

49. George Orwell, "Reflections on Gandhi", in *The Orwell Reader* (New York: Harcourt, Brace, 1956).

50. Raymond Williams, *Keywords: A Vocabulary of Culture and Society*, revised edn (New York: Oxford University Press, 1985).

51. Raghavan Iyer (ed.), *The Moral and Political Writings of Mahatma Gandhi*, vol. 2: *Truth and Non-Violence* (Oxford: Clarendon Press, 1986), pp. 211–458.

52. There are many exceptions, of course, but the critical and analytical literature on Gandhi does not even remotely begin to approximate the scholarship on Marx and Marxism.

53. D. G. Tendulkar, *Mahatma: The Life of Mohandas Karamchand Gandhi*, 8 vols. (New Delhi: Publications Division, Ministry of Information and Broadcasting, Government of India, 1951), vol. 8, p. 89; Iyer, *Moral and Political Writings of Mahatma Gandhi*, vol. 3, p. 609.

54. For the most incisive reading of this argument, see Nandy, *The Intimate Enemy*.

55. Amaresh Misra, *Lucknow, Fire of Grace* (Delhi: HarperCollins, 1998), offers a charming and nuanced portrait of Wajid Ali Shah, the deposed ruler of Awadh. Satyajit Ray's film, *Shatranj ke Khilari* (*The Chess Players*, 1981), is also an interesting meditation on the subject of rulership, sexuality, and notions of masculinity: for an extended discussion, see Vinay Lal, "Masculinity and Femininity in *The Chess Players*: Sexual Moves, Colonial Manoeuvres, and an Indian Game", *Manushi*, nos. 92–3 (January–April 1996), pp. 41–50.

56. Gandhi, who founded or edited four newspapers in his lifetime, and other Indian nationalists, such as Bal Gangadhar Tilak and Lajpat Rai, made very effective use of newspapers. Both Tilak and Gandhi, among others, were put on trial for seditious writings, and both displayed such consummate mastery in the courtroom that the British must have had occasion to think about the efficaciousness of the courtroom trial as a mode of containing opposition to British rule.
57. Carse, *Finite and Infinite Games*, p. 165.
58. Walter Benjamin, "Theses on the Philosophy of History", in *Illuminations*, ed. Hannah Arendt and trans. Harry Zohn (New York: Schocken Books, 1969).
59. Serena Nanda, *Neither Man Nor Woman: The Hijras of India* (Belmont, Calif.: Wadsworth Publishing Company, 1990); Vinay Lal, "Not This, Not That: The Hijras of India and the Cultural Politics of Sexuality", *Social Text*, no. 61 [vol. 17, no. 4] (Winter 1999), pp. 119–40.
60. Harjot Oberoi, *The Construction of Religious Boundaries* (Delhi: Oxford University Press, 1997), is an extraordinary study of the historical difficulties in drawing lines of rigid distinction between Hindus and Sikhs.
61. See Emma Tarolo, *Clothing Matters: Dress and Its Symbolism in Modern India* (Chicago, Ill.: University of Chicago Press, 1996).

POSTSCRIPT

1. I am not aware when, and why, 911 became the national number for distress, and no cultural history that I know of delves into this question.
2. "The tradition of the oppressed," Walter Benjamin wrote, "teaches us that the 'state of emergency' in which we live is not the exception but the rule." *Illuminations*, ed. Hannah Arendt (New York: Schocken, 1969), p. 257.
3. Raul Hillberg, *The Destruction of the European Jews* (New York: Harper & Row, 1979 [1961]), p. 23; Roger Eatwell, *Fascism: A History* (New York: Penguin Books, 1996), p. 149.
4. Osama bin Laden, "America Will Not Live in Peace ...", *Los Angeles Times* (8 October 2001), p. A16.
5. Barbara Ehrenreich, *Blood Rites: Origins and History of the Passion of War* (New York: Henry Holt & Co., 1997), p. 210.
6. "Islam is Peace". For the texts of Bush's remarks, see <http://www.whitehouse.gov/news/releases/2001/09/20010917–11.html>
7. Editorial, "The National Defense", *New York Times* (September 12th 2001), section A.
8. HinduUnity.Org, Press Release (New Delhi), "Islamic Terrorism Hits America", September 11th 2001.
9. Bernard Lewis, "The Roots of Muslim Rage", *Atlantic Monthly* (September 2000), pp. 47–60.
10. Francis Fukuyama, "The West Has Won", *Guardian* (October 11th 2001), also published in the *Wall Street Journal*.
11. Fareed Zakaria, "The Roots of Rage", *Sunday Times* (Singapore), Review section (October 21st 2001), pp. 34–5. See also Susan Sachs, 'Behind the

Extremism: Poverty and Despair', ibid., p. 35 (reproduced from the *New York Times*).

12. Salman Rushdie, "Let's Get Back to Life", *Hindustan Times* (October 9th 2001), p. 10.

13. Salman Rushdie, "Yes, This is About Islam", *New York Times* (November 2nd 2001).

14. I have discussed the events of September 11th with specific reference to South Asia in "Terrorism as a Way of Life", *AmerAsia Journal* 27, no. 3 (2001); 28, no. 1 (2002), pp. 103–24.

15. Karen Armstrong, "The True, Peaceful Face of Islam", *Time* (8 October 2001). Much attention has been drawn to passages in the Qur'an such as: "Fight those in the way of God who fight you, but do not be aggressive: God does not like aggressors" (2: 190). See Ahmed Ali, *Al-Qur'an: A Contemporary Translation*, revised edn (Princeton, N.J.: Princeton University Press, 1990), p. 34.

16. Rafiq Zakaria, "Islam, Muslims and the Media", *Hindustan Times* (October 21st 2001).

17. Samuel Huntington, "The Clash of Civilizations?", *Foreign Affairs* 72, no. 3 (Summer 1993), pp. 22–49; see also his "The West and the Rest", *Prospect* (February 1997), pp. 34–9.

18. See, for example, Ken Ringle, "The Nature and Nurture of a Fanatical Believer: A Void Filled to the Brim with Hatred", *Washington Post* (September 25th 2001), p. C1.

19. Thomas Friedman, "Real Clash Today is Within Civilisations", *New York Times* (September 15th 2001), and Jim Hoagland, "Moment of Truth", *Washington Post* (September 14th 2001).

20. Hoagland, "Moment of Truth".

21. Friedman, "Real Clash Today is Within Civilisations". One much less obvious reason that the terrorist actions of September 11th evoked such a strong reaction is the barely expressed feeling that the United States was dragged into an internal conflict for the soul of Islam.

22. See <http://www.whitehouse.gov/news/releases/2001/09/20010911–16.html>

23. Words attributed to Bush by Arundhati Roy, "War is Peace", Outlook (October 19th 2001). Bush's speech of September 25th at FBI headquarters does not appear to contain exactly these words: see <http://www.whitehouse.gov/news/releases/2001/09/20010925-5.html> However, since the gist of his pronouncements has been to similar effect, the precise wording is somewhat immaterial.

24. Speech of October 7th 2001, as reproduced in the *Los Angeles Times* (October 8th 2001), p. A8.

25. Ashish Kumar Sen, "Biden Gets Hell for Afghan War Remarks", *India Post* (November 2nd 2001), pp. 1, 14.

26. William Bennett, "Faced with Evil on a Grand Scale, Nothing is Relative", *Los Angeles Times* (October 1st 2001), p. B11. Here Bennett is echoing Bush: "America was targeted for attack because we're the brightest beacon for freedom and opportunity in the world." See note 19, above.

27. Joyce Appleby, "The Bad News Is, We're History", *Los Angeles Times* (October 16th 2001), p. B19.

28. Arundhati Roy, "The Algebra of Infinite Justice", *Guardian* (September 29th 2001); first published in *Outlook* [New Delhi]. Around 55 of the political cartoons that appeared in American newspapers on September 12th drew upon the image of the Statue of Liberty – a weeping Liberty, a Liberty bent over double in pain, a Liberty with severed hands, and so on.
29. On the "cult of the flag" in the United States, see Ehrenreich, *Blood Rites*, pp. 208–10.
30. Ernest Jones, "Psychology and War Conditions", *Papers on Psychoanalysis*, 5th edn (Boston, Mass.: Beacon Press, 1948), p. 187.
31. See David E. Omissi, *Air Power and Colonial Control: The Royal Air Force, 1919–1939* (Manchester: Manchester University Press, 1990).
32. "Hey, Hit the Brake: Why do Americans Refuse to Conserve?" *Chicago Tribune* (November 11th 2001).
33. The extensive connections of the Bush family to the oil industry have been the subject of numerous investigative reports: see, for example, the two-part article by Damien Cave, "The United States of Oil" and "Oily Waters", in the internet web portal, *Salon* (November 19th–20th 2001).
34. See Vinay Lal, "The Fragments of Bamiyan", *The Little Magazine* 2 (March–April 2001), pp. 23–7. The principal story in the American press through the long summer concerned the antics and political future of Congressman Gary Condit, a minor politician who appears to have had a sexual liaison with a young woman intern, Chandra Levy. A few months earlier, Levy vanished from her Washington, D.C. apartment, never to be seen again.
35. Eknath Easwaran, *A Man to Match His Mountains: Badshah Khan, Nonviolent Soldier of Islam* (Petaluma, Calif.: Nilgiri Press, 1984). Less readable, but more scholarly, is Attar Chand, *India, Pakistan and Afghanistan: A Study of Freedom Struggle and Abdul Ghaffar Khan* (Delhi: Commonwealth Publishers, 1989).
36. V. J. Patel, Chairman, *Report with Evidence of the Peshawar Inquiry Committee Appointed by the ... Indian National Congress* (Allahabad: Allahabad Law Journal Press, 1930). The wider context is furnished by Sayed Wiqar Ali Shah, *Ethnicity, Islam, and Nationalism: Muslim Politics in the North-West Frontier Province 1937–1947* (Karachi: Oxford University Press, 1999), who admits that "the most significant aspect of the whole Civil Disobedience movement was the strict adherence of the Khudai Khidmatgars to non-violence" (p. 37).
37. Ernest Gellner, *Muslim Society* (Cambridge: Cambridge University Press, 1981).
38. R. Stephen Humphreys, *Islamic History: A Framework for Inquiry*, revised edn (Princeton, N.J.: Princeton University Press, 1991).
39. See, for example, Stephen Schwartz, "Terror and Islam", and Tariq Ali, "Questions and answers", both available on the internet.
40. Edward Said, *Orientalism* (New York: Vintage Books, 1978), p. 307.
41. Ahmed Rashid, author of the authoritative *Taliban: Militant Islam, Oil and Fundamentalism in Central Asia* (reprint edn, New Haven, Conn.: Yale University Press, 2001), stated in a recent television interview (MSNBC, October 29th) that, over the last two decades, the US government has not had a single notable expert on Afghanistan.

42. The United States' difficulties with languages are legion. Lewis Lapham has written that neither of the "two senior officials formerly charged with directing the CIA's intelligence operations in the Middle East and Afghanistan" could speak Arabic fluently, and that during the twelve years of American involvement in Vietnam, "only one American university offered graduate instruction in the Vietnamese language." See "Drums along the Potomac: New War, Old Music", *Harper's* (November 2001), p. 40.
43. Aditya Sinha, 'Back to the King', *Hindustan Times* (September 30th 2001), p. 13.

Suggestions for Further Reading

Adkins, Jenny. *Whose Hunger? Concepts of Famine, Practices of Aid* (Minneapolis: University of Minnesota Press, 2000).

Alexander, George (ed.). *Western State Terrorism* (London: Routledge, 1991).

Ali, Tariq. *Masters of the Universe? Nato's Balkan Crusade* (London: Verso, 2000).

——. "Throttling Iraq", *New Left Review* (September–October 2000).

Anderson, Benedict. *Imagined Communities: Reflections on the Origin and Spread of Nationalism* (London: Verso, 1983).

Andrepoulos, George G. (ed.). *Genocide: Conceptual and Historical Dimensions* (Philadelphia: University of Pennsylvania Press, 1994).

Arens, William. *The Man-Eating Myth* (Oxford: Oxford University Press, 1979).

Arnove, Anthony (ed.). *Iraq Under Siege: The Deadly Impact of Sanctions and War* (Cambridge, Mass.: South End Press; London: Pluto Press, 2000).

Arrighi, Giovanni, and Silver, Beverly J. *Chaos and Governance in the Modern World System* (Minneapolis: University of Minnesota Press, 1999).

Ashton, Basil, et al., "Famine in China, 1958–61", *Population and Development Review* 10, no. 4 (December 1984), pp. 613–45.

Aveni, Anthony. *Empires of Time: Calendars, Clocks, and Cultures* (New York: Basic Books, 1989).

Bacevich, Andrew. "Different Drummers, Same Drum", *National Interest*, no. 64 (Summer 2001).

Banham, Reyner. *Los Angeles: The Architecture of Four Ecologies* (Harmondsworth: Penguin Books, 1971).

Barber, Benjamin R. *Jihad vs. McWorld: How Globalism and Tribalism are Reshaping the World* (New York: Ballantine Books, 1995).

Barker, Debi, and Mander, Jerry. *Invisible Government: The World Trade Organization* (San Francisco, Calif.: International Forum on Globalization, 1999).

Barsh, Russell R. "Are Anthropologists Hazardous to Indians' Health?", *Journal of Ethnic Studies* 15, no. 4 (1988), pp. 1–38.

Bauman, Zygmunt. *Modernity and the Holocaust* (Ithaca, N.Y.: Cornell University Press, paperback edn, 1992).

——. *Globalization: The Human Consequences* (New York: Columbia University Press, 1998).

Baxi, Upendra (ed.). *The Right to be Human* (Delhi: India International Centre, 1987).

Bayly, Christopher (ed.). *Atlas of the British Empire* (New York: Facts on File, 1989).

Bedau, Hugo Adam (ed.). *The Death Penalty in America: Current Controversies* (New York: Oxford University Press, 1997).

Bertman, Stephen. *Hyperculture: The Human Cost of Speed* (Westport, Conn.: Praeger, 1998).

Blaut, J. M. *Eight Eurocentric Historians* (New York: Guilford Press, 2000).

237

Bledstein, Burton. *The Culture of Professionalism: The Middle Class and the Development of Higher Education in America* (New York: W. W. Norton, 1976).

Blum, William. *Killing Hope: U.S. Military and CIA Interventions since World War II* (Monroe, Me.: Common Courage Press, 1995).

——. *Rogue State: A Guide to the World's Only Superpower* (Monroe: Common Courage Press, 2001).

Brown, David J., and Merrill, Robert (eds.). *Violent Persuasions: The Politics and Imagery of Terrorism* (Seattle, Wash.: Bay Press, 1995).

Bryant, Bunyan, and Mohai, Paul (eds.). *Race and the Incidence of Environmental Hazards: A Time for Discourse* (Boulder, Colo.: Westview Press, 1992).

Bullard, R. D. *Unequal Protection: Environmental Justice and Communities of Color* (San Francisco, Calif.: Sierra Club Books, 1994).

Burch, William J. (ed.). *The Evolution of UN Peacekeeping: Case Studies and Comparative Analysis* (New York: St. Martin's Press, 1993).

Calvocoressi, Peter, and Wint, Guy. *Total War: Causes and Courses of the Second World War* (Harmondsworth: Penguin Books, 1974).

Carse, James P. *Finite and Infinite Games: A Vision of Life as Play and Possibility* (New York: Ballantine Books, 1986).

Cesaire, Aime. *Discourse on Colonialism*, trans. Joan Pinkham (New York: Monthly Review Press, 1972 [1955]).

Chakrabarty, Dipesh. *Provincializing Europe: Postcolonial Thought and Historical Difference* (Princeton, N.J.: Princeton University Press, 2000).

Chatterjee, Partha. *Nationalist Thought and the Colonial World: A Derivative Discourse?* (London: Zed Books, 1986; reprint edn, Minneapolis: University of Minnesota Press, 1993).

Chomsky, Noam. *The New World Order*, Open Magazine Pamphlet no. 6 (Westfield, N.J.: Open Magazine Pamphlet Series, 1991).

Clark, Ramsey. *The Fire This Time: US War Crimes in the Gulf* (New York: Thunder's Mouth Press, 1992).

Clark, Ramsey, et al. *NATO in the Balkans: Voices of Opposition* (New York: International Action Center, 1998).

Commission for Racial Justice. *Toxic Wastes and Race in the United States* (New York: United Church of Christ, 1987).

Commission on Global Governance. *Our Global Neighbourhood* (Oxford: Oxford University Press, 1995).

Conquest, Robert. *The Harvest of Sorrow: Soviet Collectivization and the Terror-Famine* (New York: Oxford University Press, 1986).

Das, Bhagirath Lal. *The World Trade Organisation: A Guide to the Framework for International Trade* (London: Zed Books; Penang: Third World Network, 1999).

Davies, Merryl Wyn, Nandy, Ashis, and Sardar, Ziauddin. *Barbaric Others: A Manifesto on Western Racism* (London: Pluto Press, 1993).

des Forges, Alison. *Leave None to Tell the Story: Genocide in Rwanda* (Washington, D.C.: Human Rights Watch, 1999).

Diamond, Jared. *Guns, Germs, and Steel: The Fate of Human Societies* (New York: W. W. Norton, 1997).

Dizdarevic, Zlatko. *Sarajevo: A War Journal*, trans. Anselm Hollo (New York: Henry Holt & Co., 1994).

Dower, John. *War without Mercy: Race and Power in the Pacific War* (New York: Pantheon, 1986).

Dunkley, Graham. *The Free Trade Adventure: The WTO, the Uruguay Round and Globalism – A Critique* (London: Zed Books, 1997).

Easwaran, Eknath. *A Man to Match His Mountains: Badshah Khan, Nonviolent Soldier of Islam* (Petaluma, Calif.: Nilgiri Press, 1984).

Ehrenreich, Barbara. *Blood Rites: Origins and History of the Passions of War* (New York: Henry Holt & Co., 1997).

Elias, Norbert. *Time: An Essay* (Oxford: Basil Blackwell, 1992).

Ellis, John. *Eye-Deep in Hell: Trench Warfare in World War I* (New York: Pantheon Books, 1976; reprint edn, Baltimore, Md.: Johns Hopkins University Press, 1989).

Escobar, Arturo. *Encountering Development: The Making and Unmaking of the Third World* (Princeton, N.J.: Princeton University Press, 1995).

Fabian, Johannes. *Time and the Other: How Anthropology Makes Its Objects* (New York: Columbia University Press, 1983).

Foner, P. S. (ed.). *W. E. B. Du Bois Speaks: Speeches and Addresses, 1890–1919* (New York: Pathfinder Press, 1970).

Foucault, Michel. *Discipline and Punish: The Birth of the Prison*, trans. Alan Sheridan (New York: Viking, 1979).

Frank, Thomas. *One Market under God: Extreme Capitalism, Market Populism, and the End of Economic Democracy* (New York: Doubleday, 2000).

Franklin, H. Bruce. *Vietnam and Other American Fantasies* (Amherst: University of Massachusetts Press, 2000).

Fraser, J. T. (ed.). *The Voices of Time*, 2nd edn (Amherst: University of Massachusetts Press, 1981).

Gadgil, Madhav, and Guha, Ramachandra. *Ecology and Equity: The Use and Abuse of Nature in Contemporary India* (Delhi: Penguin Books, 1995).

Gellner, Ernest. *Nations and Nationalism* (Oxford: Basil Blackwell, 1983).

——. *The Conditions of Liberty: Civil Society and Its Rivals* (Harmondsworth: Penguin Books, 1996).

Gitlin, Todd. *The Twilight of Common Dreams: Why America is Wracked by Culture Wars* (New York: Henry Holt & Co., 1995).

Gourevitch, Philip. *We Wish to Inform You that Tomorrow We Will be Killed with Our Families: Stories from Rwanda* (New York: Farrar, Straus & Giroux, 1998).

Greenblatt, Stephen. *Marvelous Possessions: The Wonder of the New World* (Chicago, Ill.: University of Chicago Press, 1991).

Guehenno, Jean-Marie. *The End of the Nation-State*, trans. Victoria Elliott (Minneapolis: University of Minnesota Press, 1995).

Guha, Ramachandra. *Mahatma Gandhi and the Environmental Movement* (Pune: Parisar, 1993).

Guha, Ranajit. "The Prose of Counter-Insurgency", in Ranajit Guha (ed.), *Subaltern Studies II: Writings on South Asian History and Society* (New Delhi: Oxford University Press, 1983), pp. 1–42.

Haq, Mahbub ul. *Reflections on Human Development*, new edn (Delhi: Oxford University Press, 1998).

Harding, Sandra (ed.). *The "Racial" Economy of Science: Towards a Democratic Future* (Bloomington: Indiana University Press, 1993).

Hardt, Michael, and Negri, Antonio. *Empire* (Cambridge, Mass.: Harvard University Press, 2000).

Hartung, William. *And Weapons for All: How America's Multibillion Dollars Arms Trade Warps Our Foreign Policy and Subverts Democracy at Home* (New York: HarperCollins, 1995).

Huntington, Samuel. "The Clash of Civilizations?", *Foreign Affairs* 72, no. 3 (Summer 1993), pp. 22–49.

——. "The West and the Rest", *Prospect* (February 1997), pp. 34–9.

Ibrahim, Anwar. *The Asian Renaissance* (Singapore: Times Books International, 1996).

Ihonvbere, Julius O. *Africa and the New World Order* (New York: Peter Lang, 2000).

International Forum on Globalization (San Francisco). *IFG Bulletin*, "Special Water Issue" (Summer 2001).

Johnson, Paul. "Colonialism's Back – and Not a Moment Too Soon", *New York Times Magazine* (April 18th 1993).

Kaplan, Amy, and Pease, Donald (eds.). *Cultures of United States Imperialism* (Durham, N.C.: Duke University Press, 1993).

Keim, Curtis. *Mistaking Africa: Curiosities and Inventions of the American Mind* (Boulder, Colo.: Westview Press, 1999).

Kennedy, Paul. "Preparing for the 21st Century: Winners and Losers", *New York Review of Books* (February 11th 1993).

Kerr, Alex. *Dogs and Demons: Tales from the Dark Side of Japan* (New York: Hill & Wang, 2001).

Khoshoo, T. N. *Mahatma Gandhi – An Apostle of Applied Human Ecology* (New Delhi: Tata Energy Research Institute, 1995).

Klare, Michael. *Rogue States and Nuclear Outlaws: America's Search for a New Foreign Policy* (New York: Hill & Wang, 1995).

Kochler, Hans. *The United Nations Sanctions Policy and International Law* (Penang, Malaysia: Just World Trust, 1995).

Kolko, Gabriel. *The Politics of War: The World and United States Foreign Policy, 1943–1945* (New York: Pantheon Books, 1990 [1968]).

Kothari, Manu and Mehta, Lopa. *The Other Face of Cancer* (Mapusa, Goa: The Other India Press, 1994).

Kothari, Smitu, and Sethi, Harsh (eds.). *Rethinking Human Rights*: *Challenges for Theory and Action* (Delhi: Lokayan; New York: New Horizons Press, 1989).

Lake, Anthony. "Confronting Backlash States", *Foreign Affairs* 73, no. 2 (March–April 1994).

Lal, Anil, and Lal, Vinay. "The Cultural Politics of Hybridity", *Social Scientist* 25, nos. 9–10 (September–October 1997), pp. 67–80.

Lal, Vinay. "The Discourse of History and the Crisis at Ayodhya: Reflections on the Production of Knowledge, Freedom, and the Future of India", *Emergences*, nos. 5–6 (1993–94), pp. 4–44.

——. "History and the Possibilities of Emancipation: Some Lessons from India", *Journal of the Indian Council of Philosophical Research* (June 1996), pp. 95–137.

——. "Not This, Not That: The Hijras of India and the Cultural Politics of Sexuality", *Social Text*, no. 61 (Winter 1999), pp. 119–40.

——. (ed.). *Dissenting Knowledges, Open Futures: The Strange Selves and Multiple Destinations of Ashis Nandy* (Delhi: Oxford University Press, 2000).

——. "The Fragments of Bamiyan", *The Little Magazine* 2 (March–April 2001), pp. 23–7.

Landes, David S. *Revolution in Time: Clocks and the Making of the Modern World* (Cambridge, Mass.: Harvard University Press, 1983).

——. *The Wealth and Poverty of Nations: Why Some Are So Rich and Some So Poor* (New York: W. W. Norton, 1998).

Lapham, Lewis H. *Money and Class in America: Notes and Observations on Our Civil Religion* (New York: Weidenfeld & Nicolson, 1988).

Lauren, Paul Gordon. *The Evolution of International Human Rights* (Philadelphia: University of Pennsylvania Press, 1998).

Leslie, Jacques. "Running Dry", *Harper's Magazine* (July 2000), pp. 37–52.

Levine, Robert. *A Geography of Time: The Temporal Misadventures of a Social Psychologist* (New York: Basic Books/HarperCollins, 1997).

Lewis, Bernard. "The Roots of Muslim Rage", *Atlantic Monthly* (September 1990), pp. 47–54.

Loy, David R. "Buddhism and Poverty", *Kyoto Journal*, no. 41 (1999), pp. 43–56.

Luhrmann, Tanya. *The Good Parsi: The Fate of a Colonial Elite in a Postcolonial Society* (Cambridge, Mass.: Harvard University Press, 1996).

Lummis, C. Douglas. *Radical Democracy* (Ithaca, N.Y.: Cornell University Press, 1996).

McCully, Patrick. *Silenced Rivers: The Ecology and Politics of Large Dams* (London: Zed Books, 1996).

Maguire, Daniel C., and Rasmussen, Larry L. *Ethics for a Small Planet: New Horizons on Population, Consumption, and Ecology* (Albany: SUNY Press, 1998).

Mander, Jerry. *In the Absence of the Sacred: The Failure of Technology and the Survival of the Indian Nations* (San Francisco, Calif.: Sierra Club Books, 1991).

Melvern, Linda. *A People Betrayed: The Role of the West in Rwanda's Genocide* (London: Zed Books, 2000).

Miller, Marion A. L. *The Third World in Global Environmental Politics* (Milton Keynes: Open University Press, 1995).

Mingst, Karen A., and Karns, Margaret P. *The United Nations in the Post-Cold War Era* (Boulder, Colo.: Westview Press, 1995).

Miyoshi, Masao. "A Borderless World? From Colonialism to Transnationalism and the Decline of the Nation-State", *Critical Inquiry* 19, no. 4 (Summer 1993), pp. 726–51.

Muldoon, James P., Jr., wt al. (eds.). *Multilateral Diplomacy and the United Nations Today* (Boulder, Colo.: Westview Press, 1999).

Mumford, Lewis. *Technics and Civilization* (New York: Harcourt, Brace & World, 1934; paperback edn, 1963).

Naess, Arne. *Gandhi and the Nuclear Age* (Totowa, N.J.: Bedminister Press, 1965).

Nanda, Meera. "Is Modern Science a Western, Patriarchal Myth? A Critique of the Populist Orthodoxy", *South Asia Bulletin* 11, nos. 1–2 (1991), pp. 32–61.

Nanda, Serena. *Neither Man Nor Woman: The Hijras of India* (Belmont, Calif.: Wadsworth, 1990).

Nandy, Ashis. "The Final Encounter: The Politics of the Assassination of Mahatma Gandhi", in Ashis Nandy, *At the Edge of Psychology: Essays in Politics and Culture* (New Delhi: Oxford University Press, 1980).

——. *The Intimate Enemy: Loss and Recovery of Self under Colonialism* (Delhi: Oxford University Press, 1983; Oxford India paperback, 1988).

——. *Traditions, Tyranny, and Utopias: Essays in the Politics of Awareness* (New Delhi: Oxford University Press, 1987).

——. (ed.). *Science, Hegemony and Violence: A Requiem for Modernity* (Tokyo: The United Nations University; Delhi: Oxford University Press, 1988; paperback edn, 1990).

——. "Time Travel to a Possible Self: Searching for the Alternative Cosmopolitanism of Cochin", *Japanese Journal of Political Science* 1, no. 2 (2000), pp. 295–327.

Nettle, D. and Romaine, S. (eds.). *Vanishing Voices: The Extinction of the World's Languages* (New York: Oxford University Press, 1998).

Oberoi, Harjot. *The Construction of Religious Boundaries: Culture, Identity, and Diversity in the Sikh Tradition* (Chicago, Ill.: University of Chicago Press, 1994).

O'Brien, Robert, et al. *Contesting Global Governance: Multilateral Economic Institutions and Global Social Movements* (Cambridge: Cambridge University Press, 2000).

O'Malley, Michael. *Keeping Watch: A History of American Time* (New York: Penguin Books, 1991).

Padel, Felix. *The Sacrifice of Human Being: British Rule and the Konds of Orissa* (Delhi: Oxford University Press, 1995).

Pakenham, Thomas. *The Scramble for Africa 1876–1912* (New York: Random House, 1991).

Panikkar, K. M. *Asia and Western Dominance*, new edn (London: George Allen & Unwin, 1959).

Patel, Jehangir P., and Sykes, Marjorie. *Gandhi: His Gift of the Fight* (Rasulia, Madhya Pradesh: Friends Rural Centre, 1987).

Patil, Anjali V. *The UN Veto in World Affairs, 1946–1990* (Sarasota, Fl: UNIFO, 1992).

Peng, Xizhe. "Demographic Consequences of the Great Leap Forward in China's Provinces", *Population and Development Review* 13, no. 4 (December 1987), pp. 639–70.

Press, Eyal and Washburn, Jennifer. "The Kept University", *Atlantic Monthly* (March 2000).

Quigley, John. "Prospects for the International Rule of Law", *Emory International Law Review* 5, no. 2 (Fall 1991).

Raina, Vinod, et al. (eds.). *The Dispossessed: Victims of Development in Asia* (2nd edn, Hong Kong: ARENA [Asian Regional Exchange for New Alternatives] Press, 1999).

Ramet, Sabrina Petra. *Balkan Babel: The Disintegration of Yugoslavia from the Death of Tito to the War for Kosovo*, 3rd edn (Boulder, Colo.: Westview Press, 1999).

Rashid, Ahmed. *Taliban: Militant Islam, Oil and Fundamentalism in Central Asia* (reprint edn, New Haven: Yale University Press, 2001).

Readings, Bill. *The University in Ruins* (Cambridge, Mass.: Harvard University Press, 1996).

Reisner, Marc. *Cadillac Desert: The American West and Its Disappearing Water*, revised edn (New York: Penguin Books, 1993).

Renner, Michael. "Ending Violent Conflict", in Lester Thurow (ed.), *State of the World 1999* (New York: W. W. Norton, 1999), pp. 151–68.

Rieff, David. *Los Angeles: Capital of the Third World* (New York: Simon & Schuster, 1991).

——. "The Institution that Saw no Evil", *New Yorker* (February 12th 1996).

Rifkin, Jeremy. *Time Wars: The Primary Conflict in Human History* (New York: Henry Holt & Co., 1987).

——. *Beyond Beef: The Rise and Fall of the Cattle Culture* (New York: Plume Books, 1993).

Rohde, David. *Endgame: The Betrayal and Fall of Srebrenica, Europe's Worst Massacre since World War II* (New York: Farrar, Straus & Giroux, 1997).

Ross, Dorothy. *The Origins of American Social Sciences* (Cambridge: Cambridge University Press, 1991).

Rothenberg, David. *Is It Painful to Think? Conversations with Arne Naess* (Minneapolis: University of Minnesota Press, 1993).

Rubenstein, Richard L. *The Cunning of History: The Holocaust and the American Future* (New York: Harper Torchbooks, 1987).

——. *After Auschwitz: History, Theology, and Contemporary Judaism*, 2nd edn (Baltimore, Md.: Johns Hopkins University Press, 1992).

Sachs, Wolfgang. "On the Archaeology of the Development Idea", *Lokayan Bulletin* 8, no. 1 (January–February 1990).

Sachs, Wolfgang (ed.). *Development Dictionary: A Guide to Knowledge as Power* (London: Zed Books, 1992).

——. *Planet Dialectics: Explorations in Environment and Development* (London: Zed Books, 1999).

Sahlins, Marshall. *Culture and Practical Reason* (Chicago, Ill.: University of Chicago Press, 1976).

——. "Goodbye to *Tristes Tropes*: Ethnography in the Context of Modern World History", *Journal of Modern History* 65 (1993), pp. 3–4.

Said, Edward. *Reflections on Exile and Other Essays* (Cambridge, Mass.: Harvard University Press, 2000).

Sardar, Ziauddin. *Postmodernism and the Other: The New Imperialism of Western Culture* (London: Pluto Press, 1998).

——(ed.). *Rescuing All Our Futures* (New York: Adamantine Press; London: Praeger, 1998).

——. *The Consumption of Kuala Lumpur* (London: Reaktion Books, 2000).

Sardar and van Loon, Borin. *Cultural Studies for Beginners* (Cambridge: Icon Books, 1997).

Sarkar, Sumit. *Writing Social History* (Delhi: Oxford University Press, 1997; paperback edn, 1998).

Schlosser, Eric. "The Prison-Industrial Complex", *Atlantic Monthly* (December 1998), pp. 51–77.

Schor, Juliet. *The Overworked American: The Unexpected Decline of Leisure* (New York: Basic Books, 1992).

Schott, Jeffrey. *The Uruguay Round* (Washington, D.C.: Institute for International Economics, 1994).

Schwartz, Stephen (ed.). *Atomic Audit: The Costs and Consequences of U.S. Nuclear Weapons Since 1940* (Washington, D.C.: Brookings Institution Press, 1998).

Seamon, David, and Zajonc, Arthur (eds.). *Goethe's Way of Science: A Phenomenology of Nature* (Albany: SUNY Press, 1998).

Seed, Patricia. *American Pentimento: The Invention of Indians and the Pursuit of Riches* (Minneapolis: University of Minnesota Press, 2001).

Sells, Michael A. *The Bridge Betrayed: Religion and Genocide in Bosnia* (Berkeley, Calif.: University of California Press, 1996).

Sen, Amartya. *Poverty and Famines: An Essay on Entitlements and Deprivation* (Oxford: Clarendon Press, 1981).

Sherry, Michael. *The Rise of American Airpower: The Creation of Armageddon* (New Haven, Conn.: Yale University Press, 1987).

Shiva, Vandana. *Staying Alive: Women, Ecology and Survival in India* (London: Zed Books, 1988; Delhi: Kali for Women, 1988).

——. *Stolen Harvest: The Hijacking of the Global Food Supply* (Boston, Mass.: South End Press, 2001).

Simpson, Christopher (ed.). *Universities and Empire: Money and Politics in the Social Sciences during the Cold War* (New York: New Press, 1998).

Singer, Daniel. *Whose Millennium? Theirs or Ours?* (New York: Monthly Review Press, 1999).

Singh, Kavaljit. *The Globalisation of Finance: A Citizen's Guide* (London: Zed Books, 1998).

Smith, Linda Tuhiwai. *Decolonizing Methodologies: Research and Indigenous Peoples* (London: Zed Books; Dunedin: University of Otago Press, 1999).

Smith, Richard Austin. "Los Angeles, Prototype of Supercity", *Fortune* (March 1965), pp. 98–106, 200–2.

Soley, Lawrence C. *Leasing the Ivory Tower: The Corporate Takeover of Academia* (Boston: South End Press, 1995).

Srinivasan, T. N. *Developing Countries and the Multilateral Trading System: From the GATT to the Uruguay Round and the Future* (Boulder, Colo.: Westview Press, 2000).

Stannard, David. *American Holocaust: Columbus and the Conquest of the New World* (New York: Oxford University Press, 1992).

Starr, Paul. *The Social Transformation of American Medicine* (New York: Basic Books, 1982).

Stewart, Michael. *The Time of Gypsies* (Boulder, Colo.: Westview Press, 1997).

Taylor, Christopher C. *Sacrifice as Terror: The Rwandan Genocide of 1994* (Oxford: Berg, 1999).

Taylor, Philip M. *War and the Media: Propaganda and Persuasion in the Gulf War*, 2nd edn (Manchester: Manchester University Press, 1998).

Thompson, E. P. "Time, Work-Discipline, and Industrial Capitalism", *Past and Present*, no. 38 (December 1967), pp. 56–97.

Tierney, Patrick. "The Fierce Anthropologist", *New Yorker* (October 9th 2000), pp. 50–61.

Trouillot, Michel-Rolph. *Silencing the Past: Power and the Production of History* (Boston, Mass.: Beacon Press, 1995).

Tucker, Richard P. *Insatiable Appetite: The United States and the Ecological Degradation of the Tropical World* (Berkeley: University of California Press, 2000).

Uberoi, Jit Singh. *Science and Culture* (Delhi: Oxford University Press, 1978).

——. *The Other Mind of Europe: Goethe as a Scientist* (Delhi: Oxford University Press, 1984).

Udall, Stewart L. *The Myths of August: A Personal Exploration of Our Tragic Cold War Affair with the Atom* (New York: Pantheon Books, 1994; paperback edn, New Brunswick, N.J.: Rutgers University Press, 1998).

Unger, Roberto Mangabeira. *The Critical Legal Studies Movement* (Cambridge, Mass.: Harvard University Press, 1986).

United Nations. *Human Development Report 1999* (New York: United Nations, 1999).

——. *Human Development Report 2001* (New York: United Nations, 2001).

United Nations, Department of Social and Economic Affairs. *Measures for the Economic Development of Underdeveloped Countries* (New York: United Nations, 1951).

Wagner, Peter, Wittrock, Bjorn, and Whitely, Richard (eds.). *Discourses on Society: The Shaping of the Social Science Disciplines*, Sociology of the Sciences Yearbook, vol. XV (Dordrecht: Kluwer Academic Publishers, 1991).

Wasserstrom, Jeffrey N., Hunt, Lynn, and Young Marilyn B. (eds.). *Human Rights and Revolutions* (Lanham, Md.: Rowman & Littlefield, 2000).

Watson, James L. (ed.). *Golden Arches East: McDonald's in East Asia* (Stanford, Calif.: Stanford University Press, 1998).

Weber, Eugene. *Peasants into Frenchmen: The Modernization of Rural France, 1870–1914* (Stanford, Calif.: Stanford University Press, 1976).

Weiss, Thomas G., et al. (eds.). *Political Gain and Civilian Pain: Humanitarian Impacts of Economic Sanctions* (Lanham, Md.: Rowman & Littlefield, 1997).

Will, Garry. "The Dramaturgy of Death", *New York Review of Books* (June 21st 2001).

World Commission on Dams. *Dams and Development: A New Framework for Decision-Making* (London: Earthscan, 2000).

Worsley, Peter. *Knowledges: Culture, Counterculture, Subculture* (London: Profile Books, 1997; New York: The New Press, 1997).

Worthington, Richard. *Rethinking Globalization: Production, Politics, Actions* (New York: Peter Lang, 2000).

Wright, Richard. *Stolen Continents: The Americas Through Indian Eyes since 1492* (New York: Houghton Mifflin, 1992).

Young, Robert. *White Mythologies: Writing History and the West* (London and New York: Routledge, 1990).

Zerubavel, Eviatar. *Hidden Rhythms: Schedules and Calendars in Social Life* (Chicago, Ill.: University of Chicago Press, 1981).

——. *The Seven Day Circle: The History and Meaning of the Week* (New York: The Free Press, 1985).

Websites

Sentencing Project: <http://www.sentencingproject.org>
UN Peacekeeping: <http://www.un.org/Depts/dpko/dpko/pub/pko.htm>
UN Srebrenica Report: <http://www.un.org/news/ossg/srebrenica.html>
World Commission on Dams: <http://www.dams.org>

Index